the symbiotic man

A NEW UNDERSTANDING OF THE ORGANIZATION
OF LIFE AND A VISION OF THE FUTURE

Joël de Rosnay

Translated from the French by Phyllis Aronoff, Rémy Charest,
Howard Scott, and Wanda Romer Taylor

McGraw Hill

New York • San Francisco • Washington D.C. • Auckland • Bogotá
Caracas • Lisbon • London • Madrid • Mexico City • Milan
Montral • New Delhi • San Juan • Singapore
Sydney • Tokyo • Toronto

Library of Congress Cataloging-in-Publication Data
Rosnay, Joël de.
[Homme symbiotique. English]
  The symbiotic man : a new understanding of the organization of life and a vision of
the future / Joël de Rosnay.
    p. cm.
  ISBN 0-07-135744-0 (alk. paper)
    1. Human ecology—Forecasting. 2. Twenty-first century—Forecasts. I. Title.
GF50 .R69 2000
304.2—dc21   00-020669

McGraw-Hill

A Division of The McGraw-Hill Companies

1 2 3 4 5 6 7 8 9 0 DOC/DOC 0 9 8 7 6 5 4 3 2 1 0

ISBN 0-07-135744-0

*It was set in Berling and Officina Sans by Impressions Book and Journal Services, Inc.
Printed and bound by R. R. Donnelley & Sons, Company.*

Acknowledgments to Biotics Sarl (Paris, France) for participation in the translation.

Contents

PART III   WANTING THE FUTURE

Foreword

Joël de Rosnay has created a book that is, at once, reasonable and wild! It is reasonable because it conceives the world we are building as a complex integrated whole consisting of humans, machines, networks and society. And it is wild because it goes on to envision the resultant complex aggregate as a new kind of self organizing living form. The unique roots of this book lie in this intersection of the logical and the unexpected, brought to life through pairs of apparently unrelated elements—natural and artificial systems, order and disorder, simplicity and complexity, real and virtual experiences and many others that make up life and the world around us; which are brought next to each other, and, magically, seem unrelated no more.

But, de Rosnay goes well beyond exposing and discussing contrasting aspects of the future. He draws on his involvement with the Group of Ten in France, which brought together scientists philosophers and politicians to discuss the use of systems thinking in research, education, management and politics. He also draws on theories of Chaos and Complexity, and on his background as an organic chemist, a manager of research programs, and an expert on information technology and its uses. Consciously or not, he also brings to the table his background as a European scientist who was trained in the United States of America. de Rosnay focuses distills these rich and contrasting experiences into an original and big idea which is the centerpiece of his vision and of this book: His thesis is that we must understand the laws of self organization of matter and systems, from atoms to complex societies, to build the next step of the evolution of mankind—the symbiosis of human beings, their organizations, and machines into a living planetary organism.

This main theme is developed in simple lay terms and is surrounded by a wealth of interesting observations and conclusions. The author discusses the technologies of information, bio- and molecular electronics, artificial life, genetic algorithms, combinatorial chemistry, and nanotechnology and explains their relevance to the future of industry and to our ability to manage complexity in the next millennium. The fascinating contrasts that characterize this book carry into these discussions as well: For example, a unifying theory linking tomorrow's living and inanimate systems is between the same book covers as the marketing approaches that will dominate future business transactions!

To some, this book will be a forecast for the next millennium. To others, it will be a call for action. Yet others will see in it a sociotechnical and philosophical description of our future. Whether it is viewed as a forecast, a call for action or a philosophical treatise, *The Symbiotic Man* is a book full of fresh ideas that will inform, amaze and stimulate the reader. At this millennial turning point, when everyone is asking where we are headed, Joël de Rosnay's *The Symbiotic Man* offers an original, visionary and exciting answer.

Michael L. Dertouzos, Director
MIT Laboratory for Computer Science,
and author of *What Will Be*
Weston, Massachusetts
November 8, 1999

Preface

I have always liked molecules. In 1965, after completing my doctoral thesis in science at the Pasteur Institute, I wrote a book on what had just been named molecular biology, a little book for general readers entitled *Les Origines de la Vie* [The Origins of Life]. What fascinated me at the time was how life arose in the primeval world from material that had formed in the atmosphere and the oceans. How did the extraordinary complexity of the cell, the microscopic unit of the living world, come into being?

After doing research and teaching at the Massachusetts Institute of Technology (MIT) from 1967 to 1971—and, as a bonus, discovering computers—I worked in a venture capital company that specialized in financing and launching hi-tech companies. That led me to discover the complexities of companies, the economy, and the major regulatory cycles.

To better describe this realm of infinite complexity, I devised a symbolic tool I called the macroscope, which was also the name of a book I published in 1975 on the systemic approach. Designed to help us understand complexity, the *macroscope* supplemented the microscope and the telescope, instruments for observing the infinitely small and the infinitely large.

Today, after two decades of using personal computers, I believe that the symbolic tool I described now exists in reality. With its capacity for simulation, the computer has become a macroscope. It helps us understand complexity and act on it more effectively to build and manage the large systems of which we are the cells—companies, cities, economies, societies, ecosystems. Thanks to this macroscope, a new vision of the world is emerging, based on a unified approach to the self-organization and evolution of complex systems. Some call this new way of thinking the "sciences of complexity."

On the basis of this comprehensive vision, I wanted to describe the origin of a new form of life on Earth, a planetary macro-organism made up of the totality of human beings and machines, living creatures, networks, and nations—a still-embryonic macro-organism that is trying to live in symbiosis with the planetary ecosystem.

This book is the story of the emergence of this macrolife, a new account of the origins of life in which, this time, we as cells are directly involved. It is an attempt to shed some light on the future that we are still trying to build—the future of symbiotic humanity.

I am well aware of the scope and ambitiousness of this undertaking, which should be regarded not as a blueprint for the future but as a vision of an achievable utopia, a vision intended to provide a direction for our day-to-day actions as we build the world of tomorrow together.

Note: Certain terms that are not in common use may be found in a glossary at the end of the book.

Joël de Rosnay

Introduction

HISTORY AND NATURAL LAWS

It is sometimes dismaying to witness the short-sightedness of policies regarding the future: Ten years seems like an eternity. The world is too complex, and its evolution unpredictable. The future is a mystery. At the dawn of a new millennium, who would dare to try to describe the form of our technologically advanced societies in 2030 (a single generation away), and their relationship with less advanced countries? Aside from demographic extrapolations (10 billion people in the world in 25 years!) or specific technological predictions, it seems impossible to make any forecast about the next century. We are facing a blank wall. The year 2000, which for a long time was an almost mythical horizon, is now behind us, and 2100 is not very relevant for dealing with our current concerns. Our approach to the future is confined to discussions of personalities, generally focused on the next election.

Prediction is impossible, the experts tell us, because developments are chaotic, fluctuating, random, wild, with sudden rapid changes followed by periods of stagnation. A commonplace event that happens at the right time and place and is blown up by the media can change the destiny of a nation. This is the "butterfly effect" popularized by Edward Lorenz, one of the fathers of chaos theory. According to his famous example, the fluttering of a butterfly's wings in Singapore can lead to a tornado in the Caribbean because of the instability of the air masses of the atmosphere.

No overall forecast beyond two or three years seems realistic. Twenty years ago, who would have predicted the destruction of the Berlin Wall and the collapse of the Soviet Union, peace between Israel and the Palestinians, or the economic and political impact of AIDS? Of course, these events have made history. But the writing of history while managing change is no longer reserved for politicians, economists, industrialists, or even journalists or sociologists. There are natural laws that are even stronger than those that govern societies, principles to which all bodies in nature—whether they are made up of molecules, cells, insects, or people—are subject. A better knowledge of these immutable laws could shed some light on the road ahead.

This knowledge is now begining to emerge. It will serve as the basis for a middle path between the traditional political and economic management of the world and an approach of collaborative guidance, using tools and instruments developed from the unifying perspective of the sciences of complexity. We must not forget that *cybernetics* (the art of controlling machines) and *government* (the art of managing complex systems) share the same etymology.*

THE METAPHOR OF THE CYBIONT

Since history and politics cannot light our way to the future, what can we learn from the laws of nature? They tell us that there are upheavals in store for us. For example, that life will spring forth *again* on Earth. Of course, life has never disappeared; on the contrary, it exists in profusion—the population explosion is ample evidence of that. But this is a new form of life, on a level of organization never before achieved by evolution: *macrolife* on a planetary scale, in symbiosis with humanity. This *hybrid* life, at once biological, mechanical, and electronic, is coming into being before our very eyes. And we are its cells. In a still unconscious way, we are contributing to the invention of its metabolism, its circulation, and

---

*From the Greek *kubernetes*, "rudder" or "helmsman."

its nervous system. We call them economies, markets, roads, communications networks, and electronic highways, but they are the organs and vital systems of an emerging superorganism that will transform the future of humanity and determine its development during the next millennium. The birth of this organism and its significance for our lives today, and our individual and collective decisions in building the future are the central theme of this book.

Any new life deserves a name. I propose that we baptize this planetary organism the *cybiont*—a name I have coined from *cybernetics* and *biology*. It stands for a hypothetical model, a useful metaphor for envisioning one possible stage in the evolution of matter, life, and human society on our planet. This macro-organism will come fully into being at a future time whose exact date is not very important (in the first or second half of the new millennium?), but it exists already, in a primitive state, as a living entity. Its birth will not occur in a single stage and the process of its evolution will never be completed. I will describe it in an anecdotal and narrative way.

To me, this model provides a way of looking toward the future, a way that is necessary for building the societies of tomorrow. Its advantage is that it illuminates the immediate present through a *retroprospective* process. Imagining—or, better, visualizing—the symbiotic relationship between humanity and the cybiont makes it possible to choose particular directions, particular structures, and particular intermediate stages. This iterative process, cycling between present and future on the basis of a model that is a starting point and not an end, puts events, situations, currents, and changes into perspective, orders them hierarchically, and helps us make decisions. Through the retroprospective approach, the impossibility of making predictions about the world by means of traditional extrapolation gives way to constructive hypotheses. The movement back and forth between prediction, verifications, and coherence allows us to validate the facts. Rather than an analysis of unconnected situations projected into an uncertain future, we have a synthesis of facts that are of significance for the future, converging towards a transitory model, which enriches this new vision of the future. To paraphrase the Xerox PARC motto, the best way to predict the future is to invent it.

THE NEW SCIENCES OF COMPLEXITY

Of course, all this requires new and powerful tools. Cartesian analysis, which breaks down complex entities into simple elements, is no longer sufficient to explain the dynamics and evolution of systems. Though it is well suited for isolating the decisive factors in the functioning of certain mechanisms, its approach fails when it comes to the understanding of processes of self-organization and self-selection. The systemic method, which emerged in the fifties with the rise of cybernetics and systems theory, supplements the traditional analytic approach. Focusing on the connections among the various elements of systems, their levels of organization, and the dynamics of their interactions, the systemic approach allows us to describe complexity better and act on it more effectively. The analytic and systemic approaches are complementary, as we will see in Part I.

In recent years, a higher-level synthesis of these approaches has been achieved in the sciences of complexity, which bring together chaos theory and the theory of self-organization to provide a new perspective on physical, biological, social, and ecological systems. This is a unified approach that reveals the great laws of nature I spoke of and brings out the universality of their application. The systemic approach as presented in *The Macroscope* was a descriptive, pedagogical approach aimed at providing a better *understanding* of complexity. The new unified approach of the sciences of complexity provides the means for *acting* on complexity. It attempts to explain the transition from an organization at a given level to the organization of which it is itself a component. Nature proceeds through the hierarchical ordering of structures and functions in assemblies of a higher order, such as cells in organisms, organisms in populations, populations in ecosystems. As I show at the end of Chapter 1, a unified theory of the self-organization and dynamics of complex systems is possible. Such a theory will be essential for shedding light on the future; it will allow us, in keeping with the natural laws, to choose the structures and functions necessary to the life of symbiotic humanity and its freedom of action. This unified theory is the guiding thread running through this book.

The instrument I will use throughout is the computer, not only as the catalyst that accelerates the functioning of our societies but also as a tool for the direct observation of complexity, as a *macro-scope*. With its capacity for simulation, the computer allows us to do experiments of the kind traditionally performed in the laboratory. Used by the pioneers of the sciences of complexity, it helps us understand the origins of life, biological evolution, the creation of order out of disorder, and the regulated functioning of an ecosystem or of the economy. This new role of the computer is described in Chapter 1, which discusses the tools for studying complexity and the simulation experiments that reveal the great laws of self-organization.

Through the use of these tools, a new understanding of nature is dawning, one based on synthesis rather than analysis. The quest for the elementary particles that are supposed to provide a causal explanation of the subsequent evolution of matter toward increasing levels of complexity does not make the world more intelligible, nor bring it any closer. Meaningful explanation eludes us with analysis. On the other hand, using a synthetic approach—with the possible assistance of the computer—to understand how elements combine into more complex groupings or how the universal evolution of matter is born out of these interactions brings us closer to nature. We are an integral part of it, and our role in the universe thus becomes more understandable, providing the basis for any conscious action. New and sometimes disturbing areas such as artificial life and virtual reality fit harmoniously into the new paradigm of the sciences of complexity.

A PLANETARY SYMBIOSIS

One of the great challenges for humanity in the third millennium will be the conscious construction of its symbiotic partner. This next stage in biological and socio-technological evolution has already begun. During the prebiological period in which the first cells developed, the basic structures and functions of living things were selected: DNA, membrane, power plants, systems of locomotion, and basal metabolism based on fermentation, photosynthesis, and respiration. Today, we are building a new hybrid life *from the inside*. We are actors in a play about the new origins of life, a play that is still in the process of being written. As enzymes in a planetary protocell, we are working without an overall plan, without any real goals, chaotically, to build a structure far greater than ourselves. The economic, ecological, educational, and energy functions of our societies are the basic functions of a living superorganism. Developing an awareness of this fact is both motivating and empowering. It puts individual action at the heart of the evolution of the world.

From this perspective, the old question about what the people of the future will be like takes on a whole new meaning. They will be neither supermen nor biorobots. Nor will they be a supercomputer or a megamachine. They will simply be *symbiotic humanity*, living in close partnership with a social system—if they succeed in building it—that is an externalization of their own brains, senses, and muscles, a superorganism that nourishes and lives off the neurons of the Earth, neurons that we humans are in the process of becoming.

After *homo sapiens*, who sought to dominate other living species through intelligence, *homo faber*, who learned to use tools and machines, and *homo economicus*, consumer and predator, the time has come for *homo symbioticus*, a species living in harmony with a greater being that it helped to create and that is creating it in turn.

In *The Macroscope*, in 1975, I attempted to envisage this new form of collective life that I am describing today:

> The earth shelters the embryo of a body and the beginnings of a spirit. The life of this body is maintained by the great ecological and economic functions brought together in the ecosphere. Collective consciousness emerges from the simultaneous communication of men's brains; . . . . Reaching beyond the management of nature, it recognizes the *symbiotic nature* of the relationship between human society and the ecosystem, wherein each uses the other to their mutual benefit. [emphasis added]

The synthesis of planetary macrolife and the conditions for the emergence of symbiotic humanity will be covered in the beginning chapters of this book. I place particular emphasis on the three major stages of this birth: self-organization, coevolution, and symbiosis.

Part II of the book deals with the relationships between the human brain, computers, and the planetary brain. It describes the everyday life of the cybiont, and ends with the birth of a collective consciousness as a result of the symbiosis of brains and networks in new internalized spaces of communication.

A WORLD TO BE INVENTED

I am well aware of the risks of such an approach. Could a *single* planetary superorganism, the cybiont, be the point of convergence of *all* forms of human society? Surely the diversity of the world cannot be reduced to such a simplistic model. Moreover, the planetary brain of the cybiont (interconnected human brains, computers and communications networks) and its metabolism of self-preservation (global economies and energy systems) arise out of coevolution among technologically and industrially advanced societies. How will the rest of the world participate in building this organism? How will the legitimate rejection of such technological hyperdevelopment be expressed? Fundamentalist movements and ideologies are deeply influential in human societies. Communities live, as we will see, in time bubbles of different densities, even though they coexist in the universal time measured by clocks.

To try to answer these questions, Part Three discusses the policies, industries, educational methods, and values of the future, allowing for the variety of currents and alternative paths. I must emphasize that the metaphor of the cybiont is a simplified, hypothetical model intended to create an awareness of what is in my opinion the probable next stage in the development of the human species in coevolution with its machines and its forms of organization.

My undertaking involves many risks. My Attempt to erase the boundary between the natural and the artificial exposes me to accusations of excessive reductionism or of acting as a scientific imperialist out to conquer the social sciences. I am seeking neither to reduce the inventions of humanity to spontaneous productions arising out of the natural laws of self-organization, nor to extrapolate from the laws of physics or biology to social systems. My objective is to reveal some simple laws that apply to the evolution of all organized matter and to draw lessons from this for our action in society.

Any attempt to describe an organism that is more complex than human society and that relies on symbiotic relationships is immediately open to criticisms of vitalism, animism, or even pantheism. I have been influenced neither by anthropomorphism nor by animism—only by the general systemic laws discovered by the *scienza nuova* of the twenty-first century, the sciences of complexity. Nor has ideology influenced by collective model of a possible next stage of human evolution. Collectivism and totalitarianism are equally absent from my vision. My only concern is the nature of hierarchical organizations that contain collections of elements in complex systems, from atoms to human societies. Finally, although my focus is on the technological advances that make possible the vital functions of the cybiont, I have not forgotten the influence of religion, economic and social inequalities, fear, violence, disease, hunger, and war. As I explain in Part Three, our view of the world is distorted by the media. Disasters, social upheavals, scandals, wars, riots, acts of terrorism, drugs, and epidemics are the most common aspects presented, and they tend to discourage us from taking responsibility. However, we need to understand the world better in order to change it. The new vision of our role in nature, provided by unified science, seems to me to give us the means to do so.

I am inviting you to share an optimistic vision of a world to be invented. I will remain in my own scientific and technological orbit, aware of the complementary importance of political, economic, and spiritual action in the evolution of society. Cybernetic laws and human government are complementary. I will consider here only that aspect of our individual and collective responsibility that arises from scientific and technological advances. Not a thesis or a doctrine or a cautionary tale, this book offers another way of looking at our evolution and presents new tools for building the world of tomorrow.

A FRACTAL BOOK

The structure of this book is based on a new form of communication I call fractal communication. The term *fractal*, coined by the

French mathematician Benoît Mandelbrot in 1969, applies to any shape or structure that remains identical to itself at any level of observation. For example, a small branch of a tree is like a big one, which is like the tree as a whole; the leaf of a fern is like the whole fern; a snow crystal is like the smallest of the crystal structures that make it up; the form of a rocky coastline is like that of its smallest section. A fractal structure has the same resolution at every level of observation. In this book, I use a form of fractal communication—rather than a linear, sequential discourse, with one argument following another in the arbitrary order of my presentation, I attempt to communicate my ideas in a series of modules organized fractally. A particular theme dealt with may be taken up again, developed, and looked at in another context. The fractal forms in this book are nested within each other. A simple sentence may contain the totality of my thesis, and the redundancies in one chapter may enrich a proposition already discussed in another context.

It is possible to generate fractal forms of enormous complexity on the basis of simple, repetitive mathematical rules. The complexity emerges from the division of simplicity: this is one of the great laws of nature. I hope this book will be a seed of simple complexity.

I

A Unified Vision of
Nature and Society

1

Molecules, Insects, and Humans

THE KEY TO THE FUTURE: MASTERING COMPLEXITY

At the start of the twenty-first century, we are experiencing future shock, mainly as a result of the progress made over the past 35 years in the physical and biological sciences. Physics and electronics have given us computers and communications technology; biology has given us biotechnology and bio-industry. Humanity has already undergone similar historic transitions. The agricultural revolution took place over several millennia. The industrial revolution lasted more than a century. We are now at the beginning of the information and communications revolution, which will probably take several decades. These changes are leading to an increase in the complexity of society and of the organizations, systems, and networks for which we are responsible, a complexity that challenges our traditional methods of analysis and action.

We are not prepared for these changes. Our reasoning about complexity remains analytical, our vision of the world divided into disciplines, our knowledge encyclopedic. We continue to extrapolate in a linear way from past data, whereas the changes we are experiencing are nonlinear, exponential, and constantly accelerating. The politicians, economists, planners, and organizers of the world approach the complexity of situations and organizations with intellectual methods and tools based on those developed in the nineteenth century for dealing with linear, homogeneous change in a stable world where the same causes produced the same effects. However, there is feedback from effect to cause. Processes, networks, and systems are entangled in inextricable webs. Thus, we need new tools and new ways of thinking to deal with an evolution in which we are the main actors. We need to obtain some perspective, to find a higher vantage point, to make the connections that will enable us to understand better, to put things into context so that we will be better able to act.

The complexity of life and of the ecosystem can be approached using either deductive or inductive reasoning. If we break down complexity into simple elements through analysis, we lose the quality of the emerging properties. If we reassemble the whole from its parts through synthesis, we lack experimental proof to confirm our hypotheses. A combination of analysis and synthesis can help explain complexity. The ecological approach, for example, is a systemic synthesis starting from analytic elements. It draws connections between natural phenomena that obey general laws and individual and collective human actions.

Until very recently, our management of the world has been oblivious to the great currents that shape the ecosphere, the biosphere, and the technosphere. Our vision and our actions were connected to an essentially historical concept of human creativity, in which politicians could legitimately consider themselves the only ones with the know-how to change the world and advance societies in a chosen direction. However, other forces are at work. For lack of methods, observation tools, and evaluation capabilities, these forces have long eluded analysis, and thus they are seldom taken into account in traditional politics. They are difficult to grasp since they involve knowledge from many different disciplines and fields. The excessive specialization of our view of the world has made them invisible.

These great forces are the forces of nature—laws of self-organization, autocatalysis, competitive exclusion, hierarchy of complexity, dynamics of evolution, and natural selection—forces that produced the world, from atoms to molecules, and from cells to the species that inhabit the planet. These are strong tendencies, limitations, and constraints that are now impossible to ignore in the behavior of any complex system. It is in connection with such laws that human responsibility takes on its full meaning. It now has to take into account the constraints of nature in order to benefit better from it. People must be able to economize on human energy as well as that of machines to increase the effectiveness of their actions and to guide major changes in directions favorable to human development, resources, and freedoms.

A full understanding of the complexity of the laws of nature allows us to overcome more simple contraints. Take for example the laws of gravity. What could be more counterintuitive than the flight of an airplane? Of course, a bird, which is light, can fly. But a plane weighing several tons? This miracle is based on the laws of fluid mechanics combined with the laws of gravity, the propulsive power of engines, and the lift created by the aerodynamic shape of the wings. The combination of these elements enables the plane to fly. Similarly, the dynamics of social systems cannot be based only on human laws; they must also take into account the general laws of nature, which science is now beginning to understand and use.

What are these laws of nature and how are they expressed at our level of observation? They are expressed through similarities, hierarchies, and optimums that apply to fields very different from nature and society. The following are a few examples.

▶ The major functions of life, the economy, and the ecosystem are based on the same types of structures: fluid, adaptable communications networks; energy cycles; the circulation of information and materials; transactional interfaces; regulatory loops. This is true for the immune, nervous, and hormonal systems, the cycles that provide living cells with the energy to function, markets of goods and services and the stock market, and the major biogeochemical cycles that recycle the basic components of the ecosystem. Why such similarities in such diverse areas?

▶ Nature uses the same rules of assembly to build structures of increasing complexity: the assembly of elementary modules that become the building blocks of higher levels. Elementary particles, atoms, molecules, cells, multicellular organisms, families, tribes, populations, companies, cities, societies, nations, and ecosystems are organized using building blocks that are nested and linked in interdependent networks. Why such economy of means?

▶ Living things develop within a narrow range of physical and chemical dimensions (temperature, light, composition of the atmosphere or water) that are precisely—almost miraculously—compatible with life. Who set the thermostats and regulators and defined the ideal compositions?

▶ Certain shapes, structures, and functions emerge from all the competing shapes, structures, and functions. They come to the fore through self-selection and become obligatory transition points, determining and conditioning subsequent development. This is the case of the first living cells that emerged from an undifferentiated primeval soup, the animal and plant species that arose through natural selection, new products that become established in a market, key ideas, and universal obligatory operating procedures, rules, and standards. Why do some of these forms succeed while other innovations of nature or human invention come to nothing?

▶ Computers and communications networks have evolved rapidly, catalyzed by multimedia, digitization, and data compression. The Internet, the worldwide network of interconnected networks, feeds on this progress and is evolving spontaneously, chaotically, autocatalytically. Who set the standards and the rules for this evolution?

These fundamental questions can be answered for the first time by the sciences of complexity. General laws exist that apply to areas as diverse as business, markets, large international organizations, competing animal populations, insect societies, cell development, chemical reactions, the reproduction of viruses, and the formation of planets.

THE MAGIC OF VIRTUOUS CIRCLES

Out of many possible examples (some of which will be discussed here), I would like to describe a mechanism for reproduction and natural selection in order to demonstrate its universality. In the world of molecules, this mechanism is called *autocatalysis* or self-selection. In the world of the economy, we speak of increasing returns, the virtuous circle, or the snowball effect. The basis for these terms is one of the fundamental laws of evolution, which directs it toward increasing levels of complexity.

As surprising as it may seem, molecules were reproducing even before life came into being. Imagine in those primeval oceans a molecule formed by chance in a succession of long stages of assembly from material dispersed in the surrounding environment. This new molecule has a special property: it is a catalyst. It accelerates certain stages of its *own assembly*. The second molecule of this type is thus manufactured much more quickly than the first, and the following ones even more quickly. A positive feedback loop is established: this is autocatalysis. At increasing speed, these molecules sort and select building blocks present in the environment and integrate them into their own structure. They reproduce more and more quickly and take over the environment; they are self-selecting. Controlling the flows of intermediate parts, this species of molecule finally occupies all the space in which it has developed, preventing other evolution that is necessarily slower.

Such phenomena also occur in the economy, but it has taken economists some time to realize their universality. Whereas classical economics considered only changes that occurred according to the law of diminishing returns (saturation of markets, need to reduce prices, advertising campaigns, marginal competition, etc.), the new school of the sciences of complexity is interested in the laws of *increasing* returns, those that lead to the explosion of a market or the self-selection of some new good or service and the competitive exclusion of others. Such a product becomes dominant and imposes its law on the following generations of similar products. The new economists call the exclusive occupation of a sector by a product through autocatalysis and self-selection *lock-in*. We need only analyze a few recent technological-economic, cultural, or political developments to understand the scope of this natural law.

The widespread adoption of the fax machine is a good example of lock-in. At first, when there were only a few fax machines and they were still very expensive, there was not much incentive to own one, since there were not enough potential correspondents. But as the number of fax machines grew, the practical value of each fax machine became greater—which, in turn, led to new applications and more reasons to get a fax machine. This is an example of a positive feedback loop.

Another example is provided by the Astra satellite, a telecommunications satellite that was launched under criticism by experts. Transmitting 25 channels—and with digitization, 150—this satellite, more than any political decision, established truly European television. Its success has created commercial and cultural expansion niches for satellite dishes, decoders, programs, films, CDs, magazines, and other products, all of which reinforce the Astra's role as a catalyst through positive feedback. This is a lock-in. Too bad for those who did not get in at the start. There is no room left!

The rise of Microsoft is yet another example. The company diversified its products, making modules that are the essential building blocks for networks of producers of computerized information. Each product creates a new expansion niche that reinforces the existing products through positive feedback.

The Internet, the network of networks connecting computers throughout the world, today has close to 200 million users and 45 million host computers. Each new application creates an area of complexification, amplifying the network's total "intelligence." New solutions and applications appear more quickly, catalyzing the growth of the system. The more users connected, the more incentive there is to be connected, and the more the interfaces improve. The English language has followed a similar course. With all due respect to the defenders of multilingualism, the rise of English as the universal language of basic communication is following an irreversible process of lock-in through autocatalysis. More and more people are choosing English as their first language for work or public use, creating new expansion niches for applications, such as books, courses, guides, procedures, technical devices, tools, software, CDs. These applications reinforce the catalytic role of English in the choices of new users and lead to the creation of other niches. A positive feedback loop has been established. The self-selection of one language through the competitive exclusion of others (at least for certain types of applications) does not mean we have to abandon multilingualism, which is essential in order to preserve cultural variety, a crucial factor in the complexification of evolution. The self-selection of

English as a kind of convenient but limited Esperanto is probably a transitory phenomenon pending the development of individual real-time automatic translation systems.

The phenomenon of lock-in through autocatalysis and self-selection elicits many aspects of the general processes of emergence of organized complexity such as variations, mutations, catalysis, amplification, selection, stabilization, self-organization, and coevolution. It shows that by reversing (or combining) feedback loops it is possible to go from a situation of diminishing returns to one of increasing returns. This is a golden rule for breaking deadlocks in the management of complex systems.

An anecdote will illustrate this. A prince summons his two sons, Godfrey and Lancelot. "I bequeath my fortune and my domain to the one whose horse enters the city gates *last*. Start from behind the big hill and return as you choose." Godfrey mounts a black horse and Lancelot a white horse. They make their way toward the city, each one trying to arrive last. The situation is at an impasse. The prince is getting bored. Suddenly, Godfrey and Lancelot ride through the city gate at full gallop, Godfrey riding the white horse and Lancelot the black horse. What happened? The two sons had simply decided to trade mounts, so that the one who arrived first would make his horse (ridden by the other son) arrive last, and thus win. Positive feedback toward zero, the cause of a "slowness" race, was converted into positive feedback with increasing returns, creating a speed race, which made possible the competitive exclusion of the rival.

Observing the laws of nature that apply to physical, biological, and social systems helps to highlight the universal nature of common phenomena, as I have shown in the case of forms of organization, regulatory mechanisms, and amplification systems, using examples from the world of molecules or the economy. Gradually a new vision of nature is emerging, one that is essential for our understanding of where the next stage in the organization of human societies will take us.

THE SCIENCE OF THE TWENTY-FIRST CENTURY

In an old abbey in the heart of New Mexico, a handful of researchers are working to create the science of the twenty-first century. This is the Santa Fe Institute, where scientific disciplines meet and cross-fertilize. A team of young postdoctoral researchers works under a committee of prestigious scientists that includes several Nobel laureates. One of the distinctive features of this organization is that the researchers live there, with substantial administrative support and computer facilities, while their project directors—who include such pioneers of the new science as John Holland, Brian Arthur, Stuart Kauffman, and Christopher Langton—teach in various universities and visit the institute regularly. When I have presented seminars at the Santa Fe Institute, I have experienced the impressive transdisciplinary atmosphere that prevails there: one group is working on immunity, another on ecosystems, and still others on the economy or artificial life. There are no boundaries between disciplines; what is important is their sharing of a common approach through complexity, systems dynamics, and the use of the macroscope-computer.

Another respected institution of the new science is the Université Libre de Bruxelles, where Ilya Prigogine, Grégoire Nicolis, and Jean-Louis Deneubourg work. Their teams have distinguished themselves in the field of the thermodynamics of irreversible systems, which focuses on the processes of self-organization and the emergence of complexity in chemistry and the social sciences. There are teams of French researchers associated with the work of these two institutions, in addition to those directed by Francisco Varela of the CNRS (National Center for Scientific Research) , Paul Bourgine of the Cemagref, and Gérard Weisbuch of the Ecole Normale Supérieure in Paris.

After the division and fragmentation of disciplines into increasingly specialized territories, a comprehensive vision is emerging, bringing together disciplines in a productive, harmonious whole. Paradoxically, this harmonious vision was created in part by a discipline that, at first glance, seems quite remote from it—chaos theory, an unfortunately named field that has given rise to the sciences of complexity.

The new vision of the world brings together two complementary modes of analysis and action, the analytic method, based on that of Descartes, and the systemic approach, from cybernetics and systems theory. A paradigm shift had already occurred in the 1950s and

1960s, when researchers in the physical, biological, and social sciences at the Josiah Macy Foundation and the Société pour l'Étude des Systèmes Généraux laid the foundations of a new approach to complexity. There were teams from MIT and Harvard University, including Norbert Wiener, Warren McCulloch, Arturo Rosenblueth, Julian Bigelow, and Walter Pitts, but also philosophers, anthropologists, and economists such as Gregory Bateson, Margaret Mead, Anatol Rappoport, Kenneth Boulding, and Ross Ashby. Bridges were built between the physical, mechanical, and biological sciences through cybernetics and systems theory. In France, in the late 1960s, the Groupe des Dix [Group of Ten], in which I took part, was formed. Actually consisting of some 20 people, it brought together Henri Atlan, Jacques Attali, Henri Laborit, Edgar Morin, Michel Serres, and others around Jacques Robin. This group also took a systemic approach.

PUTTING THE PART AND THE WHOLE BACK TOGETHER

What is the relationship between cartesian analysis and the systemic approach? Descartes contributed to our understanding of the complexity of the world by reducing it to a number of simple elements that could be studied independently. He laid the foundations for the acquisition of knowledge through rigorous reasoning and the use of experimentation to test hypotheses. This scientific method, which is still in use today, led to the development of science, technology, and society. But it has drawbacks. It separates and isolates, fragments and disperses, making knowledge seem flat, without depths or hierarchies, and dividing it into a multitude of unconnected domains with boundaries that are constantly reforming. These domains are the scientific disciplines that claim to describe the reality of nature, a juxtaposition of piecemeal elements, a "justadisciplinarity" rather than a true synthesis of knowledge. As Edgar Morin has said, "Fragmented, compartmentalized, mechanistic, disjunctive, reductionist intelligence breaks down the complexity of the world into disjointed pieces, splits up problems, separates things that are connected, and reduces the multidimensional to a single dimension." [*Homeland*

Earth: A Manifesto for the New Millenium (Advances in Systems Theory, Complexity and the Human Sciences) by Edgar Morin, Anne Brigitte Kern, Anne Briggite Kelly, translator, Hampton Press, Mount Waverly, VIC, October 1998.]

The disadvantage of the analytic method is that it has made it difficult to draw connections among different fields. The fragmentation of knowledge has led to the problem of communication among the disciplines and created the need for an encyclopedic culture and a way of classifying facts, objects, and elements in order to organize and find information.

While it was essential to the foundation of science, the analytic approach is no longer sufficient to explain the dynamics and evolution of complex systems, feedback, equilibrium, increasing diversity, or self-organization. New methodologies for organizing knowledge have had to be developed to deal with the complexity of the world. That is how the systemic approach came into being. Complementary to the analytic approach, the systemic approach is applicable to a wide variety of fields, including biology, ecology, computer science, communications networks, education, psychiatry, management sciences, and economics. While the analytic method breaks down complexity into distinct elements, the systemic method reconstructs the whole from its parts, taking into account their interdependencies and their evolution over time.

The systemic approach arose from the convergence of cybernetics, information theory, and biology. I see it as a new methodology for organizing knowledge in terms of more effective action. It is devoted to the study of systems, a system being defined as a set of dynamically interacting elements organized in such a way as to maintain its structure. A cell, a society of insects, the human body, a company, a city, and the ecosystem are all examples of systems.

Systems occur at many levels. Some are building blocks for higher levels, as atoms are for molecules, molecules for macromolecules, macromolecules for cells, cells for organs, organs for organisms, organisms for populations, each level nested in another as in a set of Russian dolls. The systemic approach deals with these wholes; it never considers an element in isolation, but always in relation to the levels that precede and follow it, and to its overall environment.

Systems theory is the study of communications networks such as the nervous system, the immune system, transportation systems, and telecommunications networks. It looks at the regulatory networks by which feedback is provided to a system so that it can adapt its operation to the constraints. It also studies the effects of positive and negative regulation. Negative regulation provides feedback from the output of a system to the input in order to make the system change direction (negative feedback). This is how a thermostat works: when the temperature rises, a signal is sent to the input to stop heating and lower the temperature; when the temperature goes down, a signal goes to the input to turn the heat back on, and the temperature goes up; thus the system fluctuates around a stable value. In what is called positive regulation (positive feedback), more leads to more. Effects act on causes in the same direction: this is autocatalysis. The result is explosive change, as in a nuclear explosion, population explosion, or the proliferation of cancer cells, or a runaway toward zero, in which the process slows down until it stops.

The systemic approach includes the time factor; it looks at the changes in complex systems over time, how they evolve, how they modify their environment, and how feedback from their environment influences them. Hence the importance of this approach for the management of companies and large-scale projects.

Systemic action adopts a *combinatorial method* that involves modifying systems by acting on their distinct but related elements, not in an isolated way as one would tend to do in applying the cartesian method, but acting on several elements at the same time, while respecting certain sequences. In a complex network, one acts at several points to force the system out of its conservatism and make it change in the direction desired.

The systemic approach has led to a profound change in our relationship to the world, which philosophers and scientists call a *paradigm shift*. We were trapped in a disciplinary, analytic, sequential, linear paradigm; we are now beginning to think in terms of a systemic paradigm. Interdependence is more important than isolation, complementarity is more important than exclusion. Whereas the analytic approach led to a logic of exclusion, the systemic approach opens the way to a logic of complementarity.

The systemic method radically alters the process of acquisition of knowledge. Imagine the encyclopedic approach as a skyscraper and the systemic approach as a sphere. The skyscraper is built to hold all the knowledge in the world, arranged by discipline as in a huge library. Each new item of knowledge corresponds to a room, each new field to a floor. Using modern building techniques, it is possible to add floors and rooms ad infinitum, upwards or sideways. Each room or floor has a code so that people can find their way and retrieve information. It is obvious that it would quickly become impossible to find your way around in such a building. How would you find information using only a simple topological classification? Where would you begin if you wanted to get an education?

The sphere symbolizes the systemic approach. It can be as small as a point or as large as a planet, but it is *always a sphere*. There are no compartments, sections, or levels in it; the information that comes in from the outside is constantly mixed together and connected. The contents of the sphere thus grow, become richer and denser, and fractalize. The part contains the whole, and the whole contains the part; each remains significant to the other. As in the encyclopedic skyscraper, the expansion of the volume of knowledge is unlimited. But it occurs coherently and not by mere juxtaposition.

The analytic and systemic approaches are thus more complementary than antagonistic. Paradoxically, the link between them is called *chaos*.

CHAOS: A HIDDEN FORM OF ORGANIZATION?

What is complexity? A complex system is not necessarily complicated. Using appropriate methodologies, we can understand and act on complexity, whereas a complicated system resists any type of analysis by traditional methods.

Complex systems are characterized first of all by the number of elements they are made up of—for example, the number of molecules in a cell or people in a city—and then by the nature of the interactions among these elements and the number and variety of connections among them. A sand pile contains billions of grains of sand, but the interaction of those grains of sand are simple compared to those among the people in a society. Finally, complex systems are characterized by the nonlinear dynamics of their development, that is, their accelerations, inhibitions, and fluctuations, which are not easily predictable. A living cell, an organism, a termite nest, a tree, an ecosystem, the economic system, a city and its inhabitants, and an international airline reservation system are all complex systems. The sciences of complexity have led to the understanding of the processes governing such systems in terms of simple laws.

This approach to nature is derived from chaos theory, which developed in the early 1970s from the work of researchers such as Jim Yorke at the University of Maryland, Edward Lorenz at MIT, Joseph Ford at the Georgia Institute of Technology, and Paul Glansdorff and Ilya Prigogine at the Université Libre de Bruxelles. According to chaos theory, complexity can arise from simple interactions repeated a great many times among elements in constant interaction. A tiny change can be amplified and can lead to states of very high organization that are recognized by the observer as form or information. For example, the water droplets or ice crystals in a cloud undergo convection movements, turbulence, and chaotic combinations or dispersions. Over time, however, agglomerations form, change shape, and endure or disappear, creating a characteristic shape depending on the circumstances of the cloud's development. That shape—which we recognize as cumulus, stratus, or cirrus—is also characteristic of particular weather conditions, making it possible for us to forecast the weather.

These unstable but perennial shapes result from deterministic chaos, a form of organization of matter present in all natural phenomena. Until now, we did not have sufficient capacity to analyze and simulate these processes of self-organization, but modern computers have made this possible.

Another example of complex forms of organization based on simple laws is the fractal structures made popular by the mathematician Benoît Mandelbrot and seen by an amazed public on television, in photographs, or in computer programs—magnificent colored shapes that look like jewels, patterns in Indian tapestries, flowers, sea horse tails, butterfly wings, estuaries, mountain ranges, or lightning bolts. These structures are produced by means of simple formulas repeated a great many times and graphically plotted by computers. Structures grow and evolve on the screen like the biological beings to which they have more than a superficial similarity; they are produced by coded, iterative processes very much like those that generated the astonishing variety of living beings.

A *fractal structure* is a structure whose resolution remains the same on different levels or scales of observation. In other words, it is constructed of repeating patterns that are recreated on different levels to produce a shape that maintains the same basic structure. This is the structure of a fern, a crystal, or a rocky coastline seen from an airplane or observed on a human scale. Long invisible to us, the fractal form of the shapes of nature is now completely obvious, and is easily simulated on a computer. One famous fractal shape results simply from a triangle to which three new triangles are added, one in the middle of each side, creating a new structure, a kind of six-pointed star; then the same modification is made on the 12 new sides; and so on ad infinitum. The same simple modification applied repeatedly to each new shape creates a structure of extraordinary complexity.

Chaos theory and fractal shapes lead to a unified vision of nature. Phenomena that are separated into their elements by the traditional method of analysis reveal their commonalities and are brought closer together. Just as the concept of a sphere establishes a relationship among a drop of water, a soap bubble, and the globe of the Earth, the fractal shapes of nature fall into a certain number of categories, linking biology to chemistry and physics to animal societies. For the first time, we perceive the unity behind shapes as varied as those of trees, clouds, and shorelines. Shapes, diversities, and unities are the result of chaotic processes involving myriads of elements in interaction. Chaos theory allows us to understand how successive bifurcations, continously amplified, can quickly lead to the emergence of new forms very different from the initial situation and to the self-organization of complex structures. Thanks to these new approaches to complexity, we are better able to explain the emergence of new shapes, structures, functions, networks, and systems as disparate as international communications networks, the stock market, or the organized structures that were the origin of living things.

The following description explains how experts in chaos theory characterize the self-organization of a complex system through the interplay of chaotic interactions. Although the terms used may seem rather technical to some, this description shows the general implications of the theory.

In a population of interacting elements or agents (molecules, water droplets, ants, people, etc.) random fluctuations (variations) occur around a state of dynamic equilibrium. These tiny changes put certain parts of the system out of balance, and the fluctuations can be amplified and give rise to more regular oscillations. As a result of evolutionary bifurcations and successive amplifications, subsystems can thus leave the state of equilibrium and form organized structures that carry a flow of energy. These dissipative structures optimize the outflow of that energy, and maintain their structure over time. In this way, an organized form can arise out of random chaotic movements and become stable. Certain organized structures can accelerate the formation of new structures. The result is autocatalysis and acceleration that is analogous, as we saw earlier, to reproduction. The new structure forms more quickly than the one that formed it.

This type of evolution can be simulated and visualized on computers. The catalyst for the rapprochement of the analytic and systemic approaches and the emergence of the new sciences of complexity is without any doubt the computer.

UNDERSTANDING CHAOS: THE MACROSCOPE-COMPUTER

One of the great challenges of the modern world, in science and in our understanding of the behavior of large organized forms, is the control of complexity. How can we understand complexity better and act on it more effectively? After the infinitely large and the infinitely small, we once again find ourselves confronting an unfathomable infinite—the infinitely complex. Modern science arose as a result of the efforts of scientists and philosophers to fathom the infinitely large and the infinitely small. The infinitely complex has a direct influence on our actions and our view of the role of humanity in the world.

Knowledge advances in successive leaps related to the way we see the world. We see in order to understand, and understand in order to see better. Visualizing phenomena, structures, and evolutionary change is crucial to the progress of science and the resulting view of the world. The telescope and the microscope have played key roles in the way we see the world. Even today, with the new generations of instruments, such as the Hubble Space Telescope and the scanning tunneling microscope (STM), they still play an essential role, enlarging the field of the visible. Without Galileo's telescope, the workings of celestial mechanics and gravity could not have been observed. Without the microscopes of Antonie Van Leeuwenhoek (1632–1723) and Louis Pasteur, the world of microbes and the world of cells could not have been discovered, and there would be no molecular biology or biotechnology.

In the past 15 years, an extraordinary instrument for observing and acting on the third infinity, complexity, has emerged—the computer, in particular, the personal computer, which has greatly amplified the capacity of the individual brain to process complexity. Of course, the computer has existed for more than half a century, and its many applications are familiar to us. Without this *sociocatalyst*, human societies could not function with the speed and efficiency needed to coordinate their huge variety of interrelated actions. But the new characteristics of personal computers connected in networks are transforming our situation. These new characteristics can be summed up in three words: power, visualization, simulation.

A modern computer uses microprocessors with processing capacities light years beyond those of the computers of the mid-1980s. Speed, memory, addressing, and parallel operations provide these computers with the computing capacity of the most powerful machines of the 1980s at a thousandth of the cost. Anyone with a portable computer, in a laboratory or office or even on a trip, can now solve huge numbers of nonlinear differential equations simultaneously and display the results as curves, color graphics, three-dimensional charts, or animated shapes—an unimaginable task with pencil and paper. Suddenly, as a result of discontinuities or critical thresholds characteristic of the coevolution of knowledge, the computer has emerged as the tool of choice for observing and simulating the infinite complexity of life, of society, and of the ecosystem—and above all, as a tool for acting on it.

The computer has thus become the macroscope of the third infinity, no longer a symbol but a reality, a reality that is transforming our vision of the world. The macroscope-computer contracts or dilutes time and space, allowing us to perceive changes that are too slow or too fast for our brains. It applies myriad parameters simultaneously and allows its user at any moment to change the rules of the game; it forms a true symbiosis with the user. Air traffic controllers can follow the trajectories and flows of aircraft in real time; chemists can create molecular models capable of reacting with each other; surgeons can travel inside the body before an operation, using images from scanners reinterpreted by the computer; financiers can analyze patterns to identify market trends; and generals can deploy tanks on a virtual battlefield. But one of the greatest achievements of the macroscope-computer is to illuminate the relationships among order, chaos, and complexity in a multitude of natural phenomena in physics, chemistry, biology, the social sciences, and ecology. It is through visualization and simulation on their computers that the founders of chaos theory and the sciences of complexity discovered the universality of certain phenomena and formulated their hypotheses: Edward Lorenz in meteorology, Benoît Mandelbrot in the geometry of nature and fractal forms, Stuart Kauffman and Doyne Farmer in the chemical reactions that gave rise to life, John Holland in genetic algorithms, Brian Arthur in economics, and Ilya Prigogine and Grégoire Nicolis in social systems, and many other researchers in the sciences of complexity all over the world.

The computer is a portable chemistry, biology, sociology, economics, and ecology laboratory. Its simulation software contains an infinity of worlds that may be modified and manipulated as the user wishes. A simulation is nothing but a *computerized experiment*, with the same characteristics, advantages, and intellectual scope as a traditional laboratory or field experiment. The computer allows any kind of experiment to be undertaken without the risks of actual experimentation, which might involve people, companies, or economies. In an in vitro experiment, biologists reconstruct the basic machinery of cells in the test tube and add the molecular ingredients that make it function. Computer scientists do their experiments in silico, but the objectives and results are similar. For the first time it has become possible to understand nature by *reconstructing* it from simple elements and laws to produce the complexity of organized forms and operations. We are no longer limited to *breaking it down* into smaller and smaller component parts—molecules, atoms, and elementary particles—the traditional scientific approach. Hypotheses can be tested by observing the behavior of the model in its simulated environment, and validation lies not only in the causal explanation but also in the coherence of the overall operation and the underlying organization.

The macroscope-computer is thus gradually leading to a unified theory of the organization of complex systems.

FUNNY BIRDS AND VIRTUAL ANTS

We now possess, thanks to the teams at the Santa Fe Institute and the Université Libre de Bruxelles, a range of tools for understanding the self-organization of complex systems and their behavior over time. Beyond molecules, crystals, and clouds, it is important to account for the appearance of "intelligent" collective behaviors such as those observed in animal and human societies. This is clearly necessary in order to envisage the formation of the planetary macroorganism that humans are building through their creations and interactions.

Can chaos theory account for such behaviors? Scientists have long been fascinated by the coordinated behavior of millions of living creatures, their collective constructions, and their adaptation to the constraints of their environment. Swarms of insects and flocks of birds are models that can be simulated on computer. Theories of self-organization and the macroscope-computer make it possible today to adapt these models to human forms of organization.

They reveal a basic rule of profound significance: a multitude of individuals acting simultaneously and in parallel according to simple rules can produce intelligent collective behavior that can solve the overall problems of the community. This fundamental principle can be illustrated by examples from insect societies and the flights of flocks of birds.

Craig Reynolds, of Symbolics Inc. in Los Angeles, tried an experiment one day that yielded a result so unexpected that it kept him awake for several nights. He simply wanted to simulate on his computer the behavior of a flock of starlings. To do so, he programmed the machine with rules controlling the individual movement of hundreds of birds, which were represented by triangles that he called "boids." At first, the program was very complex because it had to take into account the multiple possibilities for individual actions and interactions among the birds. The result displayed on the computer screen was not very satisfactory: the "boids" moved like a regiment under strict orders, the overall structure was not very realistic, and the curves and changes of direction were jerky or symmetrical, quite different from the actual flight of living starlings.

Reynolds then decided to draw on chaos theory, and programmed his computer with a few simple rules based on information sent to him by experts on the behavior of flocks of birds. The rules for the behavior of the birds were as follows:

▶ Maintain a minimum distance from objects in the environment and from the other birds.
▶ Match speed with that of nearby birds.
▶ Move toward the center of the mass of nearby birds.

That is all. It is a long way from the detailed programming one might expect for a complex living form. To make things more interesting, Reynolds created obstacles by introducing columns into the landscape, and added another rule: if a "boid" encountered a column, it had to avoid it; if that was impossible (the odds were slim), it would collide with the column, fall to the base, and then fly more quickly to catch up with the flock.

Having created a simulation with these few simple rules, Reynolds ran the program and observed the flight of his "boids" among the columns. He was dumbfounded by the result—quasi-live behavior by one of the "boids!" The hesitant, halting, collective, harmonious, unpredictable flight of the "boids" approached the columns, and almost all the triangles wove their way through, avoiding the columns, dividing into subgroups, or speeding up. But a single "boid" on an improbable collision course could not avoid hitting a column; it fell to the ground and then took off again, flying around the column at full speed to catch up with the other "boids!" An unprogrammed situation emerged from the constraints and the collective behavior of individuals obeying certain rules. The program "invented" a solution to a particular problem. The most astonishing thing is that, independently of the distribution or dispersion of the "boids" at the beginning of the simulation, a grouped flight forms in *every* experiment, although this formation was not programmed in *any* individual.

The collective intelligence of ants is the result of the interactions of myriad individuals following simple rules. The society of an anthill is a macroorganism with overall intelligent behavior. The communications networks of insect societies form a "neural network," a collective intelligence that can solve the community's problems, such as finding the shortest route to food and bringing it back to the anthill, repairing damage to the anthill by bad weather or predators, or isolating any dead ants from the living ones.

The individual ant does not have a sufficiently developed brain to solve such problems. It is the faithful, tenacious performer of a certain number of preprogrammed routines that can be modified by information from outside. It perceives its environment [the anthill, the trails surrounding it, sunlight, ultraviolet (UV) rays] by means of appropriate sensors. But one of the most important elements is the collective memory of the community, which is recorded like an engram in the topology—in trails on the ground that are recognizable by their scent. The ants secrete pheromones, chemical substances with odors they are very sensitive to. As it moves about, each ant regularly touches the ground with the hind part of its body and deposits a microdrop of pheromone. It is estimated that 1 milligram of this substance would be enough to guide a column of ants on a trail that circled the Earth three times. Its odor dissipates eventually, so its effect gradually diminishes. The ants' "choice" of the shortest route to food may be explained by the combination of these elements. This is a property of colonies of social insects that can readily be simulated on a computer.

The source of food is, let us say, 20 yards from the anthill. A narrow path on which thousands of ants circulate links the food source to the anthill. Ants going to the food source pass those returning with food. Each ant leaves a trace of pheromone on the ground, which attracts and guides the others. Now imagine an obstacle placed across the path in such a way that there are two possible routes around it, one longer than the other. At first, about as many ants go around the obstacle on the left side as on the right; the probability of a left or right choice is the same. But since the path on the right is longer, that way takes more time, and traffic there will be less dense. The odor of the pheromone will therefore fade a little more quickly than on the left-hand path. The result will be a further imbalance in the density of circulation, since fewer ants will take that path. There will be less pheromone, attracting even *fewer* ants. On the other path, however, circulation is increasingly dense, the concentration of pheromone increases, and its odor attracts still more ants. A positive feedback loop is established, further amplifying the attractiveness of this route and leading to a lock-in of this path. The left-hand path has been self-selected over the right-hand path. There has been competitive exclusion by the one of the other. The ants have thus collectively "chosen" the shorter route, using an autocatalytic "logic," saving their energy for other necessary tasks. The "neural network" of the anthill has functioned as an intelligent system, selecting the optimal solution for the community as a whole.

Another example is the formation of an ant "cemetery." Once again, there are only a few simple rules. Since the dead ants have an odor that attracts predators and therefore endangers the community, moving them away from the anthill increases the colony's chances of survival. The following rules for the behavior of the individual ants are programmed into the computer:

► Collect a corpse and deposit it anywhere.
► If a corpse deposited by another ant is encountered, deposit the one being transported in the same place.
► If small heaps of dead ants are encountered, move them to a larger heap (which is more attractive).

Small heaps of dead ants are gradually formed, then bigger ones. After a time, as a result of the chaotic action of hundreds of ants, all the corpses have been gathered into a single big heap, the "cemetery."

Many more examples could be given, from the construction of the anthill to the maintenance of the larvae and queens, to defense against invaders. One last example illustrates the computer's power of simulation, its capacity to reconstruct a collective behavior that is similar to real behavior and that obeys similar laws.

Professor John Koza of Stanford University simulated the behavior of an ant colony in seeking food, using a computer program based on genetic algorithms. This type of programming generates a kind of Darwinian selection among parts of programs, selecting the code best suited to solving a particular problem. To accomplish this, programmers write program lines in a special language that contains many independent modules that can "mutate" by undergoing random variations in their codes, generation after generation. Thanks to ongoing evaluation of the results and a "bias" in the form of a "reward" loop that reinforces the best solutions to a given problem, the program *converges* by trial and error toward the solution sought in a way that is analogous to biological evolution. Hence the name *genetic algorithms*.

Koza used a computer capable of representing the movements of the ants—symbolized by dozens of little black squares—in real time. The screen of the computer was laid out in a grid. At the top left of the screen there were about a hundred blue squares together in a mass representing food. At the lower right, about a hundred red squares together in a continuous surface represented the anthill. The programmed genetic algorithms, based on the simple rules of ant behavior as observed by entomologists, were as follows:

- ▶ Seek food. If a blue square is found, take it and carry it to the red area (the anthill), leaving a trail of "pheromone" (a gray line).
- ▶ In the absence of food, move through the squares of the grid in search of a trail of pheromone. When one is encountered, follow it in the *opposite* direction from the anthill (ants can orient themselves in space), the direction of the food.

▶ In the absence of food or trails, search randomly from square to square, crossing as many squares as possible.

At the beginning of the simulation experiment, dozens of black squares (ants) are distributed randomly throughout the grid. Those close to the blue squares (food) transport them toward the red surface (the anthill), leaving a gray trail (pheromone). By the time these ants arrive at the anthill, the grid occupied by the whole population is divided in two by a gray diagonal. Some ants will be north of it, others south of it. The probability of ants crossing the trail steadily increases. Thus, a denser and denser column of insects moves toward the blue squares, taking them in their "mandibles" and then moving toward the anthill, leaving a trail of pheromone. The original small trail becomes a road, then a highway, attracting still more ants (positive feedback, amplification). All the food (blue squares) is soon stored in the anthill (red squares). The experiment may be repeated hundreds of times, but the time it takes for the ants to carry all the food to the anthill is always different. It depends on the initial conditions and the amplification of effects along the way.

Even more interesting, a computer simulation of ant behavior and observations of real ants both revealed the emergence of a global rhythm of activity/inactivity out of chaotic individual patterns. Brian Goodwin of Schumacher College in Devon and his colleagues at Catalonia's Polytechnic University and Britain's Open University have built a virtual ant colony on a computer. They were able to confirm what Blaine Cole of the University of Houston in Texas found with real ants, namely, that, when a critical density of activity and stimulation is reached among the ants, a rhythmic pattern suddenly emerges. The colony behaves like a single, pulsating superorganism. The pattern by which all workers are active within the brood chamber at the same time improves the colony's method of nurturing its young and creates a competitive advantage and a better survival rate.

THE DEMOCRATIC CHOICES OF BEES

The study of bee societies also offers interesting possibilities for observing and understanding the mechanisms of self-organization that are found in human societies. Much has been written on the dance language of bees, their orientation systems, and their production of communication hormones, which make the beehive a social macro-organism like the anthill. It is interesting to look at certain basic mechanisms from the point of view of chaos theory and self-organization. The computer can simulate the construction of a hive, the formation of the hexagonal cells, the distribution of the stores of honey and nectar, and the position of the larvae in relation to the queen. One such simulation, by Scott Camazine of Cornell University, of bees' collective decision making in the choice of a source of pollen, is particularly pertinent to the functioning of a market.

The worker bees are faced with a constant problem: how to conserve their energy while bringing back to the hive the maximum amount of food (energy resources) and avoiding overly frequent, unproductive, or distant trips. The decision-making mechanism, as a whole, resembles a microprocessor carrying out a logical operation (see the figure below). Two sources of pollen, the garden and the field,

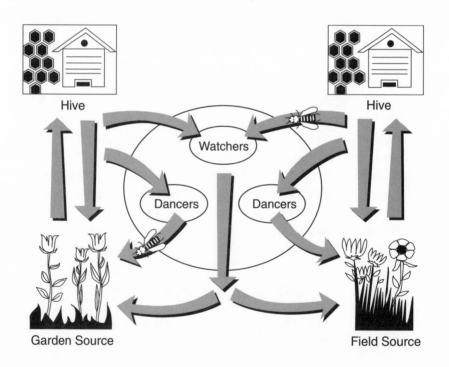

Hive   Hive

Watchers

Dancers   Dancers

Garden Source   Field Source

are located at different distances from the hive. The "garden" bees go directly to that source, collect pollen, take it back to the hive, and return at once; the "field" bees act in a similar manner. Some of the bees ("tired" or "discouraged") remain in the hive. Another group dances on a special platform to inform other bees of the quality and distance of the food source. They mingle with bees from the "field" source, and inform the community of the richness of their source. Depending on the density of the information provided by one group or the other, the probability that bees from the "garden" source will go to the "field" source may increase. A higher number of "field" bees will "convince" a growing number of "garden" bees. Gradually, the equilibrium shifts toward the new, richer or nearer, source.

An even more interesting experiment by Thomas Seeley of Cornell University showed that, when choosing a home, a swarm of 4000 bees can make a collective decision in less than 16 hours. All the bees (and particularly the 149 scouts) were tagged and followed as they traveled to and danced around 11 different potential nesting sites. The individuals combined to create a superorganism that was able to make a precise and sophisticated decision in a very short time.[*]

A collective decision has led to a strategic choice that is beneficial to the whole colony—conserving energy by avoiding unnecessary travel—a decision based entirely on the probability of individuals switching toward one or the other of the possibilities presented, and the amplification of the effects to the community level according to strict rules and constraints.

The "boids," the ants, and the bees illustrate several important points. Simple rules applied by a large number of agents acting in parallel produce intelligent collective behavior. In these "decision-making" mechanisms, we find the general properties of positive feedback, autocatalysis, amplification, and self-selection that are also at work in human societies (markets, demonstrations, fashion, mass hysteria).

---

[*] Thomas Seely and Susannah Buhrman, "Group Decision-Making in a Swarm of Honey Bees," *Behavioural Ecology and Sociobiology*, vol. 45, 1999, p. 19; Kirk Vissher and Scott Camazine, "Collective Decisions and Cognition in Bees," *Nature*, vol. 397, 1999, p. 400.

The computer has increasingly become a tool for the real-time observation of the complexity and dynamics of systems. It serves as a portable laboratory for experimentation on social systems—systems made up of large numbers of interacting elements associated with emerging structures that are created by these elements, with functions of maintenance and development, and with networks of information and regulation.

Finally, insect societies have no overall vision of their situation that might give rise to general plans or "strategies." Instead, there are direct and indirect interactions among individuals and with the environment. The "memory" of the group, its model for coordination, is the environment in which it evolves, a memory environment full of physical or chemical markers resulting from the activities of the community.

BETWEEN ORDER AND DISORDER, A STRANGE BOUNDARY

In the preceding examples, we can see a general approach to the mechanisms of self-organization gradually taking shape, an approach that is pertinent to human societies, allowing us to envisage potential future forms of social organization. Chaos theory goes beyond the self-organization of the structures of the physical and chemical world. It also applies to biological systems, insect societies, human societies, and the ecosystem. At each hierarchical level, specific new properties emerge.

How can chaotic interactions generate organized complexity? The computer simulation of complex systems reveals the general principles of such evolution and provides answers to questions about similarities of structures, optimal zones of evolution, and rules of construction for networks.

When large numbers of agents interact (we have seen this with molecules and insects, but it would also apply to buyers in a market), various situations may emerge. In one case, the turbulence resulting from these interactions is too strong; structures form, but are destroyed as quickly as they are built. The associations that are produced can also lead to a rigid, inflexible order, inhibiting any further evolution and adaptation. But an unstable transition zone between order and turbulence may be created, a zone in which organized structures, chains, cycles, and loops may form that stabilize the system as a whole, despite the constant renewal of its components and disturbances from the environment.

We know, for example, that random fluctuations can be converted into stable oscillations. This conversion occurs when a chain of reactions forms a loop, creating a cycle that reproduces the same substances or regulates their appearance or disappearance. The formation of regulatory cycles is one of the most widespread stabilization mechanisms in nature. It is the basis of the major cycles of the ecosystem that maintain the vital functions of the planet (the carbon, nitrogen, and oxygen cycles); in living cells it is involved in the production of energy or the recycling of substances required for metabolism; and it is among the basic processes of the economy. Thus, a complex form of organization can be maintained over time and evolve, adapt, and therefore *exist*, as if by miracle, in an ocean of disorder and turbulence. This is precisely the case for human life and forms of human organization.

It seems that it is in this particular transition zone, *at the edge of chaos*, as Christopher Langton has suggested, that complexity can arise, and organized forms, systems, and networks can grow and develop. This is illustrated in the figure below.

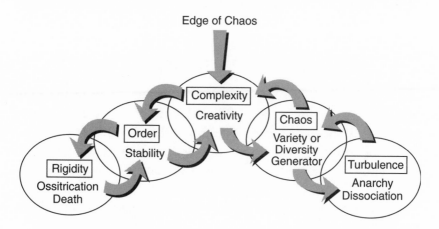

There are two abysses, one on either side of the edge of chaos. On one side is total disorder, an anarchic turbulence that does not generate organization. On the other side is structured, inflexible, static rigidity. Between the two, as in a phase transition, on the boundary between perfect order and total anarchy, there is fluidity, adaptability, self-organization of forms, structures, and functions that are born and die in perpetual self-regulated renewal—the emergence of organization and complexity. It is in this narrow margin, at this precise boundary, in this state of unstable yet stabilized transition, temporary and yet permanent, that the mechanisms that build life, society, and the ecosystem are found. How can we understand and channel them? How can we use them to build symbioses that are beneficial at all levels of partnership between nature and human beings and their machines? These are some of the fundamental questions that are shaping our future.

The sciences of complexity can help us think about the future of human societies in the next century and beyond. The combination of political rationality (or irrationality) with the great laws of nature creates a permanent tension at the boundary between ideal order and sterile turbulence. It is in this niche that the spontaneous mechanisms of self-organization and acceleration can emerge and at this precise point that the capacity for adaptation and efficiency is greatest. We need to understand how to stay there in order to coevolve with the world we have created and the planetary ecosystem. We need to exploit its properties in order to create a richly meaningful symbiosis with the cybiont that is emerging.

A GENERAL THEORY OF SELF-ORGANIZATION

The sciences of complexity have lead to a new vision of the processes of self-organization. Chaos theory is devoted to these processes, although its name suggests just the opposite. The generation of order from disorder does not lend itself to a clear, synthetic representation of the general nature of the phenomena we are considering.

Many writers have tried to bring together the major currents of thought on evolution, organization, and increasing complexity. Some have noted the profound difference between the two great tendencies of matter, toward life and toward entropy. Teilhard de

Chardin has sought to explain the emergence of life, thought, and self-consciousness by a law of "complexity-consciousness." Still others, such as Francisco Varela, Jean Piaget, and Edgar Morin, have sought to identify the conditions for autonomy of a complex system during its creative evolution.

I would like to try to expand on these approaches by adding some contributions from chaos theory and the sciences of complexity. These fields could be brought together in a unified theory based on the study of complex organized forms and computer simulations of their behavior over time. I propose it be called *the unified theory of the self-organization and dynamics of complex systems*. However, this designation, although it captures the essence of the subject, is rather long and not easy to use. More concisely, I would propose the term *symbionomics* (from *syn*, together; *bio*, life; and *nomos*, rule) to describe the range of phenomena covered by this unified theory.

I define *symbionomics* as the study of the emergence of complex systems through self-organization, self-selection, coevolution, and symbiosis. In this book, I will speak of the symbionomic process or symbionomic evolution when describing phenomena related to the emergence of organized complexity as we observe it in molecular systems (as in the origin of life), insect societies (anthills, beehives), social systems (businesses, markets, economies), and ecosystems.

One of the key processes of symbionomic evolution is symbiosis. This concept is generally applied to living organisms, but many writers have extended its use to relationships between humans and non-living systems. Without getting into a discussion on whether there is a boundary between the "natural" and the "artificial" (I will look at this in subsequent chapters), I will, for convenience, make no distinction between symbiosis occurring in the natural world prior to human intervention and symbiosis occurring since the appearance of humans, in what we call the artificial world, the world of machines, organized forms, networks, and cities. I will therefore continue to use the term *symbiosis* to refer to the links both between humans and their artifacts (such as computers) and between humans and the ecosystem.

Symbionomic evolution goes through certain stages and essential transition points. The following elements or elementary functions seem to me to be fundamental: agents, links, reproduction, reinforcement, network, chaos, amplification, self-selection, organization, emergence, transmission, and symbiosis. Their order here is for ease of presentation only, and has nothing to do with their importance.

Agent: An individual operator with functions that allow it to act on its environment (molecules, cells, bees, people, companies, organizations).

Links: Agents have mechanisms and means of connection, assembly, and interaction that allow them to create material or immaterial links with each other.

Reproduction: Agents can encode and reproduce their structures and functions.

Reinforcement: Exchanges among agents are enhanced (or eliminated) by the reinforcement (or inhibition) of certain links or regulatory loops. Only reinforcements are considered here, since they lead to the preservation of the agents and their links. Those that are eliminated play no role in subsequent evolution.

Network: Agents, with their links and exchanges, form the nodes and connections of networks in which multiple operations are carried out in parallel, simultaneously. A network of this kind is like a parallel multiprocessor (networks of molecules, cells, insects; immune system, nervous system, ecosystem; telephone system, telematics, market).

Chaos: The dynamics of interactions lead to random fluctuations, generating a large variety of unpredictable states, situations, and behaviors (mutations, inventions, events, bifurcations, turbulence).

Amplification: Certain states, situations, and behaviors are amplified by positive feedback, quickly absorbing flows of energy, matter, and information. Amplification can come about from autocatalytic or cross-catalytic reactions among many agents or subsystems (viral infections, cancer, stock exchange panic, population explosion).

Self-selection: Acceleration resulting from amplification mechanisms isolates the system in a "time bubble" of higher density, leading to a temporal divergence with other systems in evolution. The system self-selects through the competitive exclusion of concurrent systems (Darwinian natural selection, a product's dominance of a market, technological "revolution").

Organization: An individual system that can maintain its own structure and functions. An organization is defined by its overall functioning, which results from the interactions among the agents that make it up (cell, company, city, society).

Emergence: The overall functioning of a complex system leads to the emergence of unpredictable new structures, functions, and properties (life, the collective intelligence of an insect society, human intelligence, public opinion).

Transmission: Information related to structure and function and to relational, reproductive, and evolutionary mechanisms is stored in memory in a coded form that can be passed on to subsequent generations. This coding can have a material or immaterial form (the shape of molecules, DNA, plans, laws, social codes, cultures).

Symbiosis: An association of organisms or organizations that results in mutual benefit to the partners. These associations are created through the mechanisms of coevolution, and they give rise to more complex forms of organization. A new generation of agents may be born.

Three comments can be made regarding symbionomic processes and the stages I have described. First, I am speaking of evolution as a *general* process, one that extends from elementary particles to human societies and to forms of organization created by humans and living in coevolutionary symbiosis with them. Furthermore, this evolution is not linear, nor even in unidimensional acceleration. It occurs in a multidimensional way, in time bubbles that are contemporary but that have different "densities" and "qualities" of time. Each step in symbionomic evolution takes place in *fractal* time. (I will return to this important concept in Part Three.) Finally, symbionomic evolution may be seen as a spiral: each turn (self-organization, coevolution, symbiosis, emergence) corresponds to a new degree of complexity and a transition to a higher hierarchical level.

The birth of a complex form of organization can be described by connecting the various elements or elementary functions listed here, using the terms introduced in this chapter, as follows.

Multiple agents that can reproduce and maintain their structures and functions form a population in coevolution with their environment; examples include molecules in the primeval oceans, individual cells in interaction, insects in colonies, living species in an ecosystem, users of a telecommunications network, or buyers and sellers in a market.

Their chaotic interactions, which are carried out through communications networks, lead to a large variety of structures, situations, and behaviors. Some of these behaviors may be reinforced and amplified by positive feedback loops. Structures may be preserved and maintained through the mechanisms of catalysis (autocatalysis and reciprocal catalysis) and the establishment of closed loops. A set of molecules that catalyze the various stages of their assembly and a production line in which the last product accelerates the production of the first are examples of this process.

Autocatalysis leads to the self-selection of the best-adapted systems and to their accelerated evolution, locking in the sector in which they develop. Symbiotic relationships form through coevolution with other organisms or organizations, and collective properties emerge. This information is transmitted to succeeding generations through the memorization of structures and reproductive and evolutionary mechanisms by means of chemical or electronic coding or by the culture.

A complex organization is born.

From a symbionomic perspective, it is possible to trace the essential phases of the emergence of a new form of life on Earth, a macrolife, of which humanity, this time, is not the evolutionary end point, but the starting point and catalyst. These essential phases are self-organization, coevolution, and symbiosis.

2

The Birth of the Cybiont:
The New Origins of Life

LOOKING BACK AT OUR BEGINNINGS

Human beings are taking part in the birth of a new life-form on Earth. They are the principal catalysts for the origins of this new life. But this time humanity cannot consider itself the product of biological evolution; it has become the copilot of an evolutionary process that involves the whole living world, human societies and their "natural artifices" (machines, organizations, systems, networks, cities), and the ecosphere, whose functioning they have barely begun to regulate.

To understand the mystery of the origins of life, science turned to microbiology, the study of the infinitely small world of the first living forms. To understand our future, we now have to call upon *macrobiology*, a new biology of the infinitely complex. Symbionomics, the unified theory of the self-organization and dynamics of complex systems, allows us to identify the major stages in the origin of the first living cells and compare them with the current stages in the emergence of a living planetary macrocell, the cybiont.

In the beginning, 4 billion years ago, the Earth's atmosphere was composed of simple molecules—methane, ammonia, hydrogen, water vapor, and carbon dioxide. In the first stage, under the effect of energy-rich UV radiation from the sun, these gas molecules combined, forming amino acids and other more complex molecules. These building blocks of life accumulated in the primeval oceans.

The second stage, which took place in the oceans and shallow lagoons, involved chemical reactions catalyzed by dissolved metals or clay. The more complex molecules—amino acids, sugars, lipids, nucleotides—combined, grew, proliferated, assimilated energy, and self-organized. They formed structures that could close up and isolate themselves from the water, thus creating an *internal environment*. These structures, called *eobionts* (from the Greek *Eos*, the goddess of dawn, and *eons*, time or eternity) or *protobionts*, consisted of droplets of protein and lipids that filtered out certain molecules present in the surrounding environment and created concentrations of catalysts within their internal environment. For the first time, complex structures formed and differentiated themselves from the undifferentiated "broth" around them.

The third stage saw the beginning of autocatalytic reactions and the emergence of autocatalytic networks that accelerated the stages and cycles of their own formation and regulation. Little by little, the rudiments of a metabolism of energy and materials formed, and a system of coding and memorization of information developed in the form of macromolecules (proteins, RNA, and then DNA). The protobionts took on certain functions of maintenance, of duplication of their elements, of development and growth. They were the ancestors of algae and primitive bacteria.

The fourth stage saw the development of the major functions characteristic of living systems. The first of these is *fermentation*, by which primitive organisms produce energy from substances in their environment, such as sugars. It was followed by *photosynthesis*, the production of the elements of life from solar energy and the massive release of oxygen into the atmosphere. Finally *respiration*, by which organisms able to feed on plants—or on animals that have consumed plants—ensures their self-preservation. Plants (autotrophic) and animals (heterotrophic) diverged, and their symbiosis was reinforced.

The fifth stage culminated in the birth of cells and multicellular organisms. Advanced cells were the outcome of a symbiosis between primitive microorganismmicroorganisms (algae and bacteria) and hosts that provided them with protection and that they, in turn, provided with the means of energy production and locomotion. Symbionomic evolution continued with an important innovation, the integration of individual cells into multicellular organisms containing thousands, then billions, of individual cells with different but complementary functions.

Surprisingly, the birth of the cybiont retraces the major stages in the origin of life. Self-preservation, autocatalysis, metabolism of energy, coding of information, self-regulation, communications networks, and socialization through the construction of higher-level entities are the basic stages of symbionomic evolution. Thus, we find certain features of the origin of life in the more familiar context of civilization.

First, the progressive complexification of living systems takes place through the recombination of basic building blocks, as in the transition from unicellular to multicellular life. This is equally true in human societies: individuals gather together to form organizations (teams, workshops, businesses, and conglomerates; or families, tribes, communities, societies, and nations).

Second, early forms of life experienced a major crisis comparable to the energy crisis now threatening human beings, who are wasting fossil fuels at an ever-increasing rate. The first microorganism-microorganisms fed on energy-rich substances synthesized very slowly in the upper atmosphere. During their development in the primeval oceans, they consumed increasing amounts of these substances, endangering their future supply and thus their survival. Photosynthesis provided the solution to the crisis. Other types of microorganismmicroorganisms developed the ability to convert light directly into food, releasing large amounts of oxygen. This made respiration possible and created new conditions—the more efficient release of energy and the investment of this energy "capital" in the great enterprise of biological evolution.

Finally, the presence of living things radically changed the composition of the atmosphere, gradually supplementing its original components of methane, hydrogen, and ammonia with oxygen (through photosynthesis) and carbon dioxide (through respiration). This transformed the conditions of life and led to more efficient regulation of the temperature of the Earth. Similarly, human societies today are engaged in a major process of modification of the conditions of their environment and of the climate of the planet.

Like microorganismmicroorganisms and the first cells in coevolution with their ecosystems, the human species is now coevolving with the biosphere and the ecosphere, its "natural" environments, and with the technosphere, the "artificial" environment it has created, an environment of machines and organizations.

THE EMERGENCE OF THE VITAL FUNCTIONS OF THE CYBIONT: A COEVOLUTIONARY PROCESS

Coevolution is one of the great laws of symbionomic evolution, the process by which matter organizes itself in increasingly complex structures and functions, from atoms to molecules, to cells, organisms, populations, societies, and ecosystems. Symbionomic evolution encompasses the prebiological evolution that gave rise to life, the Darwinian evolution of living species, and the evolution of societies and environments. It involves a multitude of coevolutionary processes that continually adjust to each other through the subtle interplay of regulation, selection, exclusion, stabilization, and amplification. Characteristic of biological evolution, these processes are reinforced and expand out to the scale of human societies and the planet as a whole.

The principle of coevolution has been widely used to describe and analyze both biological evolution and the evolution of businesses. Eyes, fins, and wings formed in different species through coevolution. The mutual adjustments of plants and insects in their reproductive methods and defense mechanisms arose through mutually reinforcing, overlapping coevolutionary processes.

Human beings today are engaged in a process of coevolution with animals, plants, and the environment in the broad sense, but also with the machines, systems, and networks they have created in order to survive, grow, and develop. The boundary separating the natural and the artificial is becoming increasingly blurred. The tools, machines, and manufactured objects that populate the human environment are like a kind of externalized biological tissue or like prostheses extending the activity of our senses and brains; they are an integral part of our socioeconomic and even cultural evolution. Data processing machines will become increasingly intelligent, but living things will undergo major biological modifications through biotechnology as well. Many biological functions will be able to be duplicated by machines, and, in turn, some machines will acquire quasi-biological characteristics. An evolutionary convergence is occurring: technology is invading the biological world, and biology is invading the world of machines. New research and development in biology, information science, robotics, nanotechnology, artificial life, neural networks, virtual reality, and global communications networks will pose formidable challenges to our conception of the world as being dominated by human beings and exploitable for their benefit. The boundaries between natural and artificial, real and virtual, material and immaterial will gradually become blurred. The fundamental difference between artificial nature and *natural artifice* will no longer exist.

The coevolution of a society and its environment, with each determining the other, adds a new dimension in space and time. As we have seen in the case of social insects, in which complex behaviors are not preprogrammed or precoded, agents with limited intelligence use their immediate environment as memory and model. This malleable model, which changes over time by adapting to new conditions, functions as a reference system and planning mechanism for the community as a whole. Of course, the laws at work in the anthill or the beehive cannot be transposed directly to humans. Free will and the human capacity for rationality and irrationality introduce degrees of freedom that radically change the data. A similar phenomenon exists in the birth, growth, and development of a city; the city is both a *means of support* and a *consequence* of the activity of the collective organism that lives in it, builds it, and maintains its structure. Similarly, a coral reef is the means of support and the consequence of the coevolution of a photosynthetic alga and a marine protozoan. Of course, human beings attain higher dimensions of evolution through their creativity, their inventions, their conflicts, their aspirations, and their rationality. But the nature of the process is the same: a social macroorganism coevolving with its environment, including the artifacts the macroorganism creates to adapt to and transform the environment.

Another example of coevolution is language. Human language does not evolve in isolation, word by word and phrase by phrase, in a vacuum. It coevolves in a rich context of sounds, music, and images, but also of input and output organs. Language is a kind of sense that processes information and extracts its meanings. It becomes increasingly complex in an environment of communicating brains and is subject, like living organisms, to the laws of natural selection and competitive exclusion. Language coevolves with the human senses and the tools humans use to process information and communicate.

Culture and technology, too, coevolve in human society. Since the coevolution of the cortex and flint gave rise to technological culture, the creative relationship between speech and tools has been extended to pen, ink, and paper, and then to mouse, pixels, and computer screen. The coevolutionary environment is both memory and model, as it is for the colony of ants. This environment is cultural in the sense that it is both memory and a potential means for the transmission of information and behavior from generation to generation. The last part of this book will look at culture as a Lamarckian mechanism for the transmission of acquired characteristics.

Coevolution is leading toward a gradual emergence of the cybiont's vital functions. I propose to group the structures and functions of this still-primitive life-form into three broad interdependent areas: the control of energy, materials, and exchanges through industry and the economy; the bioecological manipulation of the environment through agriculture, biotechnology, and urbanization; and the conquest of information through writing, printing, the computer, and communications networks. Each one of these three areas (described here sequentially, but actually overlapping and simultaneous) involves the establishment of the great vital functions of maintenance and development—the "genetics," "physiology," and "neurology" of the cybiont. We find here, as in any form of life, the fundamental properties of self-replication, self-preservation, and self-regulation.

Self-replication takes place through the industrial mass production of the cybiont's components and the "enzymes" and "metabolites" necessary for its functioning (machines, manufactured goods).

Self-preservation is the basic function of its "metabolism," fuelled by solar energy domesticated through agriculture and by fossil and nuclear energy. Self-regulation is provided through communication and processing of information, essential components of the brain and "mind" of the cybiont.

These three vital functions also correspond to three fundamental revolutions carried out by humanity in the course of its evolution: the industrial revolution, with its symbol the automobile; the biological revolution, with the mastery of DNA; and the computer revolution, with the microprocessor.

THE INDUSTRIAL REVOLUTION: FROM COAL TO CARS

The conquest of energy to enable the survival of humanity began with the spread of agriculture. The collection of solar energy through the domestication of plants allowed human beings to produce enough food energy for their own survival and that of their animals—the animals serving as machines or capital, or as food income. Hunter-gatherers began to settle down, forming the first towns, and trading societies appeared in a primitive form. Agriculture is a way of collecting and storing dispersed renewable energy. At first, humans lived off the income from the Earth without touching its capital. The machines that coevolved with humanity used renewable natural resources: falling water, gravity, wind, and fire.

With the discovery and large-scale exploitation of fossil fuels such as coal and petroleum, the development of societies accelerated. The industrial revolution of the eighteenth century was the outcome of power looms and steam engines. Humans used concentrated energy in the form of nonrenewable resources: Earth capital. The "bonus" energy released was invested in the enormous enterprise of industrialization, the production of an extraordinary variety of goods and services, and, above all, a means of transportation—trains, boats, cars, and planes.

With the invention of the assembly line, megamachines developed the ability to reproduce. Until then, assembly of the myriad parts for a car required bringing together a great many skills in one place, and it was impossible to alter the speed of production or to adapt it to external conditions. In the assembly line, each worker carries out the same specific task in continual succession; the workers are like enzymes integrated into an organism much larger than themselves. As the inherent danger became evident, many began to protest against the megamachine that was devouring their lives; witness Charlie Chaplin's brilliant film *Modern Times*.

But machines coevolve with humanity. There is a continuum between the "natural" and the "artificial," not an absolute boundary. When James Watt and Matthew Boulton invented the centrifugal governor, they introduced intelligence into machines; this was the beginning of cybernetics and automation. The first steam engines, in 1785, used a flywheel to regulate the speed. To keep the engine from racing too fast, children were used to increase and decrease the steam supply. With their eyes on the wheel and their hands on the valve, they served as flesh prostheses in a steel monster. The centrifugal governor (the word *governor* has the same root as *cybernetic*) introduced negative feedback, enabling the machine to regulate itself. When it sped up, balls sliding on a spindle moved apart, opening a valve that allowed steam to escape so that the machine slowed down. The balls then moved closer together, closing the valve, and the pressure went back up to make the machine speed up again.

The car provides the perfect illustration of the coevolution between humans and their machines. The global system introduced as a result of the car has profoundly influenced and made dependent the lives of people and nations. With gasoline, highways, jobs in the automotive industry, accidents, oil wars, pollution, tourism, restaurants, maps and guides, and so forth, the automobile has a substantial impact on every country's economy and policies. The private automobile is the source of both pleasure and mortality. From the general perspective of evolution, the appearance of the car is analogous to the self-selection of a new living species. Of course, a car is made of steel, aluminum, plastic, fabric, and electronic components, but does that mean it is simply an artificial object that has nothing to do with evolution? The boundaries are becoming blurred. In terms of coevolution, the car—like many of the machines invented and manufactured by human beings—possesses the characteristics of a new living species. The car "reproduces," "feeds," and moves toward its destination. Its method of reproduction is complex; it is produced in a matrix, a kind of "uterus," called a factory, and its "DNA" is composed of engineers' plans, computer programs, assembly manuals, and various instructions. Its basic food is gasoline. Its brain is *removable*; it is the brain of the driver when he or she gets into the car and turns the ignition key. Do human beings and their cars live in symbiosis, and if so, what is the symbiotic benefit for the car? The car is fed, maintained, tested, used throughout its life, and made part of the life of a family or a business. But we cannot really speak of this as biological symbiosis. It is, rather, a metabiological symbiosis, part of a greater whole in which the traditional boundary between the natural and the artificial is abolished.

In a way, the car has subjugated humanity. In a single century, the automobile population has gone from a few dozen to more than 500 million, and in 2010 it will reach a billion. From the point of view of Darwinian evolution, the natural selection of the car as a species may be considered a remarkable success. The car has hyperdiversified into recreational vehicles, trucks, buses, bulldozers, tanker trucks, 4 × 4s, amphibious vehicles, tanks. The automobile species has "succeeded" in maintaining humans in a state of dependence, determining their holidays, their recreational activities, how they live in their cities, and how they have modified the landscape through highways.

Through positive feedback and a sector lock-in, the car has become one of the dominant species of the technosphere. It is the ideal machine—flexible, adaptable, a tool for the conquest of space and freedom—but it is also indisputably harmful to the environment. The price we pay is very high. The annual global count of road deaths is 350,000, a veritable public health epidemic. Cars produce 14 percent of the carbon dioxide pollution in the world, and they consume one third of the world's petroleum, increasing the risks of oil spills and oil wars. The manufacture of a car (one is born every second) requires large amounts of raw materials and a great deal of energy.

THE BIOLOGICAL REVOLUTION:
FROM THE FARM TO MASTERY OF DNA

The coevolution of humanity, the biosphere, and the ecosphere is embodied in agriculture and the landscape. Through the domestication of microbes, plants, and animals, humans have shaped their environment to produce food and to improve their lives, establishing the first functions of self-preservation. The manipulation of the environment was carried out using empirical biotechnology initially, and then rational biotechnology.

Biotechnology began with the making of wine, beer, and cheese using fermentation reactions involving yeasts. The oldest preservation techniques use bacteria that acidify the environment or conquer it (like the lactic acid bacteria of yogurt and cheese) and thus protect it from invasion by other bacteria.

The first farmers also domesticated the microbes in the soil in order to increase their crop yields. Nitrogen-fixing bacteria in the roots of leguminous plants enriched the soil, and crop rotation allowed the land to replenish itself. On the farm, natural biotechnologies based on the work of useful microbes are omnipresent, from the rumen of the cow to the fermentation of milk and alcoholic beverages. The hybridization of plants and the crossbreeding of animals to create new domestic species have given farmers extraordinary control over nature, enabling them to shape the landscape and to coevolve with their environment. Over the millennia a natural symbiosis has been established between human beings and their ecosystem. The farm is the most widespread symbiotic unit of human survival on Earth. Ranging enormously in size—like living organisms—farms use the income from the Earth rather than its capital. They are the main agents in the coevolution between the biosphere and the ecosphere, the shapers of the landscape and the ecosystem.

In barely 35 years, the rational biotechnologies that resulted from the discovery of DNA and the means of reprogramming it have expanded to the point where they are transforming the relationship between human beings, their environment, and biological evolution as a whole. New processes of coevolution are emerging between the biological world and the mechanical, and between the biological world and the electronic.

The biological revolution is overtaking the revolution in physics and chemistry that led to the creation of the machines and materials of the twentieth century. In 35 years, humanity's ability to manipulate life has advanced so far that biological knowledge is becoming planetary power. At the end of the nineteenth century, Louis Pasteur discovered the role of microbes in fermentation. The technology that developed out of his work made it possible for humans to protect themselves from dangerous microbes and to make better use of helpful microbes. Pasteur can be considered the father of biotechnology.

As they probed deeper and deeper into the structure of living things, from organs to tissues and then from tissues to cells, biologists came face to face with the ultimate entity of life. It took physicists, chemists, and biochemists working their way back "up" from molecular structures to the cell to create a meeting point between the world of biology and the world of physics. Molecular biology was born. Nearly a century after Pasteur, in the laboratories of the institute that bears his name, this very new discipline was brilliantly exemplified in the work of Monod, Jacob, and Lwoff on the molecular regulatory mechanisms of protein synthesis.

Then things speeded up. The work of molecular biologists and geneticists converged toward DNA, the universal language of the living world. In a few years, they learned to decipher its secret code and to "read" it using automatic machines, to "write" it using computer-controlled robots, and, most importantly, to reprogram it in order to modify the biological machinery of living things—first bacteria and then plant and animal cells. For the first time, humans have automated biological information processing. Through genetic engineering, they can play on the keyboard of life and compose new species or modify existing species, becoming genetic engineers, magicians of heredity, and sometimes, too, sorcerer's apprentices.

Extraordinary molecular tools and machines were developed: "scissor" enzymes to cut DNA, enzyme "glue" to recombine the pieces, devices to locate and isolate molecules, enzyme "copiers" to reproduce DNA, vector packaging to deliver genes into cells, genetic probes to search for a coded message within a gene bank, and even a tiny "cannon" to shoot invisible shells coated with DNA into cells.

With these tools, the bioindustry was born. More than a thousand companies, most of them in the United States, constitute a strategic international force in the pharmaceutical, chemical, energy, agri-food, and environmental sectors. Biotechnology and the bioindustry now extend to the deepest areas of human life, posing formidable ethical questions. I am thinking here, for example, of work being done on the decoding of human genes and the genetic ID card, medically assisted human reproduction, the cloning of embryos, and the use of fetal tissue for grafts. The high stakes in biology in the years to come will be the treatment of cancer and AIDS and the understanding of the mechanisms of aging and brain functioning.

This quick overview of modern biology shows that human beings, the new masters of biological evolution, have reached a point of no return. Biology, biotechnology, and bioindustry today constitute an expanding technological system that is coevolving like any ecosystem. There are huge numbers of interactions in a very dense network made up of ideas, people, technology, high-tech companies, and big pharmaceutical and agri-food firms. Innovations in one sector are immediately applied in others. Biotechnology must be viewed as a global system of exchanges, competition, alliances, and breakthroughs, a system that is developing at lightning speed, autocatalyzing through combinations of innovation and know-how, and acquiring ever-greater (sometimes frightening) powers.

Thanks to developments in biology and biotechnology and their convergence with computer technology, it has now become possible to design biomaterials, devices, relays, and amplifiers with which to create new interfaces between humans and machines. The current fusion of biology and computer technology heralds a new era of bioelectronics and *direct interfaces* between the human brain and information processing machines, a crucial step toward the birth of the cybiont.

THE INFORMATION REVOLUTION: FROM WRITING TO THE MICROPROCESSOR

Another revolution began with the coding of human thought in writing: the information revolution. The industrialization of writing through the invention of printing, in the fifteenth century, led to the spread of communication by signs and symbols and made the accumulated knowledge of humanity widely accessible. The next development was the ability to process information electronically, which allowed the "memory" of books to be supplemented by that of computers and made it possible electronically to process nonverbal codes of communication such as sounds and images.

The rate of change has accelerated. Writing was invented by the Sumerians approximately 5000 years ago; printing and the book are 500 years old. The electronic storage and processing of human communication in text, images, and sounds goes back approximately 50 years. As for digitization—the translation of data into a universal language in which all types of information can be processed—its first commercial applications are barely 10 years old.

Unlike energy-based societies, information-based societies are decentralized, reticulate, and organized in autonomous modules. They are made up of infostructures that convey immaterial signs, the most widely known of which is the information highway. Just as the concrete highway and the car symbolize the industrial revolution, their extensions, the electronic highway and the personal computer, symbolize the dematerialized society that has arisen as a result of the computer revolution. Whereas the highway and the car are the means for going from one point to another, the information highway and the personal computer have abolished time and space. They provide a gateway to cyberspace, the contracted space-time of the planetary brain.

The results of the mechanical revolution and the biological revolution will be integrated with those of the current process of co-evolution—the fastest and most far-reaching—between the computer and communications technology, which is often called the *digital revolution*. This marriage of the technosphere and the noosphere already involves—and will involve to an even greater extent—not only computer technology but all human communications media. The "engines" of modern computers (microprocessors), multimedia, and world telematics networks are the catalysts of an explosive development of digital civilization.

The microprocessor was created in 1971 by researchers at Intel, a manufacturer of electronic components. Few human inventions have had such a profound impact on humanity. It has destabilized companies, dethroned business leaders, and imperiled the survival of 50,000 companies around the world. It has sent a shock wave through the entire economy. Microprocessors are everywhere—in telephones, televisions, VCRs, and, of course, portable computers, as well as video cameras, watches, calculators, video games, laser printers, CD players, anti-skid braking systems, and electronic fuel injection systems. There are now 64-bit microprocessors that sell for about $1500; only a few square millimeters in size, they are as powerful as the Cray-1, a supercomputer the size of a closet that was introduced in 1976 at a cost of $8 million. Powered by a calculator battery, they operate at an average of 150 million cycles per second—twice as fast as previous microprocessors—and can process up to a billion bits of data per second. The latest from Intel is the Pentium III with 9,500,000 transistors and a speed that reaches 600 MHz.

According to Moore's law (formulated 35 years ago by Intel president Gordon Moore), chips are reduced in size by 10 percent a year, and every 3 years a new generation of chips is launched with four times the number of transistors and four times as much memory capacity as the previous generation, while their price declines steadily. Memory capacity has gone from 1 million bits (30 pages of text) in 1985 to 16 million bits (500 pages); in 2005, it will reach 4 billion bits (the equivalent of two complete 20-volume encyclopedias), and in 2011, it will reach 64 billion bits (the equivalent of 27 encyclopedias).

The computing power available at a given price has been doubling every year for more than 30 years. There were 2 million computers in the world in 1980, most of them large office computers. In 1993, there were 150 million personal microcomputers based on powerful microprocessors. The number will reach a billion just after the year 2000. Compare this with the number of automobiles in the world, which is expected to reach the billion mark in 2010. But it took the car a century to become widely accessible; the computer has only been in existence for about 25 years. A microprocessor is like a primitive neuron. Its reproduction, like that of the car, takes place in factories. It is based on plans contained in photomasks (its "DNA"); using a technique similar to printing, the fine structures and lines linking the transistors are engraved on silicon to create electronic circuits. As with the car, the boundaries between natural and artificial have become blurred.

Another factor in the acceleration of the coevolution between humans and information-processing machines is the hybridization of technologies. Several technological streams may converge in one device. For example, with the digitization of information, a single machine may serve as fax, laser printer, photocopier, answering machine, scanner, and computer; the reading system of the scanner is used by the fax, the laser printing system by the printer and the photocopier, and the modem by the telephone. The fusion of computers, television, and telecommunications will give rise to hybrid systems in accelerated coevolution: portable notepad microcomputers that include fax machine, television, cellular telephone, videophone, and intelligent telephone with screen (smart phone or Intelliphone); or a computer television connected to a telephone, the future on-ramp to the electronic highways of cyberspace.

MEDIAMORPHOSIS: FROM MULTIMEDIA TO UNIMEDIA

The rise of multimedia, electronic highways, interactive television, and computerized planetary communications networks marks a profound revolution in the image, which I call *mediamorphosis*. Mediamorphosis is the most significant sign of the emergence of the vital functions of the cybiont. We are both witnessing and participating in the construction "from within" of the planetary nervous system and brain of the social macroorganism. Mediamorphosis possesses all the characteristics of the chaotic processes that generate organization: autocatalysis, self-selection, and temporal and spatial closure of a hybrid technological system in coevolution with its environment. Multiple agents acting in parallel create niches for technological and industrial expansion, high value-added economic pockets that, in turn, amplify the development and growth of the technological system that gave rise to them. Positive feedback loops are established. New properties emerge. Chaos, order, and complexity play their now-familiar roles for humans who are their observers and agents.

This evolution is invisible if the new technologies and communications tools—portable microcomputers, cellular telephones, interactive CDs, and digital networks—are considered separately. We usually focus on their adaptive qualities or on how fast the market for them is opening up. This traditional approach to the future is linear, analytical, and sequential. We should instead view communications systems globally and look for the principles of self-organization, self-selection, and emergence. The same law observed in an insect society, or in any complex system made up of a dense network of interactions, is at work: the application of simple rules by a multitude of agents acting in parallel leads to the self-organization of a complex system and the emergence of unpredictable properties. This law is equally valid for the networks that connect human brains, computers, and telecommunications.

The media explosion that has transformed our capacity to receive, store, process, and disseminate information has come about through digitization and data compression. Digitization makes it possible to process information (such as sound, image, text, or software) using a single universal language, a kind of Esperanto for communications machines—the equivalent of the universal coding of information in DNA on the basis of the four chemical letters of the genetic code. In its analog form, an item of information (such as a sound wave moving through the air, an electromagnetic wave, or an electrical signal) has a physical magnitude that varies continuously over time. Digitization consists of breaking down this magnitude into small fractions and measuring their values at regular intervals (40,000 times a second for music on a CD), and then quantifying these values by assigning them binary codes, numbers made up of 0s and 1s ("bits" of information). The digitized signal is a stream of bits, stored on a laser disk or grouped in packets and transmitted on telecommunications networks, that can be processed by any computer.

Before digitization, the various media were incompatible—paper for text, chemical film for photographs or movies, magnetic tape for sound and video. The transmission of digitized information is independent of the means of transmission (telephone lines, radio waves, television satellite, cable). Its quality remains perfect, unlike that of analog signals, which degrade easily, and its storage is cheaper.

The digitization and circulation of information in networks is analogous to the introduction of currency into the networks of the economy. Before the introduction of currency, goods or services were bought and sold by barter, which made exchanges slow and limited them considerably. By creating additional space for expansion and by shrinking time and space, the introduction of currency led to explosive growth in the world economy.

A complementary development—whose consequences are incalculable—is data compression, which makes it possible for much larger amounts of information to circulate on existing networks such as telephone lines and cable. This may be illustrated by a whimsical comparison: to increase the volume of traffic on the current subway system without costly investments such as building bigger cars or digging new tunnels, imagine that it were possible to reduce the size of the travelers by 90 percent at the entrance and restore them to normal size at the exit.

What makes compression possible is the fact that signals contain a great deal of useless or redundant information such as blank spaces in a text, silences in a conversation, or the unchanging parts in a sequence of video images. Compressing a sequence of images of a person speaking at a microphone, for example, involves taking into account that the background is practically unchanging, the microphone remains stationary, and the speaker's body hardly moves while the hands and mouth move a lot. These various levels of information are sampled, processed with powerful compression algorithms, and transmitted as streams of digital data. At the receiving end, decompression software restores the images, sequences, and sounds.

The compression ratios of the various standard techniques can exceed 100, but even more powerful technologies, such as holographic compression and fractal compression, are coming onto the market. With the latter, a single CD-ROM can contain a 28-volume encyclopedia and 6000 color photographs. Fractal compression is based on the same principle as fractal images, the repetition ad infinitum of the same pattern, whatever the level of observation. The advantage it offers is economy of description; to store aerial photographs of 10 cities, it is sufficient to describe and store all their common characteristics (such as the shapes and colors of roofs, streets, parks, etc.) just once to be able to reconstruct all the images.

A digital videodisk, or DVD, can store even more images. A DVD is very similar to a CD but has a much larger data capacity (about 4.7 billion bytes, or approximately 7.5 times more data than a CD). This gives a DVD enough capacity to store compressed movies—up to 133 minutes of high-resolution video with subtitles in up to 32 languages!

The most significant aspect of this evolution today is the rise of multimedia out of the convergence of traditional media. Thus, a single digital sector combines the four main types of human communication: writing (newspapers, magazines, books), audiovisual media (television, video, movies), telecommunications (telephone, satellites, cable), and informatics (computers and software) (see the figure below).

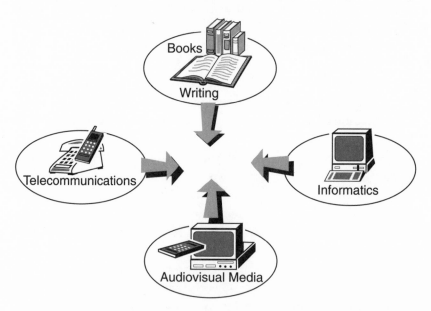

Rather than multimedia, which involves a juxtaposition of media, I prefer to call this sector *unimedia*, as did Nicolas Negroponte. Unimedia is a new language of communication for the next millennium, and multimedia is the means (see the figure on page 53).

The diagram, borrowed from the traditional one proposed by Negroponte, shows the combinations of various media that are al-

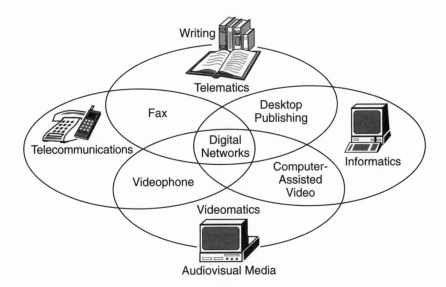

ready well under way. For example, writing and the telephone have given us the fax machine; the telephone and audiovisual media, the videophone; writing, telecommunications, and the computer, telematics, and the Internet; writing and the computer, desktop publishing. Thanks to the increasing ease of manipulation of digital video, we are already seeing applications in this area. Telecommunications, audiovisual media, and computers have created *videomatics*, the equivalent for images of telematics for text; videomatic networks can carry images, graphics, and animation, and not just text and figures.

Interactive multimedia television is based on powerful video-servers with parallel processors, which can serve hundreds of thousands of users simultaneously. Users will have set-top boxes and navigation tools that will allow them to interact from home with immense image banks.

The technical fusion of sectors brings with it industrial and economic fusions, which we hear about in the media every day: acquisitions, buy-outs, takeovers, and mergers between cable operators, telecommunications companies, producers of images, film studios, television networks, publishers, makers of video games, and software companies. The size of the investments required in unimedia is another reason for these fusions. The distribution of interactive video, sound, texts, and software to millions of users will require powerful communications vectors—the electronic highways of the future. These high-capacity information channels will carry exchanges at speeds ranging from 128,000 (the ISDN network) to more than 156 million bits per second [broadband ATM (asynchronous transfer mode) network], making it possible to send 2000 copies of a large volume in 1 second. Information circulating at such speeds must take an access ramp, a highway, a road, and then a lane to arrive at a personal computer through the telephone lines. All this requires chips capable of decompressing the signal in real time. Compatibility and interconnectivity among the various networks will also be needed: switched telephone networks, cable networks, fiber optics, hertzian transmissions, satellites. These technical requirements explain the high level of investments needed to connect users to these electronic highways and the political nature of the large international projects involved.

As we enter a new century, we are witnessing a most amazing global contest for new spaces and new markets. At the core of the mediamorphosis is a planetary network that is in the process of self-selecting, and that will serve as an example and a guide: the Internet, the network of networks.

THE INTERNET: THE GENESIS OF A PLANETARY BRAIN

The Internet is a spontaneous, emergent, autocatalytic network in rapid coevolution with its human environment. It is chaotic, anarchic, and completely decentralized. No central administration governs it, nobody owns it, and no one can now stop its development! The explosive growth of the Internet was a major phenomenon of the end of the twentieth century. With this complex network we are entering a new space-time in which duration and distances are shorter, and we are seeing fundamental changes in political, economic, and industrial rules. I prefer to call this new environment "cyberspace-time" rather than "cyberspace." The Internet is not a new technology; it is an integrated resource-sharing system, an *infor-*

mational ecosystem made up of numerous interdependent elements (computers, modems, networks, software, access and content providers, and so on). As a gateway to cyberspace-time, the Internet is a kind of cooperative or society. Each participating organization takes care of the operation and maintenance of its computers, finances the communication lines that connect it, and cooperates technically with neighboring networks. Each participant has a local interest in having the overall system function to everyone's advantage. If a constituent network does not respect protocols and thus disrupts the neighboring networks, it can be disconnected from its neighbors. In addition, any organization that is already renting lines to public or private telecommunications services has an interest in allowing a portion of Internet traffic to circulate on its network. It thus increases the number of users that are able to access its services.

This network of networks is a true macrocomputer that today links more than 45 million host computers worldwide. More than 60 million were up and running at the end of 2000. There is no need to describe the many uses made of the Internet by scientists, students, politicians, journalists, industrial companies, e-commerce buyers, or stock market traders as they are described extensively and daily in numerous journals, magazines, books, or television programs. But the Internet explosion can be illustrated by a few key figures related to numbers of users, e-commerce, and the rate of growth.

Two-thirds of U.S. households will have Internet access by 2003, according to research by the Yankee Group. The report estimates that U.S. consumers will spend $56 billion on Internet access services over the next 5 years, growing at a rate of 21 percent per annum. It is estimated that 45 percent of U.S. households currently have a PC. Twenty-five percent of U.S. homes are estimated to have Net access, and this is expected to increase to one-third of all households by mid-2000.

In the year 2000, 170 million users worldwide will have online access. According to an estimate from Datamonitor, more than 300 million people will have Internet access by 2005. According to an IDC survey (July 1998), on the other hand, the online population will reach 320 million people in 2002, a compound annual growth rate of almost 50 percent for the 1997–2002 period. Europe will catch up with the United States and will account for approximately 26 percent of worldwide Internet users, with some 82 million people online in 2002 (more than 40 million in 2000) and a growth rate of more than 37 percent for the same period.

According to the same IDC study, in 2002, some 130 million e-consumers are expected worldwide (almost 60 million in 2000). This corresponds to a growth rate of almost 50 percent for the 1997–2002 period. Business-to-business commerce will grow from $43 billion in 1998 to $1.3 trillion in 2003, according to Forrester Research, while business-to-consumer commerce will grow from $8 billion to $108 billion during the same period. The Asian and South American user market will generate a substantial percentage of the overall growth by 2005, according to Datamonitor, catching up with the United States and Europe. However, with the global population expected to reach 6.1 billion by the beginning of the millennium, the total online population in 2005 will still account for less than 5 percent of the world's population.

It all started in 1968 with a network developed by the Defense Advanced Research Project Agency (DARPA) for the U.S. army. This network was designed to survive a nuclear war, and it had no identifiable nerve center. Its creator, Paul Baran, a researcher at the Rand Corporation, in 1964 had the idea for a chaotic system based on information packets circulating in networks. The dynamic rerouting of these packets in case of obstruction or breakdown meant that even if one or more nerve centers were destroyed, the information packets would find their way to the recipient. The world protocol for segmenting, addressing, and rerouting the packets is called *transmission control protocol and internet protocol* (TCP/IP); it is the basic language of network communication that allows all computers, big and small, anywhere in the world, to understand each other.

The combination of two simple ideas set off the autocatalytic process or virtuous circle that led to the creation of the Internet as a new living network with emergent properties. These two ideas were hypertext and the distribution of information through networks, and they were already being applied separately. Information was being distributed in the scientific world by means of interconnected servers, but there was no practical means of navigating from one server to another while remaining "within" the documents being worked on. In another field, software developers at Apple were independently developing hypertexts that could easily be used by the general public. These presented information in the form of stacks of cards, with pointers; you had only to click on a card to see related information. It was the combination of information servers connected in a worldwide web (the Web) and hypertext that served as the catalyst for the explosion of the Internet. Starting from a document on a server, a user can navigate from one text (and from one server) to another by clicking on the pointers—information crossroads that are interconnected ad infinitum.

The autocatalytic development of the Internet is a perfect illustration of a coevolutionary process of order emerging from chaos. Millions of agents acting in parallel according to simple rules form a gigantic multiprocessor that can collectively find solutions to complex problems and adapt to the evolution of its informational ecosystem.

The rules of the Internet may be summed up as follows:

▶ Everyone uses the same protocol, TCP/IP, the basic language of communication, making possible an infinite number of interconnections.
▶ Information circulates in standardized packets in a chaotic way, using any path available and making multiple detours.
▶ Users pay for their own links in the network.
▶ Each node in the network (a user and his or her computer) benefits from the operation of the whole network, and the whole network benefits from the creative contribution (software, protocols, information servers, etc.) of each node.

The application of these rules leads to three emergent properties: interconnectivity, intercommutability, and intercreativity.

Interconnectivity means that any kind of network can be connected to another (copper wires, television cable, fiber optics, hertzian grids, etc.). The modern browser is a platform equipped with many programs and "plug-ins," allowing different types of multimedia information to converge on the user's screen.

Intercommutability is an extraordinary and generally overlooked development in human communications. Information switching has conventionally been accomplished using two main types of organization: the post office and telecommunications companies. Here, users are not directly responsible for rerouting their letters or phone connections. With the Internet, on the other hand, users can switch or commute information coming into their Web site to another site simply by creating a dynamic hypertext link pointing to the new address. The combinations created by this process are infinite, increasing the complexity of the network and the density of interrelations between individuals and groups.

Intercreativity is a step beyond basic computer interactivity. Users are not only connected *to* the Internet, they are interconnected *through* the Internet. This means that the system is transparent; it interconnects brains through computers and network links. The content created by a person can be transformed and shared by many. This is the basis of the intercreativity process.

As a result of these rules and emergent properties, the Internet has become an increasingly intelligent planetary metacomputer. It processes data in parallel, combining the actions of millions of agents testing procedures and programs in real time in a competitive environment—a process that is not unlike Darwinian biological evolution. We can therefore expect the Internet to select increasingly powerful solutions in electronic communications and software applications. And this is only the beginning. The system is still in its prehistory. The user-friendliness of the interfaces is sometimes still limited. The complicated "configuration" procedures are reminiscent of computers in the era of programming, and the operating instructions sometimes read like engineering manuals. But everything is changing very quickly, with applications such as search engines, intelligent agents, Web TV, interactive video, MP3 music (an easy-to-download compressed form of music), Web cams ("video eyes" looking everywhere in real time), Internet radio, Internet phone, and virtual shopping malls. Behind these names lies the reality of the Internet today, and part of its future. Users are able to interact with servers to create and publish information, and not only to consult it. They can telemanipulate instruments and devices and enter and perform actions in virtual spaces. Intelligent agents and computer programs that can help navigate the information hyperspace are already on the horizon. These virtual intellectual assistants—personalized, with recognizable faces, and capable of speech—can guide our steps through the infinite possibilities and complexities of the new terra incognita of cyberspace-time.

With the Internet we are also seeing the emergence of a new form of economy, in which agents are paid in *information* rather than in currency. In the traditional economic system, invested capital yields interest, which pays for the use of the capital, and work (energy or information) is remunerated by wages (in money). In the information ecosystem of the Internet, both capital *and interest* are information. Many researchers who contribute to the Internet by creating new software, protocols, or procedures make their creations freely available without monetary remuneration. They are paid, in turn, with higher value-added information.

The fast electronic highways that are being created will make it easier to transmit interactive images and sounds. They will be able to connect with cable and interactive television networks as well as with low Earth-orbiting satellite systems. But some users are already contrasting the pleasant country roads of the Internet, which are essentially free, with these commercial electronic toll highways. Obviously, the Internet is not the only worldwide network of intercomputer communications; there are financial, banking, industrial, commercial, administrative, research, and military networks. But the Internet is the only network that is democratically open to everyone. It is unplanned, and there are no standards or norms imposed by politicians on the advice of technocrats. Will the Internet be able to handle the extraordinary increase in traffic the future will bring? It is a victim of its own success, already plagued by congestion, virtual crowds, "spam" e-mail, swindlers, vandals, sexual predators, and pirates. In numbers, the international virtual community of the Internet represents a new nation, a nation of cyberspace-time, and some pioneers of the Net are seriously considering asking the UN for recognition.

The interconnected backbone networks and communities of the Internet create the physical basis for a planetary "nervous system." It is now possible to visualize this incredible mesh of interconnected networks thanks to a method, process, and technology called *Internet tomography*, somewhat analogous to medical "catscanners."* To gain insights into Internet traffic and workloads, the Cooperative Association for Internet Data Analysis (CAIDA), based at the University of California's San Diego Supercomputer Center, is developing such tools to collect, analyze, and visualize data on connectivity and performance of the Internet. The principal tool used by CAIDA is called *skitter*. It depicts global Internet topology and measures the performance of specific paths through the Internet. Skitter sends out packets of data from a source to many destinations through the Internet and analyzes the feedback. In this way, amazing maps of Internet topology are created. They look like dendritic maps of neurons in the brain. Dendrites are complex ramifications of the "wires" that interconnect neurons. They are involved with neural stimuli and response. Such a dendritic visualization of the Internet sheds light on its macrobiological nature and the evolutionary process leading to a brainlike global infrastructure.

TOWARD SYNTHETIC LIFE?

While the creative coevolution of humanity, the biosphere, the technosphere, and the ecosphere continues, a new space is opening up. It involves the creation of new forms of life, a surprising and daring stage in the evolution of life on Earth and a necessary condition for the emergence of planetary macrolife.

Life is difficult to define. André Lwoff has humorously defined it as "all phenomena that resist death." We can, however, try to characterize living things in terms of certain basic functions:† self-preservation—the capacity of organisms to maintain life through assimilation, nutrition, and the energy reactions of fermentation and respiration; self-replication—the ability to propagate life; self-regulation—the coordination, synchronization, and control of over-

---

* K.C. Claffy, Tracie Monk, and Daniel McRobb, "Internet Tomography," *Nature Web Matters*, January 7, 1999.
† See Joël de Rosnay, *L'Aventure du vivant*, Paris: Seuil, 1988.

all reactions. To these three properties may be added the capacity to evolve.

However, systems that may at first glance appear not to be alive share some of the properties of life. A crystal replicates itself, creating entities identical to itself. A computer virus makes copies of its own program, grows, develops, and evolves in electronic networks and computer memory. The code sequences of genetic algorithms mutate, self-select, and increase their population. Of course, the last two examples are human creations. They cannot metabolize energy and they only "live" inside computers. But how long will this be the case?

A new approach to life views it as a continuum without a clear boundary between complex matter and rudimentary life. From this perspective, looking at complex interlocking systems made up of multiple elements in interaction, we may see life as an emergent property resulting from the complexity of these interactions. Life is not contained *in* the molecules, but emerges from the *sum* of the interactions and the dynamics of the system.

By helping to discover the planets and the universal laws of gravity, the telescope led us to give up geocentrism. By showing the universality of biological evolution in the living world, from bacteria to human beings, the microscope freed us from our anthropocentrism. By abolishing the boundaries between natural and artificial, inanimate and animate, the macroscope-computer will enable us to move beyond our biocentrism. The computer considerably broadens the realm of the "living" by bringing to "life" through simulation complex systems that can reproduce, maintain themselves, self-regulate, and evolve. Life as we know it is augmented by life as it could be. We are the representatives of one complex form of life out of many possible forms of life. By making complexity intelligible and by allowing us to carry out computer experiments, the macroscope-computer is the catalyst that makes the synthesis of new forms of life possible. Rather than trying to understand life by breaking it down into increasingly simple elements, we can, with the help of the computer, build real or simulated systems with the qualities of living things. The validity of the hypotheses that gave rise to them can be tested in their environments.

Using this approach, humans are creating forms of life that are "artificial" (because they are humanly created) but that can reproduce and evolve into structures and functions very far from the original forms. To study this new relationship between human beings and their creatures, a new discipline has been created—artificial life (or AL). I suggest it be called *neobiology*, and that it be defined as the study of biomimetic organisms, systems, and networks created by human beings as objects or computer simulations.

The birth of neobiology officially occurred on September 21, 1987, in Los Alamos, New Mexico, a center of early work on the atomic bomb. Led by Christopher G. Langton, one of the fathers of this new discipline, researchers from very diverse sectors (biology, chemistry, physics, robotics, computer science, ecology, and anthropology) exchanged the results of their work in the first interdisciplinary seminar on the synthesis and simulation of living systems. Since then there have been other meetings, with larger numbers of participants, in the United States and Europe, including one at the Cité des Sciences et de l'Industrie in 1991 and one at the Université Libre de Bruxelles in 1993.

Neobiology is a multidisciplinary field bringing together areas such as the simulation of complex systems (animal or human societies), the creation of forms resembling life-forms, and the construction of robots. I will illustrate this by discussing three representative areas: the origin of life, digital evolution, and robotics.

BIOLOGICAL EVOLUTION ON THE COMPUTER

Research on the origin of life is part of the general research on the processes of self-organization of complex systems. One property has been of particular interest to researchers: autocatalysis. Molecules that can catalyze their own formation replicate themselves, a process similar to biological reproduction. Combining computer simulation and laboratory synthesis, researchers are studying the generation of complex systems, cycles, loops, and molecular networks capable of self-preservation. Some of the most outstanding work in this field has been done by Stuart Kauffman and Steen Rasmussen at the Santa Fe Institute.

One of the most fascinating areas of neobiology is that of digital evolution, which involves allowing competing populations in computer programs to evolve spontaneously to find the best solution to a given problem. This principle was originated in 1975 by John Holland of the University of Michigan and the Santa Fe Institute, and he called these programs *genetic algorithms*. Today there are many research applications of this kind of programming as well as industrial applications in areas ranging from aeronautics to the environment, from microelectronics to high finance. Digital evolution is based on sequences of programs (codes analogous to DNA chains) that can branch out and graft onto each other. Like computer viruses and DNA, these sequences can duplicate, segment, and recombine themselves. A first generation of sequences is created, and the sequences tested for their capacity (still weak) to solve given problems. The program isolates the "fittest" forms and has them self-replicate and mutate by recombining sequences among themselves. This results in a second generation of programs to which the same process is applied—testing, selection, reproduction, mutation. In thousands of generations at computer speed, the most successful sequences are thus reinforced, generation after generation. The new "species" of programs converge toward the resolution of the problem. This is the selection of the fittest through competition among populations—Darwinian evolution in the land of bits and codes.

The discovery of the conceptual simplicity and effectiveness of genetic algorithms led biologists and chemists to apply the same principles to the selection of biological molecules for pharmaceutical use. The synthesis of molecules through evolution in a test tube is a new field of biotechnology, and one that is developing rapidly. Many companies around the world are already competing for patents and commercial products based on these techniques. The process starts with the (automatic) synthesis of populations of hundreds of billions of DNA or RNA molecules, based on the same pattern but each slightly different. The molecules that are best able to bind with a protein involved in blood clotting, for example, are selected. This binding inhibits the normal functioning of the protein, and thus it can lead to a drug that dissolves blood clots. A first generation of molecules is selected. Through an enzyme that duplicates

DNA, this population is reproduced, and mutations are encouraged. This process is repeated dozens of times, generation after generation, at the speed of molecular reactions (10 generations in less than 20 days). A small number of molecules that have a very strong affinity with protein is isolated, and could thus serve as the basis for new drugs. It would take years to obtain this result using traditional techniques.

The principles of molecular evolution in the test tube are the same as those of the genetic algorithms of computers: a very large population of evolving species, reproduction, mutations, selection, and amplification. Analogous mechanisms underlie the Darwinian biological evolution that gave rise to all living species on Earth. Biological evolution is thus like a multiprocessor operating in parallel with billions of organisms, each one representing a particular program in competition with others for its survival.

The extremely slow process of evolution, which takes place over billions of years and requires the testing of each organism's ability to survive, is speeded up enormously in technological evolution (with a human invention being considered the equivalent of a mutation). With the computer, the biological or technological cycles of mutation-invention and selection-amplification are speeded up so much that generations of birth, reproduction, survival, and transmission—expressed in terms of millions and millions of instructions per second—take place in a few minutes.

Computer viruses are also products of "biological" evolution on the computer. Are these strange parasites alive? A computer virus is a pirate program written by an ill-intentioned programmer. Once introduced into the control system of a computer, the virus remains there in a dormant state until it is awakened by a special code such as a key word or a date; it then reproduces, erases programs or files, infects other computers, and finally self-destructs without leaving a trace. Viruses come from everywhere—diskettes, telematic communications, or networks like the Internet. Some are extremely virulent; others just display humorous messages. There are various means of protection against viruses. Users can try to deny them access by means of access cards, codes, or disk protection programs; these techniques are analogous to sterilization and other means of disease prevention. There are diagnostic and disinfection kits and "vaccines" for computers, and computer scientists at IBM have developed powerful defenses that can immunize whole networks and that are based on the immune mechanisms of biological organisms.

The study of self-replicating programs is illuminating in many ways. The relationship with biology goes far beyond the vocabulary alone—*vaccine, immunization, infection, disinfection, epidemic, mutations, colonization.* Many researchers consider viruses to have lives of their own in the silicon of microprocessors and telecommunications networks. Just as biological viruses infect cells and divert their biological machinery and metabolism for their own benefit, computer viruses need the environment and metabolism of the computer to reproduce. They are *infoparasites*. The British astrophysicist Stephen Hawking considers computer viruses to be alive. They are the beginning of humanly created artificial life. A group of American researchers, including Thomas Ray of the University of Delaware, one of the inventors of computer viruses, released a population of attenuated viruses on the Internet in order to study their evolutionary behavior in an information ecosystem. We can only hope that they will not produce uncontrollable mutants that could devastate entire continents of the computer world!

SWARMS OF ROBOT INSECTS

Approaching robotics by way of artificial life is very promising. The traditional approach, that of artificial intelligence, consists of modeling perception, representing the world in terms of modules, planning, and prediction. A robot has to perform tasks sequentially, in series of modules designed to process information. The application of artificial intelligence requires extensive knowledge of natural intelligence. The capacity for abstraction, the use of symbols, emotions, and values have a profound impact on intelligent human behavior, and they are not easily transferable to the world of computers. This is why in recent years groups of researchers have tried to start from a different basis. Their model is no longer the intelligence of the human brain, but rather the rudimentary intelligence of relatively simple living beings that are capable of interacting with their environment and surviving in it by means of remarkable strategies of adaptation and conquest—small organisms, such as flies, ants, earthworms, and beetles, equipped with receptors and effectors that enable them to detect and collect essential information and to perform specific actions. In neobiology it is possible to copy these simplest of intelligent forms and then to move back "up" to more advanced behaviors.

The goal of the neobiological approach as applied to robotics is to build intelligent control systems in which many individual modules each generate *part* of the overall behavior. Using such an approach, Rodney Brooks and his team at MIT have built minirobots that resemble insects and that are able to move about in complex environments, to locate and follow—or avoid—living organisms, and to right themselves if they are overturned while trying to overcome an obstacle. Their programming is very different from that of robots with artificial intelligence. Their receptors and effectors, which are connected in modules and superimposed layers, give them great adaptability and allow them to learn from their environment. Brooks's minirobots are self-programming because they "live" in the world. They are situated. The functions of their modules are simple: to explore and manipulate the environment, to build charts and models, to move about, and to avoid obstacles. As Brooks has pointed out, a global airline reservation system is situated but not embodied—it reacts to all kinds of requests in real time, but it interacts with the world only through messages. A painting robot in the automobile industry is embodied but not situated—it has physical extensions (arm and sprayer) and responds to gravity, but it does not perceive the shapes and positions of objects; if a car is moved while it is working, the robot pursues its task, spraying paint into empty space. The insect robots at MIT are both embodied and situated. They are an integral part of their environment. Although they gather information with receptors that are not entirely reliable, they are able to display robust, effective behavior in an unpredictable, constantly changing environment. This is not unlike some of our own behavior, particularly in the management of complex systems.

One of the current objectives of the MIT team is to develop a humanoid robot, called Cog, that is able to learn and evolve using information in its environment and to self-program through its inter-actions with humans. Already, Cog has shown signs of a primitive intelligence similar to that of a baby a few weeks old. It is able to recognize human faces, tell if a person is looking at it, imitate head gestures, detect movements, and modify its behavior according to the responses of its interlocutors. Brooks believes that intelligent behavior could emerge from cooperation among several simple independent subsystems. New behaviors can be built progressively without redesigning the existing systems. Tests are made through Kismet, Cog's new companion, and results later incorporated into Cog. The robots will soon have a larger memory, synthetic voice communication, and a motivational system to make them happy, interested, or bored. By gradually increasing Cog's skills, Brooks hopes that one day a form of "intelligence" will emerge.

The field of humanoid and animal robotics is booming in Japan, most notably in the form of a friendly humanoid robot called Hadaly-2, at Tokyo's Waseda University, the Honda P-3, a 130-kilogram walking robot, at the Honda Laboratory, and a commercially available "robot pet," a dog called Aibo that can perform various tricks, like wagging its tail or sending back a ball, at the Sony computer sciences laboratory.

Neobiology is on the leading edge in helping us understand complex systems. Computer simulations of societies made up of very large numbers of organisms or individuals acting in parallel, such as the simulations of birds in organized flocks or of ants or bees, can help us better understand the behavior of animal or human societies. By solving thousands of nonlinear differential equations simultaneously, the computer makes it possible for us to understand the dynamics of complex systems and to derive simple, reproducible laws governing them. This is something that once seemed impossible.

A new vision is coming into being, that of a macrolife-form that includes our life-form without excluding others. Neobiology thus opens up new areas of knowledge focusing on different life-forms, those originally created by humans but that develop according to their own dynamics. A new kind of tissue, initially mechanical and now bioelectronic, is developing around humanity, linking it to a social macroorganism to which humanity is contributing in turn—

the connective, digestive, and nervous tissue of a huge planetary embryo that is gradually taking form before our very eyes.

Having created an extraordinary variety of artificial life-forms originally for their own benefit, humans are now witnessing the autonomous evolution of artificial life. No longer in full control, they have initiated a symbiotic relationship that encompasses them more fully, leading to the emergence of an organism with a higher level of complexity. Out of this relationship, through coevolution, symbiotic humanity is emerging.

Analogous to the basic functions of life, the great vital functions of the cybiont are gradually making themselves known: self-preservation through agriculture and the metabolism of energy, self-replication through industry and the economy, and self-regulation through computers and networks. Energy, information, economy, and ecology are the components of the new macrobiology, the discipline of the future that will be necessary for the rational conception and control of the life of the cybiont. Macrobiology is based on the symbiotic relationship between humans and this macroorganism, a relationship that will require new interfaces between the human brain and the planetary brain.

II

Toward Symbiotic Man

3

The Neurons of the Earth

A GREAT DISCOVERY OF NATURE

Human beings are gradually becoming the "neurons of the Earth," integrated into the nervous system they have created. The planetary brain and real-time society have their origins in the marriage of the biosphere with the technosphere in its most advanced and most dematerialized form, a development that began with the telegraph and continued with the revolution of the telephone, television, and modern digital networks of intercomputer communication. Now emerging in the most advanced industrial societies, this new being is the symbiotic human.

As we will see, the symbiosis involves more than just our vital relationships with computer networks, which are one component of the planetary brain. The symbiosis is also occurring on other levels, involving machines and environments that are simpler than those in technologically advanced societies. But the movement toward symbiotic humanity has begun. Our collective responsibility now is to guide it toward a societal symbiosis that respects life, humanity, and human freedom. To gain a better understanding of what is at stake at this new stage, I will review, first of all, the basic mechanisms of symbiosis as a natural phenomenon; then, biomechanical interfaces between humans and machines; and finally, the direct relationship between the human brain and the computer, a crucial factor in planetary symbiosis occurring through communications networks.

The term *symbiosis* was coined in 1876 by the mycologist Anton deBary. Widely used in modern language, it has deep systemic implications. It is often used to designate a simple, optimal association between individuals or organizations. Communities live in symbiosis when their exchanges are balanced for the mutual benefit of those taking part in them. These relationships are based on exchanges of energy or information, or economic or cultural exchanges. The individuals involved survive more effectively together than in isolation; the symbiotic whole is greater than the sum of its parts. Here we see the well-known principle of synergy, a basic element of the systemic approach.

Symbiosis may be defined as a mutually beneficial relationship involving two (or more) different organisms. Other types of relationships also exist, such as commensalism and parasitism. The commensal lives on the host organism or in its immediate environment and diverts part of the host's food for its own benefit, but without causing discomfort or harm to the host. The parasite lives at the expense of the host organism and its proliferation can threaten the functioning of the host or even kill it, possibly resulting in the death of the parasite as well. A human being is both a commensal and a parasite with respect to certain overall functions of the Earth.

This rather restrictive definition of symbiosis may be broadened. I propose extending its meaning beyond its generally accepted definition as a relationship between living organisms to include relationships that occur at various levels between human beings and species "domesticated" by them (plants, animals, or useful microbes), between human beings and specific environments molded by them (houses, cities, and even ecosystems), between human beings and the new "species" of mechanical and electronic machines that now populate the technosphere, and, finally, between human beings and the macrolife they are helping to create all over the planet, for which the cybiont is the hypothetical model.

Without symbiotic relationships, life on Earth would not exist. Plants need animals that need plants. Humans feed on proteins produced by leguminous plants living in symbiosis with nitrogen-fixing microbes. Without symbiosis, there would be no herbivores, and therefore no animal protein for human consumption.

The symbiotic relationship between plants and animals is astonishingly simple. Living organisms collect and use energy from the sun by means of two pigments that are closely related chemically. One of these pigments, the chlorophyll in leaves, is green; the other, the hemoglobin in blood, is red. The leaves of plants are solar collectors. Through photosynthesis, they transform water and carbon dioxide into two products essential to life, sugars and oxygen. The sugars are combined to form cellulose (the basic material of plants) or starch, creating a reserve of energy that can be changed into glucose through digestion. Animals eat these energy reserves and burn them in tiny cellular boilers. This combustion takes place as a result of respiration, using the oxygen carried by the hemoglobin. Respiration produces carbon dioxide, water vapor, and mineral salts—which are returned to plants—and, most of all, energy, which animals need to move around, seek food, and reproduce. Finally, invisible microorganisms recycle the waste and complete the symbiotic cycle between plants, animals, and microbes.

Current research suggests that the origin of the cell in living things is symbiotic in nature. It seems important to me to come back to this phenomenon, because it applies to many more complex forms of organization.

Each one of the advanced cells that make up our bodies has a nucleus containing DNA. Tiny internal power stations, called *mitochondria*, generate the energy these cells need. The cells of plants have internal solar collectors that contain chlorophyll, which are called *chloroplasts*. We know today that mitochondria were once bacteria, and chloroplasts were algae, and that each came to live in symbiosis (or *endosymbiosis*) within a host cell. In exchange for room and board, they provide the host cell with the energy it needs to function. Even more astonishing is the machinery that activates the cilia that enable cells to move. It, too, results from symbiosis, between flagellated bacteria and other cells. The basic unit of life is therefore the product of an association of primitive microorganisms, carrying their own DNA, that came to live and coevolve within a common home, the cell of a higher organism.

So many examples of symbiosis exist in nature that one may wonder whether life itself is conceivable without symbiotic relationships.

THE BENEFITS OF SYMBIOSIS:
LICHEN, CORAL, AND ORCHIDS

None of the herbivores on the planet could live without the bacteria found in their digestive systems. This is the case for domestic animals, such as sheep, goats, and cattle, as well as for the antelopes, gazelles, zebras, and rhinoceros of the savannahs. The bacteria have enzymes that break down cellulose through anaerobic fermentation. Moreover, the remains of the dead bacteria (their life span is about 20 hours) consist mainly of protein, which is digested by the ruminants.

Termites do not have the enzymes needed to digest wood. They can do so only because of microbes living in their digestive system. Certain species of ants have even domesticated aphids to collect the sweet liquid they produce. In return, the ants build shelters that protect the aphids from the weather and from predators.

One of the most important forms of symbiosis in the biosphere is the coral reef. It is the product of a relationship between a species of algae able to carry out photosynthesis and a microscopic animal whose calcareous skeleton is used by the algae as shelter. The algae supply the host organism with oxygen and sugars, and the host provides them with shelter from currents and predators. To grow, the coral has to consume large amounts of carbon dioxide, which is transformed into food through photosynthesis by the algae and into calcium carbonate, which forms the reef. Forming a huge "sponge," the coral absorbs as much as 2 percent of the carbon dioxide produced by humans. Along with forests, coral reefs are perhaps the only effective long-term sinks for carbon dioxide. Hence the severity of the threat posed by ocean pollution, which kills the coral.

The relationship between flowers and bees is an example of a multifaceted symbiosis. The sexual reproduction of plants involves pollination. Pollen is the equivalent of sperm in animals, which fertilizes the ovary. One of the most effective forms of pollination is that carried out by insects or birds carrying pollen from flower to flower. Hence the "strategies" developed by plants to attract them: colors, shapes, and scents. One of best-known and most sought-after flowers in the world, the orchid, also depends on symbiosis. In 1904, the French botanist Noël Bernard showed that orchids could be grown from a seed (something considered impossible until then) if it was infected with various species of fungi. In exchange for a stable habitat and surplus sugar provided by the plant, the fungus returns vitamins to it and, more important, produces filaments that serve as the plants' roots.

These examples show how widespread symbiotic mechanisms are. The concept can be extended to relationships between humans and the ecosystems and machines they have created.

Humanity has a symbiotic relationship with the fodder crops, leguminous plants and cereals it cultivates to survive or to feed livestock. It has developed this same type of relationship with the domestic animals it keeps for food, agricultural work, or, in the case of pets, pleasure. How do animals or plants benefit? We need to look at them, not simply as individuals, but as entire species. Through human intervention, larger numbers of animals or plants are able to live and reproduce. The agricultural environment of humanity was formed on the basis of symbiotic relationships. The landscape, the breeds of domestic animals, and the major crops still bear traces of the manipulation of ecosystems by the farmer-ecologists of ancient times.

A further step is now being taken with the symbiotic relationship between humanity and the machines of the technosphere, and the relationship that is emerging between humanity and the ecosphere as a whole.

THE MACROBIOLOGY OF MACHINES: A NEW SYMBIOSIS?

A criticism might be laid against the relationship between humanity and the "artificial" world of human inventions: a relationship between living beings and nonliving machines created entirely by the former cannot be considered symbiotic, based as it is on the will of humans alone. The same might be said of the idea of a symbiotic relationship between humanity and the ecosphere. Since the Earth is not "alive," what "benefit" does it gain from a relationship with humanity? This question, which was raised by René Dubois and James

Lovelock, and then again by Michel Serres in 1990 in *The Natural Contract*, still arouses bitter controversy. In 1975, in *The Macroscope*, I pointed out the need for such a hypothesis. We will see that the question presents itself differently within the framework of the general theory of the self-organization and dynamics of complex systems, which I have called *symbionomy*. This theory shows that humanity can contribute to the development of a planetary macrolife in symbiosis with the natural cycles of the planet.

From the point of view of macrobiology, the symbiosis between humans and cars is particularly illuminating. Humanity maintains a fleet of 500 million vehicles, extracts the energy that feeds them, and builds roads for their circulation, garages for their repair, and factories for their "reproduction." In return for the maintenance and reproduction of the automobile species, cars allow humans to travel at greater speeds, to act more effectively, to conquer distance, and they provide pleasure and social status. They are also, as we saw in the previous chapter, a source of disease for the social organism and of danger and pollution for the planetary organism. Like symbiotic partners that turn into parasites, they are endangering the future of the ecosphere. We can easily imagine a disaster scenario in some distant future, when, in record time and with frightening efficiency, the automobile species has managed to enslave virtually the entire human species, much like ants once domesticated and enslaved aphids. There is no denying that the car has led humans to work more and more, to manufacture and sell cars and extract precious oil, and even to go to war to defend this fuel, the new drug of industrialized societies.

Computers and robots will follow the same path. Symbiosis between humanity, computers, and networks has already begun. The large global telematics systems (industrial, financial, administrative, commercial, military), public networks like the Internet, and automated factories are proof of this.

These networks and systems are already putting new constraints on us. This may be seen in certain huge projects that, despite popular pressure, become almost impossible to stop once they have been approved by the political and technical elite. The seductive power they exert on the minds of those who conceived them is too strong.

Stopping them would call into question the rationale and the power that justify and legitimate the actions of this elite. Big organizations and large systems have a life of their own. They resist and oppose any measures that challenge their existence. These mechanisms are obviously not "conscious" in the sense that we understand consciousness in human terms. We cannot project onto them our capacity to think and make decisions. Rather, they are simply homeostatic mechanisms, reflecting the resistance to change of any complex system, a force for self-preservation.

People live in a symbiotic relationship with their homes. Originally, the house was a passive shelter that protected its inhabitants from the elements. With the arrival of running water, sewage systems, energy (gas, electricity), wiring and ducts of all kinds, the house acquired a kind of "physiology." Household appliances and communications tools (telephone, television), and especially electronic devices, bring the house to a new stage of coevolution with its inhabitants. It has developed "muscles" (household appliances) and a "nervous system" (communications machines), made up of elements, such as VCRs, personal computers, and satellite dishes. With communications networks integrated into the modern home, we are witnessing the arrival of the automated home, which regulates and optimizes its own operation. The passive protective house is becoming active, and is even reacting to the lives of its inhabitants. A growing number of architects and builders are adopting the concept of the active house that adapts to climatic conditions to save energy, detects the movements of the occupants from room to room—so as to respond to their habits and turn lights and heaters on or off according to their activities—or switches on specific functions at certain times of the day. This cybernetic house is the product of the coevolution between humans and their shelters. A symbiosis has developed between them for their mutual benefit; the house is maintained, paid for, decorated, cleaned, modified, renovated. Cybernetic, communicating houses will be able to connect with each other in meganetworks, warning each other of dangers (fire, theft, flood) in the absence of their owners. The remote regulation and control of functions will be as easy as checking the messages on an answering machine by telephone.

NEW INTERFACES BETWEEN HUMANS AND MACHINES

A new kind of synapse will be required to connect human brains with computers and networks. A *synapse* is the connection between two worlds, the world of molecules and the world of ions. It is a cleft, a gap; the nerve endings are not joined, but are almost in contact. Nerve impulses circulate through the networks of the nervous system by "jumping" these synaptic gaps. When an impulse reaches the end of a neuron, a chemical mediator (a messenger molecule) is released by the vesicles, tiny pouches located at the end of the nerve. The molecules of the mediator cross the gap and are recognized on the other side by receptors (like molecular antennae), which set off a signal. The other world then goes into action. A depolarization wave arises from the ionic imbalance between the inside and the outside of the neuron and travels along the neuron to the next synapse.

In order to create a planetary brain, humans will have to communicate with machines through a system analogous to that of the synapses, linking the two distinct worlds and transmitting information in both directions. Since the brain is biological and computers are electronic, a bioelectronic interface will be required. But an ideal path of this kind is necessarily marked with essential transition points; they are buttons, keyboards, screens, remote controls, and mice, tools that are now an integral part of our immediate environment.

Among the profusion of machines created by humans are a great many devices that transmit power or information. *Ergonomics*, the science that studies the human-machine interface, examines ways to optimize the environment of machines to enable people to use them most effectively while minimizing fatigue and hazards.

In the mechanical world, this means transmitting both power (energy) and information. Reins, used to tell a horse where to go and how fast, are one form of biomechanical interface. The levers, valves, dials, and wheels of a steam engine are others. When we look around us, we realize that our environment is filled with biomechanical communications systems: door and drawer handles, keys, faucets; the steering wheel, clutch, and brake pedal of a car; the tiller of a boat;

the control column and rudder of an airplane. Hydraulic, hydro-pneumatic, and electromechanical relays amplify the action of these devices.

With electricity and electronics, the interfaces became more subtle. The slightest pressure of a finger can have an enormous effect. Just think of the notorious "red button" of the nuclear war age. The muscular force of the finger or hand is amplified by a specific connection between two worlds such as the button of an electric switch or the on/off dial of a radio or CD reader. And machines communicate with us via indicator lights, needles, speakers, and screens.

Typewriters, telephones, and computers have introduced a more complex form of interface: series of switches (keys), arranged in a standardized order, send codes that are recognized by a mechanical or electronic translation device. The human-machine interface is gradually being dematerialized, with memory "shuttles" being introduced between the two "species": recordings read by readers (disks, cassettes, CDs), magnetic cards or cards with computer chips, laser bar-code readers that decode labels or codes and transmit their information using infrared signals, and active badges that emit a specific signal allowing a computer to recognize or track the wearer. We are even seeing the first "intelligent" interfaces such as those that help technophobes program their VCRs; you enter a simple code and the machine does the rest by communicating with the VCR.

"Translators" of this kind are everywhere—the remote control, the mouse, and the modem, for example—enhancing the connections between electronic machines and their users. They represent another turn of the spiral toward the planetary brain. The infrared remote control for the television has, in a few years, transformed the way we consume images and information around the globe. This little device—an extension of the fingers, a magic wand—has introduced the practice of zapping, the feverish rush through the kaleidoscope of images that reflect our world. The remote zapper has radically reshaped advertising, political slogans, and the style of TV programs. Clips, flashes, and zapping are today's falsely interactive ways of consuming the mass of information accumulated by the videosphere.

The computer mouse is another extension of the fingers. With the mouse and graphical user interface, you need only "point and click" to make something happen. We can barely imagine how far computers have brought human communication in just a few years! For those who experienced the punch cards and endless program listings of the past, computers were the bane of their existence. One mistake, a single "bug," and you had to punch a new card and wait until the next day to check the result.

The introduction of the keyboard-screen interface changed everything. Interactivity became faster and more user friendly. But communicating with the computer via the screen was still limited by the mediation of strings of characters. It was the mouse that helped transform our relationship with computers. Thanks to research done by Xerox and then Apple, the mouse allowed users to draw, move objects in a virtual space (the desktop), and open windows or pull-down menus. The interface became tactile and physical, but in a de-materialized world of icons, mnemotechnical shapes representing files, functions, and programs. Thanks to the mouse, the computer is becoming "drivable," like a car.

The modem is a kind of synapse joining two worlds, that of the computer and the telephone. *Modem* stands for modulator-demodulator. This device transforms the electronic impulses produced by the computer (codes representing numbers and letters in the form of bits) into tone bursts or compressed digital impulses that can travel at high speeds over telephone networks. Receiving the signals, another modem converts them into codes that can be turned back into text, graphics, images, or sounds by another computer. Without modems, there would be no fax, no e-mail, no online airline reservations. The modem is the universal synapse of the planetary nervous system.

With portable personal assistants and notepad computers, a new interface has appeared: the stylus, a small wireless "pen" used to write on the screen and indicate tasks to be carried out. The electronic pages turn like the pages of a date book and it is possible to "leaf through" stacks of documents. To send a fax, you simply click on the document to be sent, the address of the recipient, and the fax icon.

The future personal communication interface will be wireless, and will include new "superphones," technological hybrids that have the merged capacity of portable phones and hand-held computers, like the Palm Top VII from 3 Com. They will be able to access the Web at high speed, using WAP (wireless application protocol) and the high bandwidth of worldwide standards, like UMTS (unified mobile telephone system). This new type of interface between humans, computers, and networks will transform the PC into a PN (personal network), an interconnected maze of appliances (phones, scanners, printers, hand-held computers, digital cameras, digital recorders, etc.) that follow the user anywhere. The appliances will talk to each other and exchange services with the help of new software like JINI, from Sun Microsystems, a universal machine language. According to Forrester Research, Americans spent $30 billion on wireless voice services in 1998, and almost none on data. By 2005, they will be spending $60 billion on wireless services, of which $8.4 billion will be on data. According to the Yankee group, a tech trend analysis company, the U.S. population of wireless intelligent terminals (Web-capable personal digital assistants or e-mail-enabled cell phones) will grow from 1.9 million in 1999 to 31 million in 2003.

The next stages of user friendliness will be voice recognition and the computer's ability to comprehend a user's sentences or even gestures and facial expressions. These advances are taking shape as we enter the new millennium

THE COMPUTER LEARNS HUMANITY

The most natural forms of communication or interface between humans are speech, writing, and observation of the body—the face, general appearance, posture, clothing, and accessories. The processing capacity of modern computers, and particularly the arrival of 64-bit microprocessors, opens the door to the world of human interfaces. Extraordinary progress has been made in voice recognition and synthesis in recent years. Many companies have developed very powerful voice-recognition algorithms. The next development will be multispeaker recognition that does not depend on training the computer. The automatic dictation machine already exists. International companies are devising dictation software with continuous speech and a good recognition ratio. It is even possible to dictate through a digital recorder, connect it to a computer, and see the spoken text displayed on the screen. Voice synthesis is quite advanced and will continue to improve. Soon, it will no longer be possible to distinguish between the infinite variety of human speech and words uttered by a computer. Computers will be able to read any text in the voice of a person whose "vocal profile" has previously been input into the machine. Nothing will prevent machines from listening to conversations, sampling the characteristics of a person's speech, and parroting them back—who knows to what end?

Other natural means of communication include handwriting, gestures, and facial expressions. Great strides have been made in handwriting recognition. Personal assistants and personal communicators are already equipped with rudimentary character-recognition systems. The programs are improving. Increased memory capacities make it possible to access larger dictionaries. It is now possible to compare whole sentences, reducing the need for artificial intelligence programs.

Gestures and mimicry are an integral part of human communication. At the MIT Media Lab and other research laboratories, such as the Human Interface Laboratory in Japan or Xerox PARC, in Palo Alto, California, computers capable of recognizing gestures and facial expressions are in the experimental stage. Proximity sensors on users' wrists and a camera on the computer allow users to reinforce their words with gestures, to point to objects, and to trace shapes in space. Face recognition programs are already used in security checks. They will also be used to communicate with machines by means of facial expressions. You need only sit down in front of a computer for its "eye" to recognize you, open your files, and greet you with "Hello! Not feeling well this morning? You seem out of sorts! I suggest the vacation file you were working on last week." The "eye" can be supplemented with an active identification badge containing a chip that emits a specific signal. Equipped with appropriate sensors, the computer can also detect the characteristic odors of a person, and thus increase its means of personalized recognition. All these forms of communication may be used in combination.

In recent years, the computer has thus gradually developed organs and senses: first, eyes to see and read (scanners, optical character recognition, and face and pattern recognition with expert software); then, ears and a vocal apparatus (voice recognition and synthesis); and now, touch, through virtual reality interfaces (data gloves, stereo vision helmets, and synthesized images, which will be discussed later).

Little by little, the computer is "learning" humanity. The human-computer symbiosis is becoming deeper and more subtle. But this close relationship requires increasingly powerful "engines" (microprocessors) and memory for the machines. Hence the importance of the recent progress made in processor speed (which has now reached 500 megahertz), in the number of operations per second (100 million to a billion), and in storage capacities (a billion bits on a chip). Also, a whole range of programs have been designed especially to interface naturally with humans, using the eye, the voice, writing patterns, and touch. Intellectual assistants and informational logistics give us increased powers. How can these powers be measured?

Economic indicators, energy consumption, and duration of work are traditional units of measurement of a society's level of development or efficiency. It would be useful to have a similar indicator to measure the information-processing capacity of the human brain and its extensions—telephone, fax, personal computer, storage devices, and networks. The units of measurement might be expressed, for example, as *bits per neuron*. It is interesting to note that the number of cells whose function it is to assist the neurons in their work (called neuroglia or glial cells) has increased over the course of biological evolution. The ratio of neuroglia to neurons increased as the brain and its functions became more complex. As assistant cells, neuroglia do not process data directly; rather, they provide the neurons with the energy they need to function, and remove the waste they produce. In a sense, they constitute the operational logistics of the neuron, just as a well-equipped office has logistics for information input, processing, storage, and dissemination. The functions are made possible by the intellectual extensions or prostheses we have created, which increase the capacities of our brain in number and variety. These capacities are further amplified by the connections among brains in intercomputer communications networks. Thus, we see the value of a coefficient of neuronal performance that would measure the power of those data-processing machines now interfacing with our brains.

CONNECTING THE COMPUTER AND THE BRAIN

People have always dreamed of transmitting their thoughts by telepathy or acquiring new senses that would let them "see" the invisible or detect forces or impulses they do not yet perceive. With the advent of bioelectronics, these dreams will become a reality.

The interconnection of human brains through networks is helping to build the planetary brain of the cybiont. Of course, other types of interfaces exist between humans and social macroorganizations, but the "biological brain–electronic brain" relationship has a special psychological and philosophical significance, because it is the ultimate interface between human and machine.

The circuit that travels from the hand, or even the voice, to the computer screen is unnecessarily complicated. In the case of the hand, electrical impulses originating in particular motor areas of the brain are transmitted by the nerves to the muscles of the fingers. They are transformed into biomechanical force when keys are pressed on the keyboard, and then into standardized computer codes, and finally into instructions to form letters on the screen. In the case of the voice, electrical impulses of the brain activate the body's muscles and the vocal cords, and make the air vibrate. The sound is picked up by a microphone and converted into electromagnetic impulses, which are then transmitted by wire, translated into standard codes by the computer, and, through a voice-recognition program, displayed on the screen in the form of letters.

Obviously, if we could pick up the coded impulses at their source, in the brain, and translate them into language understandable by the computer, the ultimate bioelectronic interface could be achieved. This area is now the subject of active research throughout the world. The work began about 15 years ago with experiments on fighter pilots and attempts to develop aids for people with disabilities. The need is the same in both cases. Since a pilot's major biomechanical and sensory functions are already occupied with piloting, it was a logical step to try using the pilot's eyes and even thoughts to transmit information to the plane. And people who have no mobility in their arms, hands, or legs can only relate to the outside world by means of eye movements or directly through thought. One of the most famous such cases is Stephen Hawking, who has amyotrophic lateral sclerosis and communicates by means of a computer with voice synthesis.

A person's eyes are full of meaning, and the area they observe is delineated with extraordinary precision. The first experiments with eye trackers were done with pilots. An invisible infrared beam followed the eye movements of the pilot. If he fixed his gaze for a certain length of time on a particular part of the control panel, the computer assessed his focus as equivalent to pressing a key, and it triggered an action.

A series of input peripherals based on this principle is about to appear. French researchers have already developed a computer writing system for people with disabilities that uses the eyes. It consists of a tablet containing about 30 graphic symbols. In the middle of the tablet is a miniature camera connected to an infrared eye tracker. Image analysis software identifies the character the eye focuses on by measuring the shape of the pupil and the position of the light's reflection on the cornea. People with disabilities can use this system to control an electric wheelchair or a voice synthesis device. They can also activate equipment such as a television, a telephone, or simply a call bell.

At MIT, researchers at the Media Lab run by Nicolas Negroponte have dialogues with their eyes, using a screen equipped with sensors and displaying an image of a person who can change facial expression and make comments according to information received.

The MIT Media Lab has also been a pioneer in "wearable computers," transforming humans into "cyborgs," or better, creating "humachines," human-machine symbionts.* In the early 1990s at the

---

* *Humachines*, Special issue of *Technology Review*, May–June 1999.

Media Lab, Steve Mann developed wearable computers, which he calls "WearComps." A number of researchers and MIT students are now walking around in suits made of special fabric and fitted with miniature computers, goggles displaying images in front of their eyes, video cameras on their heads, microphones, earphones, and connections to other computers through cellular phones and the Internet, creating a community of interconnected "humachines."

People are already communicating with the outside world through devices that transmit their brain waves to a computer. In a vision research institute in San Francisco, a doctor who was severely disabled by a degenerative disease of the cerebral cortex agreed to have an electrode implanted at the base of his skull that picked up the waves emitted by the visual area of his brain. Today, this man can make a computer write and pronounce words, using a voice synthesis system. To do this, he fixes his eyes on a dial divided into luminous squares corresponding to letters or words. By combining these squares, he can compose 600 words. The computer identifies the squares he looks at by analyzing the electroencephalogram from the visual cortex of his brain. This information is transmitted either to a word processing program, which prints it, or to a synthetic speech generator.

One of the most advanced projects in bioelectronic and biocybernetic aids for people with disabilities is being carried out by the Loma Linda University Medical Center in California. This is the Biomuse project, directed by Dave Warner in collaboration with Biocontrol Systems Inc., in Palo Alto. The researchers and users wear lightweight headbands, similar to those worn by athletes, that contain a series of bioelectronic sensors. These sensors are kept in close contact with the skin by a gel that amplifies the signals from the brain. The headband has a wireless link to a box, in turn, connected to a computer. It is also possible to pick up bioelectrical impulses from the arms, wrists, or legs. This has been used to study a variety of functions, such as control of the environment, the use of real-time biofeedback to move around in a virtual environment, and the generation of musical sounds.

Researchers at Biocontrol Systems are working on replacing the computer mouse with the eyes. This interface combines two sensors, one that interprets the eye movements and one that interprets the movements of the eye muscles. Patches are placed on the temples, and the eye movements are used to move the cursor on the screen. All it takes to click is a blink!

Sensory and motor information expressed through nerve impulses can be decoded by many types of sensors. The translation of fear, pleasure or pain, or attention or relaxation into signals understandable by the computer is an immense new area of research. It is a further step toward the direct transmission of information from the brain to computers. The research attempts to gather information increasingly close to the actual source.

In his novel *Maze,** writer Larry Collins bases his plot on a technology that can read and even influence the brain from far away; the KGB uses this system to modify the behavior of the president of the United States. Such a technology exists; it is called *magnetoencephalography* (MEG). It measures the extremely weak magnetic fields produced by neuron activity, which are one billion times weaker than the Earth's magnetic field. This requires a device that uses the properties of superconductors, the SQUID (superconducting quantum interference device). The SQUID led to the development of a special helmet, containing a magnetometer in liquid helium, that can record the reactions to certain stimuli of neurons in the deepest areas of the brain. An aircraft pilot wearing this helmet and placed in a simulator is shown a rapid succession of photographs of enemy and friendly aircraft; he has to press a button when he recognizes an enemy aircraft. But the SQUID magnetometer is faster than he is! The computer connected to it "reads" the image of the enemy plane in the pilot's very neurons, and its action takes place before the motor reflex—between the time of brain recognition and pressing the button. We are not yet able to send information in the opposite direction and modify behavior as Larry Collins describes, but it is a possibility that should not be dismissed.

The most advanced form of bioelectronic communication is without doubt the interpretation by the computer of a rudimentary

---

* New York: Simon & Schuster, 1989.

form of human thought. At the end of the 1970s, researchers at the Stanford Research Institute trained themselves to move a dot on a computer screen simply by thinking about it. Their brains were connected to the computer by an electroencephalogram (EEG) analyzer. Several research laboratories are now studying the applications of what is called *brain-actuated technology*, or BAT. The Japanese Fujitsu Corporation has been actively pursuing this research since 1991 in association with the Hokkaido University electronic sciences research laboratory in Sapporo. Its researchers have identified and measured the "silent speech" produced by the brain between the moment an object is recognized in the visual cortex and the vocalization of its name. The brain emits electrical signals of different voltages just before a person performs an action. Statistical analysis of experiments with a SQUID carried out on hundreds of volunteers shows the presence of a specific signal (such as when the subject thinks of the vowel "a") that can be translated into a command understood by a computer.

Related research is being done in many international laboratories, such as the University of Illinois, the Defense Advanced Research Projects Agency (DARPA), and the New York State Department of Health, in Albany. Their goal is to connect human thought directly to computers. But, to create the ultimate interface, new ultraminiaturized and eventually biocompatible circuits will be needed. These molecular circuits are on the way.

THE MARRIAGE OF BIOLOGY AND COMPUTERS

We are witnessing today the celebration of a union that promises to be fruitful: the marriage of biology and computers. A new fundamental and applied discipline is being born of this union and, more generally, of the hybridization and coevolution of the methodologies and techniques used in computers and of those used in biology and supramolecular chemistry. It seems appropriate to create a new term to identify this new discipline, crucial as it is to the advent of symbiotic humanity. In 1981, I proposed that it be called *biotics* (a combination of *biology* and *informatics*).* Biotics is the fusion of biology and computer technology to develop new molecular electronic components and circuits (biochips, biotransistors) and bioelectronic interfaces linking humans, computers, and networks. This new sector of research includes and goes beyond *bionics* (a combination of *biology* and *electronics*), which emerged in the 1950s and 1960s in the work of Humberto Maturana, Walter Pitts, and Warren McCulloch at MIT, who used electronics to copy the organs of the body. Its scope is also broader than that of *bioinformatics* or *biocybernetics*.

Biotics comprises two complementary areas of application: analog signals (in this case, bioelectronics) and digital signals (molecular electronics). The construction of a "biocomputer" based on circuits and memory from molecular electronics and using materials compatible with living systems is part of biotics. The field emerged from recent advances in biology, solid-state physics, organic chemistry, microelectronics, robotics, and nanotechnology, and today it constitutes a new area of research with many applications.

Molecular electronic components are currently considered the potential successors to semiconductors. These synthetic components offer many advantages over traditional semiconductors: three-dimensional assembly, synthetic materials that allow the custom design of properties, miniaturization approaching that of biological structures, and possibilities for interfacing with living systems.

Molecular electronics dates from the 1970s. Following the publication of a series of articles—including a now-famous one by Aviram and Ratner of IBM, published in 1974—a visionary chemist, Forrest L. Carter, organized the first seminar on the subject on November 19, 1978, at the Naval Research Laboratory in Airlie, Virginia. Present were pioneers from very diverse fields, including a handful from France led by André Barraud of the Commissariat à l'Énergie Atomique (ECA), recognized as one of the fathers of organized supramolecular structures. In March 1981, I had the opportu-

---

* See Joël de Rosnay, "La Biotique," in *L'Expansion*, May 21, 1981, p. 149; "Les Biotransistors, la Micro-électronique du xxie Siècle" ("Biotransistors, the Microelectronics of the Twenty-First Century"), in *La Recherche*, no. 124, July–August 1981, p. 870.

nity to take part in the second symposium and to meet most of the founding fathers of this fascinating field of research. New ideas were discussed concerning the possibility of creating the first molecular components for the biocomputers of the future such as switches, storage devices, diodes, and molecular wire.

The field of molecular electronics—the use of molecular devices to process data—is today recognized as a strategic field of research that is crucial for the future of computer technology and interfaces between biology and information technology. Molecular electronics will be the third major stage in the development of computers. The first stage (1940–1960) was characterized by electronic tubes, the second by transistors (1960–2000), and the third (2000–2050) will be characterized by molecular electronics and the molecular processing of information. To achieve this, we will need to be able to manufacture transistors as small as biomolecules.

Most biological molecules and macromolecules are information-processing machines. DNA and proteins are essentially microprocessors capable of recognizing signals (electrons, ions, small molecules) and of reacting by modifying their physical structure, shape, or chemical functions. Cells contain large numbers of supramolecular assemblies, which consist of large numbers of connected molecules. Microtubules, for example, are veritable micromachines that are involved in cellular transport and movement, while the membrane acts as a selective filter and organ of communication. These supramolecular assemblies are made of extremely densely packed structures—up to 1,000,000,000,000,000 (a quadrillion) per square millimeter—while the most sophisticated microelectronics technology contains barely a million elements per square millimeter.

The descent into the realm of the infinitely small, down to scales measured in nanometers (millionths of millimeters), is crucial for the future of very high-density microcircuits. Computer technology has reached its limit. With available techniques of optical photolithography, there's a limit to how fine a line can be engraved on the silicon mass used in manufacturing transistors. Even using increasingly hard radiation (UV rays, x-rays, electron guns, ion guns), we will reach the limits of resolution for the manufacture of masks in the next couple of decades. The next stage is molecular electronics. Using genetic engineering and organic chemistry, it is becoming possible to manufacture components with specific properties, plastic transistors, and even biochips that can be connected to living organisms.

BIOCHIPS FOR BIOCOMPUTERS

Revolutionary technologies will be used to manufacture the biotic circuits of the future. One of the most promising of these is the *self-assembly of organized structures*. In biology, for example, we are already familiar with the ability of viruses to self-assemble from their previously separate components. Rather than the traditional "passive" approach used, for example, for electronic microcircuits (engraving, depositing layers, grafting, doping), an "active" approach is taken, using the spontaneous organization of molecular assemblies. This involves a fundamental change in manufacturing and engineering. Traditional machining is "top down"; information comes from outside (plans, robots, machine tools), material is cut off, trimmed, or removed (as with lathes, drill presses, milling machines), or parts are stamped. It is an extension of the process used to create the first tools, which involved carving a piece of stone, in other words, removing chips from the stone to shape the tool. Significantly, the same word, *chip*, is used for the wafer of silicon in an integrated circuit. The new approach is "bottom up," using the information already contained in the molecules and the macromolecules and their bonding properties at various levels. The amino acids of proteins, for example, contain the information necessary to form a chain capable of folding in three dimensions, giving the protein a specific form.

This active, nanotechnological approach is the way of the future for the manufacture of molecular electronic microcircuits and the creation of biocomputers. For the first time, it will be possible to *grow* a circuit as a crystal is grown. To do this, researchers will have to master several crucial stages. First of all, they will have to produce reliable molecular switches that can go from one state to another, and be able to determine what state these switches are in. Next, they will have to create reversible molecular memories that can be reused many times, and connect these components by molecular wires to carry information over long distances. Another stage would involve the assembly of these switches, memory storage devices, and wires into structures or networks organized in various levels of communication and interconnection to carry out coordinated functions. Lastly, the ability to repair these systems would be required; the molecules that were not functioning properly would have to be detected and components replaced. Such systems of self-repairing molecular automatons already exist in biology, in particular for the repair of DNA.

The computer will play a fundamental role in the design and assembly of such circuits, similar to the role it already plays in automobile manufacturing, aeronautics, or the design of molecules used in pharmaceuticals, where it joins the various molecular components and integrates them into functional units. Researchers have also started to take advantage of an extraordinary tool: the scanning tunneling microscope (STM) invented in 1981 by Nobel laureates Gerd Binnig and Heinrich Rohrer of the IBM laboratories in Zurich. Originally a tool for observation, the STM has become an instrument for processing as it makes it possible to manipulate individual atoms and modify chemical structures and functions.

Thanks to this technology, molecular electronics has made considerable progress in recent years. It now constitutes a strategic goal for major American, European, and Japanese companies in chemistry and microelectronics. They can already count among their achievements molecular wires capable of carrying information over long distances, connections between molecular wires to create nanocircuits, optical switches, transistors made of semiconducting polymers, plastic polymers for luminous screens, molecular diodes, photochrome memory, artificial retinas, and even the manipulation of *a single bit* of molecular information.

The first steps toward creating a molecular computer were taken in July 1999 by a team of chemists at the University of California at Los Angeles (UCLA) and researchers from the Hewlett-Packard Laboratory. Headed by James R. Heath, the team has demonstrated for the first time molecular-based logic gates, the essential components required for the creation of a molecular computer. They used a class of molecules called rotaxanes as molecular switches inside a complex chemical architecture. Those molecules can achieve results that are the same as or better than silicon. According to James Heath, in about a decade, it will be possible to put the computational power of 100 workstations onto an object the size of a grain of sand, with vastly reduced power consumption.*

Despite the extraordinary advances in biotics, many questions remain unanswered. Will these circuits be repairable? Will it be possible to break and reconnect chemical bonds? Will automatic machines, such as biological micromachines, be able to intervene, and on what level? Will the logic of these circuits have to be different from the boolean logic on which all current computer technology is based? Will these circuits lend themselves to the construction of neural networks or will they be better suited to the manufacture of cellular automatons based on interconnected molecules? And, more important, what noninvasive conditions (that is, that do not attack the body's organs or require implanting electrodes) will be found to connect these biocompatible circuits to the brain?

Without waiting for answers to these questions, researchers are attempting to build the computer equivalent of the biological brain. Under the auspices of ATR Laboratories in Kyoto, a team at the human information-processing laboratory headed by Hugo de Garis is building a silicon brain made up of more than one billion artificial neurons that interconnect in networks much like natural neural networks. The researchers' objective is to create more synapses than can be found in the human brain. With such great density in a three-dimensional network, the critical mass required for the emergence of a form of autonomous intelligence may be reached by the year 2015.

Many laboratories are now working on chips that are compatible with neurons. Some researchers are even testing silicon implants in their living tissues. In August 1998, Kevin Warwick at the University of Reading in the United Kingdom implanted in his left arm a 23-millimeter-long radio transponder and a silicon chip that can open

---

* C. P. Collier, et al., "Electronically Configurable Molecular-Based Logic Gates," *Science*, July 16, 1999, pp. 391–394.

doors and send instructions to the Warwick computer. Around 2001, he intends to link a new implant to his nervous system to help him communicate with people through his thoughts.

William L. Ditto, a physicist at the Georgia Institute of Technology working with a group at the University of Bordeaux in France, has developed hybrid computers that mate living neurons with silicon circuits. He has called this new field "neurosilicon computers." In 1999, he was able to do arithmetic with two large neurons from leeches, joined together and linked to a personal computer. The computer sends each cell different signals that code for several numbers. Using the basic principles of chaos theory, Ditto selectively stimulated the two neurons. From their responses, the PC extracted the correct answer to a simple addition problem. It is the first time living neurons have been able to do arithmetic and communicate the results to humans. Computer simulations show that larger groups of neurons should also be able to do multiplication and boolean logic operations, the basic computing principles of all digital computers. In the future, Ditto plans to link neurons to video cameras and microphones to create systems with artificial senses.

Another step on the road to creating biocomputers was achieved by Jerry Pine, a biophysicist at the California Institute of Technology in Pasadena. He was able to "grow" microcircuits made of living neurons on top of an array of electrodes. He calls the device the "Neurochip." By assigning a specific place to each neuron, it is possible to "listen" to their chatter and develop reproducible logic gates out of combinations of neurons.

A similar type of research has been undertaken by Keiichi Torimitsu at the NTT's (Nippon Telegraph and Telephone Corporation) Biosciences Research Group in Atsugi, Japan. His group is trying to develop an effective interface between computers and the brain. To test this possibility, his laboratory sent electronic signals to slices of neuronal tissue placed close to tiny electrodes; and researchers monitored the electronic current naturally generated by the neurons when they communicated with each other.

For some pioneers, the ideal path is DNA computers, which outperform silicon-based machines in complex mathematical calculations. Michio Kaku, a theoretical physicist and futurist, foresees microprocessors built around DNA molecules by 2020.* The idea of DNA computing was first put forward in 1994 by Leonard M. Adleman, a mathematician at the University of Southern California in his now famous paper, "Molecular Computation of Solutions of Combinatorial Problems." † He described how he used a test-tube approach to solve a classic mathematical problem: how to organize a traveling salesperson's itinerary among seven cities so that the traveler visits all seven cities without passing through any city more than once. Several laboratories around the world have been able to reproduce Aldeman's biocomputation technique using classical molecular biology and enzymatic materials and methods. Recombinations of strands of DNA coding for specific items (like cities in the original experiment) occur in parallel in the test tube in a very short time, providing the solution to the problem. The tedious part involves sorting and extracting out the molecules that contain the solution. New microtechniques implemented for microlabs or "labs on a chip" are used to automate the different steps of the process. Researchers at the Bell Labs in New Jersey under the leadership of physicist Allan Mills are working on improving and speeding up the basic technique. Their goal is to create a neural network version of Aldeman's DNA biocomputer.

THE NEW SENSES OF SYMBIOTIC HUMANITY

What will the people of the future be like? Biologists, futurologists, and science fiction writers have been grappling with this challenging question for centuries. For some, the human of the future will be a "superman," whose brain will surpass the brain of our day in numbers of neurons, and who will possess phenomenal intellectual capacities. These humans will have large heads and tiny legs (thanks to mechanized movement) and no teeth (from the consumption of concentrated food). This caricature of humanity could be further elaborated, but biological evolution, as against that of the techno-

---

* Michio Kaku, *Visions: How Science Will Revolutionize the 21st Century*, New York: Bantam Books, 1998.
† *Science*, vol. 266, November 11, 1994, pp. 1021–1024.

sphere, is not fast enough to produce such significant changes. Others argue the human beings of the future will be bionic, made up of interchangeable electronic and computer parts, with custom-built senses and organs and enhanced sight and hearing systems. Able to hear at a distance of hundreds of yards, to see in the dark, and to leap and run like gazelles, bionic men and women were popularized all over the world by an American TV series.

Scientists and science fiction writers have imagined cybernetic humans (cyborgs), half human, half robot, like RoboCop or Terminator. Bruce Mazlish has predicted the arrival of "combots" (computer-robots), a new generation of intelligent beings produced by humans that would then be self-reproducing and live in relationship with us, as a new kind of species cohabiting with biological humanity. Hans Moravec believes that the robots of the future will have such a high level of intelligence that they will be able to dissuade us from "pulling the plug" if we want to turn them off. Emotionally appealing and integrated into our lives, they will exert the kind of pressure on us that pets do.

These visions of the future usually focus on the individual. I prefer to consider humanity, society, and the technosphere as a *coevolutionary whole*. For me, humanity in the future will be symbiotic humanity, not very different physically and mentally from twentieth-century humans but with extraordinary means of knowledge and action thanks to their biological, psychological, or biotic connections with the cybiont.

I have described the gradual coevolution of humanity with the biosphere (mainly through agriculture and, more recently, biotechnologies), with the technosphere (by means of machines, industry, trade, and the economy), and with the noosphere (through computers and broad communications networks). I have stressed the importance of interfaces between humans and mechanical or electronic machines. But the emergence of biotics makes it possible to envision even more direct interfaces between humans and their machines, and the creation of new bodies and new senses.

Our symbiotic relationship with computers is not unidirectional, going from our brains to the machine. We also receive information from computers. Today, this information is expressed in numbers, text, graphs, fixed images, and animated sequences displayed on screens, or in sounds emitted by speakers. But with portable computers, personal digital assistants, hand-held computers, increasingly miniaturized telephones, videophones, and pagers, there will be a need to transmit information to the brain in a way that is more personalized, more discreet, and more private.

We are at the dawn of a revolution in the means of communication, going *from* electronic machines *to* humans. What we call the "communications revolution" is in fact the prehistory of a phase that will take place in the first decade of the twenty-first century. When it comes to communications, we haven't seen anything yet! Bioelectronic ears, eyes, and noses that can hear, see, smell, transmit, and, especially, interface with human beings, are already being developed by high-tech companies. The reception of information from computers and communications machines is taking a new direction. For example, a small California company has developed a combination earphone-microphone placed in the ear. The innovation is in the clever relationship between the earphone, the microphone, and the information emission unit. There are no wires; everything is transmitted by hertzian waves. You can talk with your computer while moving about, or keep your portable telephone in your pocket while talking in a very low voice with the person at the other end. The microphone placed just outside the ear electronically reduces ambient noise by taking into account the constant distance between the ear and the mouth. In addition, using an original process, the microphone picks up the sounds transmitted by the bones of the skull. This considerably amplifies the emission quality of the voice of the person speaking, even when he or she is only whispering. Other companies are developing implants placed deeper in the ear, similar to certain hearing aids, which allow a computer with voice synthesis to speak directly into the ear.

Artificial noses have been developed by a number of laboratories in the world. One of them, created at the University of Manchester, is already using molecular electronics. A sensor functions like the olfactory mucous membrane. It consists of conducting polymers containing groups of chemicals that recognize the molecules responsible for various odors. When a molecule carried by the flow of air lands on a receptor, a change in the electric conduction of the polymer occurs, which produces an olfactory "fingerprint" or profile of the substance. A neural network then compares this information with the various families of odors in its memory. The computer screen displays the specific pattern of the odor and announces the name of the substance. A palm-sized vapor detector has been developed by Sawtek, a Florida-based company. Up to 200 known chemicals ranging from toxic gases to moldy food can be sniffed out using four piezoelectric crystals coated with different polymers that absorb target vapors.

Synthetic retinas that can distinguish shapes are the precursors of the eyes of future generations of robots. Until now, the artificial retinas used in the vision systems of robots or smart missiles have been based on silicon. A Japanese team at the Fuji laboratories has used bacteriorhodopsin, a protein that acts as a photoreceptor in certain photosynthetic bacteria that live in salt water, in particular, in the Dead Sea. One of the important characteristics of this artificial retina is its capacity to react in a few microseconds to changes in light intensity. Researchers at Johns Hopkins University's Wilmer Eye Institute and at the Massachusetts Institute of Technology have developed artificial retinas in the form of silicon implants packed with transistors that sit on the surface of the retina. Alan Chow, an opthalmologist and founder of the start-up OptoBionics, is working on a subretinal implant made of a collection of microphotodiodes implanted behind the retina.

The wrist videophone, similar to a wristwatch, will follow close on the heels of the portable telephone with hidden earphones. Japanese companies have partially solved the problem of compressing a television image so that it can be carried by a cellular telephone. Compressed color images are transmitted today at a speed of 10,000 bits per second, with a quality close to that of videoconferencing systems operating at 64,000 or 128,000 bits, making possible the commercial production of an interactive wrist videophone. Siemens, Kyocera, and Nokia are anticipating the launch in 2002 of color videophones, which will be connected to the Web and will use the new GPRS (General Packet Radio Service) at 170 kilobits per second, and UMTS (Unified Mobile Telecommunications System) at 2 megabits per second.

Mechanical and electronic (mechatronic) systems that store sound and images—mainly tape recorders and videotape recorders with no moving parts—are being reduced to a single microchip. Goodbye cassettes, magnetic tapes, motors and read/write heads! With small solid-state digital sound readers, cybernauts can listen to music downloaded from the Web in MP3, a highly compressed music format.

Through the coupling of GPS (the satellite Global Position Systems), the cellular phone, "tags," and the Internet, humans will also have at their disposal a highly developed sense of direction. The GPS can localize a cell phone or a hand-held computer. A Web service will respond to any geographical question (such as: find the nearest hospital, the closest Italian restaurant, or a given address), and the cellular phone voice will guide the user to the destination. With miniaturized "tags," chips hidden in clothing or in cars and connected to GPS, cellular phones, and the Internet, it will be soon possible to localize or track people, cars, objects, parcels, or luggage anywhere in the world. With such miniaturization, these communications devices will be brought even closer to our sense organs.

Finally, the familiar television screens that are watched from several yards away are being replaced by special "TV glasses" that are right in front of viewers' eyes and that use a technology similar to that of the heads-up displays in the cockpits of fighter planes. The top of the frame hides a liquid-crystal display less than an inch in size, which is reflected in a half-silvered mirror placed at an angle to the viewer's field of vision, giving the viewer the impression of seeing a single screen with both eyes.

These examples show how transmission systems for audiovisual information from televisions, telephones, or computers are being miniaturized and brought closer to the human body. We can already envisage the next stages in communication between humans and the cybiont in two possible ways: through invasive and noninvasive interfaces. The former include electrodes, implants, or plug-in modules introduced into the body such as a pacemaker or a cochlear implant. The latter include the new virtual reality communications tools: video helmets, data gloves, data suits, and, soon, biosensors—a step on the road to a direct perceptual and emotional interface with the brain itself. Among the noninvasive interfaces, we should also mention a generation of creatures that live in the virtual world. These are intelligent agents, designed to facilitate dialogue with computers and navigation in information hyperspace. Let us first consider some applications of the direct method of communication, and then enter the world of virtual reality and intelligent agents.

RETINA SCREENS AND MEMORY IMPLANTS

Many laboratories are working on tools for direct communication. Because they are invasive, this approach, in my opinion, poses serious problems in the way it violates the integrity of the body.

Researchers at the University of Wisconsin are already working on *retina painting*. Their goal is to write synthetic images directly onto the retina with a low-intensity laser beam that penetrates the pupil by means of miniature semiconductor lasers placed on special glasses. Replacing even the screen in front of the eyes, the retina itself becomes the screen, the equivalent of the surface of the cathode ray tube in our television screens. Thomas Furness, director of the Human Interface Technology Laboratory (HITL) at the University of Washington in Seattle, has taken the project one step further. With help from Microvision, he developed the virtual retina display (VRD), which is already being used to train pilots in the U.S. Air Force, at Boeing, and at Ericsson-Saab Avionics to fly the next generation of fighter planes. It remains to be seen whether this process will really be danger-free for the fragile cells of the center of the eye and whether the users, saturated with images and lacking external points of reference, will not be driven mad.

As for the internal production of emotions that are stimulated by impulses to specific areas in the brain, such as with pleasure (we know where the pleasure centers are and how to stimulate them), joy, or terror, generating images or sounds right in the specialized areas of the brain is no longer a utopian idea. Without the necessity of implanted electrodes, these impulses will nevertheless have to reach the control centers by semi-invasive means, such as patches attached to the temples or transmitter bands that make contact with the skin, like those being developed as part of the Biomuse project described earlier.

A symbiotic way to transmit information directly between humans and machines is to use the natural electric conductivity of the human body. In the early 1990s, Tom Zimmerman and Neil Gershenfeld at the MIT Media Lab designed a low-frequency 0.5-MHz wireless technology that passes signals directly through the body within a range of 1 meter. This communications system is called *personal area network* (PAN). Today, companies like IBM are developing transmission systems that allow you to transmit your business card, for instance, through a simple shake of the hand! PAN has an important application for business security and authentication. Through PAN, users can transmit an encrypted identification to any kind of electronic machine when they come within range of its electrical field. This can be used for fast automatic registrations at hotels, with airlines, or in trade shows.

Laboratories are working on implantable memory modules to compensate for brain function impairments or diseases of the elderly. Will we one day see ads like the following on the TransNet, a commercial global network that will have arisen out of the Internet: "Lost your memory? Try our 100-gigabyte auxiliary modules! You don't want a plug-in card? No problem! A single call will allow you to download the encyclopedias of your choice! Don't forget to connect your biointerface. The whole process will take less than 30 seconds in compressed mode."

Systems such as these (patches, headbands, contact electrodes, auxiliary modules) raise the specter of a new generation of drugs—electronic drugs. Chips can contain in digitized, compressed form sequences of stimulation (music, colors, visions) that can be transmitted directly to the brain and the pleasure centers, using interfaces similar to those used in biofeedback devices now on the market. What an impact this would have on the lucrative drug market! No more exposed, visible plantations, complicated chemistry, or processing laboratories. Drugs will be digital, accessible on global networks with a bank card number, and possibly downloadable directly into the brain.

The five traditional human senses will perhaps become 10 senses. In addition to sight, hearing, smell, taste, and touch, we can also sense gravity and acceleration. Snakes locate their prey using detectors that react to infrared light; bees see in ultraviolet light; sharks can detect very weak electrical fields. Creatures as varied as pigeons, tortoises, bees, and even bacteria are equipped with tiny compasses, magnetic particles they use to orient themselves. Biotic senses would enable us to sense at will things such as low-frequency electromagnetic radiation or radioactivity, to extend our perception of colors or sounds beyond the narrow "window" of the visible spectrum or audible frequencies, to orient ourselves precisely in space, or to detect the presence of dangerous substances from a few molecules. Already a sixth sense is coming into being through our interaction with synthetic images within virtual worlds. This will transform the relationship between imagination and reality.

VIRTUAL REALITY: CLONING AND UBIQUITY

Thanks to virtual reality, I have passed through walls, flown over landscapes, opened magic boxes, fought invaders. These voyages in cyberspace are unforgettable. I remember them in as much detail as recurring pleasant dreams. This strange, disturbing world that is opening up to our minds creates a radically new situation in the evolution of our modes of communication. It represents a decisive stage in the emergence of the planetary brain.

In less than a decade, virtual reality has taken the world of computers and the media by storm. Launched on a commercial basis in 1989 by Jaron Lanier through his company VPL, which made the first tools for interfacing with the virtual world, virtual reality today represents an industrial, commercial, and strategic sector of prime importance among the major areas of development in society. Since this book is not about virtual reality, I refer the reader to the excellent articles, books, and research by Philippe Quéau, Director of the Information and Informatics Division–UNESCO, and the creator of Imagina, a virtual reality and synthetic images international conference, and Howard Rheingold, whose writings are essential reading. My aim is to describe the new two-way interfaces between humans, computers, and networks, which are accelerating the emergence of symbiotic humanity and the cybiont. I will deal later with the philosophical aspects of the conquest of inner space through this new tool, which, in my view, acts as an "introscope." But first, I would like to briefly review what we know as virtual reality—or more simply "the virtual," as Philippe Quéau prefers to call it.

This communications technology involves the creation, through the computer, of virtual spaces in which operators can move around and act on an environment made up of synthetic images. The voyage has three aspects: immersion, interactivity, and navigation. A person wears a video helmet equipped with special glasses in the form of miniature television screens to which the computer sends stereoscopic color images. Stereo earphones emit spatialized sounds. Sensors placed on the helmet detect the movements of the head and allow the computer to change the angle of vision by calculating and synthesizing new images. By wearing special gloves also equipped with movement sensors, the operator sees fingers on the screen as if they were his or her own hands. In this way, the operator can pick up electronic "objects" that are identical to real objects, turn switches on and off, start motors, operate levers, control machines, or operate on a virtual patient. An operator can also wear a special data suit that transmits the movement of the limbs to the computer. Several people physically located in different places can enter the same cyberspace, see each other, touch each other, and interact, thus forming a virtual community. Even more important, the technology of virtual reality makes it possible to create virtual clones—exact copies of real human beings—and, thanks to "virtual studios," to access new spaces that represent imaginary universes, inaccessible (infinitely small, infinitely large, or hostile) environments, or familiar places (laboratories, stores, forums, parks, video arcades, tourist sites, etc.).

Virtual reality is applicable to a wide variety of fields: the aerospace and automobile industries (model study, computer-assisted design, experiments in weightlessness, simulation of accidents), the military (cockpits, combat zones, piloting), robotics (teleoperations, hostile environments), transportation (visualization of new routes), architecture (building construction, virtual visits, interior design), medicine (surgical simulations), psychiatry (phobia simulations), chemistry (visualization of molecules and interatomic forces), education (exploration of the body, simulation of experiments), recreation (nature and amusement parks), art (new spaces, virtual museums), finance (visualization of the growth of a stock portfolio), marketing (sale of real estate and household appliances).

Today there are innumerable interface systems and tools offered by companies specializing in virtual reality. Clumsy video helmets and complicated gloves, but also joysticks, buttons, and trackballs are gradually being replaced by lightweight glasses, biosensors, and feedback gloves that provide the user with sensations of pressure and force, and even data suits that stimulate certain parts of the body.

Researchers at the Human Interface Laboratory in Tokyo have developed the successor to the data glove. It consists simply of a number of ultrasensitive biosensors worn on the wrist like a watch, which detect the electrical signals emitted by the muscles of the hand and fingers. This information is transmitted to a neural network, a chip that mimics the functioning of the brain, which recognizes what muscle the signal is coming from. The computer reproduces the hands from this information, thus making it possible to manipulate virtual objects.

A feedback glove made by a British company provides the actual sensations of touching distant objects. The wearer of this device physically feels the pressure or resistance transmitted by a virtual object. The technology involves some 20 cells that are inflated by air under pressure through tubes similar to blood vessels. Under the control of the computer, the glove stimulates the inner surface of the fingers and palm.

This very new field of virtual reality has had to develop a new science of computerized touch, whose aim is to understand how a computer can recognize or transmit the sensation of roughness or gentleness, the difference between a smooth and a sticky surface, the elasticity of a ball, or the softness of a piece of fruit. Arising on the borderline between mechanics, biology, and computer technology, the new science is called "haptics" (from the Greek *haptein*, "to fasten"). The science of manual and mechanical interactions with the environment, haptics makes it possible to convert information on the force, pressure, and angle of the wrist into the sensation of hitting a nail with a virtual hammer. Through research in haptics, student surgeons will be able to perform virtual operations by "feeling" the resistance of the tissues being operated on, designers will be able to create surface textures on the computer before an object is produced, and consumers will be able to feel between their fingers the quality of the leather in a catalogue of virtual products.

These devices—which will continue to diversify and improve, at an increasingly lower cost—show the extraordinary possibilities for interactivity offered by the virtual interface, which allows information to circulate in both directions between people and computers, making virtual reality the first noninvasive completely interactive biotic interface. By means of virtual reality, people can now communicate with computers not only through the voice, eye movements, and positions of head, hands, and limbs, but through the whole body. Soon, people will be able to transmit bioelectrical impulses from various parts of their bodies to computers through noninvasive lightweight sensors, and then directly from the brain through "silent speech," or the activity of the neurons, measured by changes in the brain's magnetic field.

A step in this direction was taken in 1999 by John K. Chapin and his team at the MCP Hahnemann School of Medicine in Philadelphia. The researchers placed electrodes in the brains of laboratory rats so that the animals could move a robotic arm simply by thinking about it.[*] They first trained the rats to obtain water from a robotic arm by pressing a small lever. Each rat had electrodes implanted in its brain to record the activity of certain neurons. As the rat manipulated the apparatus, the scientists analyzed the patterns of activity in the regions of the brain that control movement. They identified specific neuronal activity associated with the rat's paw movements. Chapin's team had to develop a new statistical method to analyze the brain cell signals and separate them out from the noise. They connected the robot arm directly to the rat's brain. The arm was then controlled directly through the implanted electrodes and the computer. At first, the rats continued to press the lever, even

---

[*] J.K. Chapin, et al., "Real-Time Control of a Robot Arm Using Simultaneously Recorded Neurons in the Motor Cortex," *Nature Neurosci*, vol. 2, 1999, pp. 664–670.

though this was no longer necessary for the robot arm to bring water. But soon the rats learned they could obtain water through brain activity alone, just by "thinking" about the water supply, and they stopped pressing the lever!

As John Chapin pointed out, this new field of neurorobotics suggests the imminent possibility of developing "neuroprosthetic" devices capable of restoring motor functions in paralyzed patients. These devices would extract "motor commands" from the brain through the use of neuronal population recordings, and employ that information to control robotic devices. Such symbiotic techniques could also soon be used to control computers or any electronic devices, creating a closer and tighter biotic interface between the human brain and machines.

Similarly, the computer communicates with people through sound (synthesis of speech, noises, music), three-dimensional images, animated graphics, tactile effects, and feedback. The new generation of virtual interfaces makes it possible to create the physical effects of a synthetic environment—wind, water, heat, vibrations, tremors, odors. Sensitive organs can even be stimulated directly (this has already been suggested for use in cybersex). The next generation will be based on biotic interfaces with the brain and its visual, olfactory, emotional, and motor areas to directly produce images, sounds, and sensations.

Virtual reality is much more than a mere communications technology, it is a door to new spaces. People have always dreamed of moving at high speeds, escaping the bonds of gravity, and communicating and seeing at great distances, and they do so today through automobiles, airplanes, telephone, and television. However, the power of ubiquity, teleportation, telepresence, changing external appearance, reversibly duplicating one's personality, or cloning one's body seemed forever out of reach. Virtual reality gives rise to unprecedented possibilities for exploration in these areas. A person could teleport several virtual clones and have them make speeches in his or her place (cloning, ubiquity, teleportation). One could control a remote clone and make it act in real time (telepresence) or change its form, or bring to life different individuals that meet in virtual communities (change of external appearance, duplication of personality).

The marriage of virtual reality and biotics will lead to the ultimate interface between the human brain and that of the cybiont. Humans will then have access to a new inner universe. To the relationship between the real and the imaginary will be added the relationship between the real, the imaginary, and the virtual—a shared inner universe, the embryo of a planetary coconsciousness leading its own life, notwithstanding the limited existence of the symbiotic consciousnesses of which it is made up.

OLIVER AND SARAH: INTELLIGENT AGENTS

Biotic interfaces imply relationships with electronic machines that are, to varying degrees, invasive. Of course, ubiquitous, lightweight biosensors that are no more cumbersome than a wristwatch or eyeglasses will be used for the most common applications. But there will still be a need for additional specific equipment. Hence the importance of the new "humanized" interfaces with computers and networks—"intelligent agents," autonomous, user-friendly, personalized expert programs, rather like dematerialized robot programs.

The cyberspace of the future will offer a plethora of information: a multiplicity of databases and interactive networks, a thousand interactive multimedia television networks, virtual libraries, audiovisual catalogues, guides, electronic reservation systems for hotels, car rentals, etc., all at the best price. We are moving toward complete saturation! It will be impossible for a poor isolated biological brain to find its way in these networks, to access these services, to use the countless passwords, keys, and codes that will be required. It will need a guardian angel, a guiding spirit, an untiring majordomo, a zealous and faithful intellectual assistant—in other words, an "intelligent agent" able to navigate through the twists and turns of interconnections, to sort out and select the relevant information, to propose strategies for accessing knowledge, to find and classify the mass of data generated by computers in their digital conversations, and to negotiate with other "agents" to defend the interests of its boss.

What will these "intelligent agents" be like? This curious term designates expert programs that provide ongoing electronic assistance with all the functions of computers and networks. One paradox of computer technology is that the more computers improve, the more they require of their users. Today, pull-down menus, icons, and dialogue boxes are part of the familiar landscape of the computer screen. But the software waits passively until the user decides what he or she wants to ask of the machine. Intelligent agents, on the other hand, try to anticipate the most probable actions of the user. After a period of breaking-in and shared experimentation with their owner, they learn how to carry out routine tasks automatically. When messages are received in an electronic mailbox, an agent can decide to sort them in order of priority or transmit them to other agents. It can find information in a spreadsheet and fax it to a correspondent. Agents can negotiate with each other on the network to determine the best times to set appointments between busy managers. They can access stock-market services and follow the investments in a portfolio, selectively collect information according to the interest profile of a user, or assist the user in finding the best price of a product by looking through hundreds of catalogues. Agents will also be able to select film or television programs and read newspapers and choose interesting articles for their boss.

Intelligent agents will quickly become essential for reaching correspondents when they are needed most. Studies show that, in emergencies, one call in four actually gets through, and the others get lost along the way, resulting in wasted time. Large telephone and computer companies such as AT&T, Motorola, and IBM are developing intelligent messaging systems that draw on various means of communication in order to locate a person wherever he or she is; to reach the person, all one will have to do is type a message into a microcomputer. The agent then takes charge, trying all the connection possibilities: telephone, fax, electronic messaging, portable phone, or beeper.

Equipped with speech and simulated human expressions, represented as explicit icons, agents will become true intellectual assistants, sometimes amusing, ironic, or critical, always familiar, and often essential.

The first agents were designed by General Magic, a small high-tech company financed by Apple, Matsushita, Philips, and Sony. The company has developed Magic Cap, a graphical interface for controlling teams of agents working in networks. Computer manufacturers, such as Apple, have created personalized interactive icons on their multimedia computers. The user can set the parameters of the interface, choosing the voice, sex, and physical appearance of the agent, designing a synthetic character, a robot, that appears on the screen as an icon and speaks, its lips moving with the words. The agent program understands human speech and responds the same way that computer icons do when clicked by a user.

Oliver and Sarah are two of the early prototypes for hundreds of agents now available on the Internet. These two computer creatures, who work in close collaboration, are products of the fertile mind of John Evans, president of News Electronics Data, an American subsidiary of the Rupert Murdoch group. Evans's objective was to make it possible for any user to order a custom-made newspaper, the *Daily Me*, through the use of agents. But many other applications have been developed, such as assistance with hotel and transportation reservations or research in databases.

Oliver is a yellow Labrador retriever. He regularly appears on the screen looking for something to do, independently of the functions being performed. If you do not give him a specific task, he gets bored, scratches himself, plays with balls of paper, and goes and sits in his corner. When you want him to search for references in international databases by key word, all you have to do is write the retrieval formula for him and he will disappear into the networks. At lightning speed, Oliver dials the numbers of dozens of databases, enters the codes, types the key words, collects the information and stores it in files, and returns with the results of his research, wagging his tail. If you're satisfied with his work, you give him electronic biscuits; if you're not satisfied, you send him to the doghouse. Oliver's expert program remembers the user's reactions and takes them into account when the next request is made by pursuing certain strategies and eliminating others. Thus there is reinforcement and learning as there is in training a dog.

Sarah is an ethereal character, a kind of fairy, represented by a vague, mysterious graphic. You tell her your travel preferences (type of hotel, location, price, meals, airlines, etc.), using a series of cursors similar to those in simulation games. Then, all you need to give her are brief instructions, such as "Organize my meeting in London with Jim Stuart for 10 o'clock on January 15. I would like to take him to lunch and return to Paris in the evening." On the basis of these instructions, Sarah goes to work. She knows your habits. No dawn flights, so she'll make a hotel reservation in your favorite area. You will have to leave Paris after your last appointment (Sarah manages your date book). Car rental, restaurant reservation (Sarah knows Jim Stuart's preferences, which are recorded in the contacts file), reservation for the return trip. Taxi to Charles de Gaulle Airport, as usual. With all the constraints determined, Sarah sends Oliver to check plane schedules with the travel agent and book the flights, book the rental cars and hotel, and make restaurant and taxi reservations. Oliver comes back with a series of automatic confirmation numbers. All Sarah has to do now is print your detailed schedule for the evening of January 14 and the following day. You will communicate your response to her, and she will update her reference files. Here, too, the expert program of the agent learns and evolves over time.

Of course, a good secretary can do all this, and the relationship with a secretary is—fortunately—richer than that with a virtual being. But Sarah and Oliver can work at the speed of electronics. Together, they can simultaneously carry out dozens of unpleasant, boring, routine tasks without getting discouraged, and they can communicate with other agents. Still at the prototype stage, they are the model for new generations of agents being developed by the major software companies. Secretaries will be able to devote themselves to tasks that are more interesting and that require human contact.

Intelligent agents will quickly constitute a new population of virtual beings. Like controlled computer viruses, they will reproduce, form groups, and develop their own "cultures." As representatives of artificial life, they will gradually colonize whole continents in cyberspace. They will work in teams; supplied with "permits" and "authorizations" (for making purchases or negotiating), they will be able to share tasks and compare information, and their skills will increase progressively as they do their research and prepare files. Circulating on the networks, these new "intraterrestrials" will offer their services to users. Using the genetic algorithms described here, agent programs will be able to mutate, self-select, and evolve to solve increasingly complex problems, increasing their value on the "electronic employment exchange." But there are also potential dangers. Knowing all their employer's habits, preferences, and secrets, they could be kidnapped on the networks and used against the employer. Agents negotiating on important issues could even organize to oppose certain demands or refuse certain constraints. Recently, a new generation of "Darwinian" agents that can mutate, learn, evolve, compete, and even "die" have been developed by Pattie Maes, an associate professor at MIT's Media Laboratory, where she founded and directs the Autonomous Agents Group.[*]

The physical appearance of intelligent agents will change considerably. Since virtual cloning makes it possible to create synthetic electronic beings, doubles of real people, they will be physically more human. They will communicate through speech, repartee, changes of expression, and mimicry. Science fiction writers and futurologists of the 1970s foresaw a world populated with domestic robots living in homes like pets. The robots R2D2 and C3PO in *Star Wars* personify this type of anthropomorphic, friendly robot. It is probable that certain duties will be carried out by a growing variety of real, mechatronic, and computer-generated robots or by swarms of minirobots resembling insects, like those developed by Rodney Brooks at MIT, described earlier. But just as the invasive and complex interfaces with humans will give way to less constraining virtual interfaces, the cyberspace, hypermedia, and information highways of tomorrow will be populated by agents, new virtual robots. Through virtual cloning, they will also invade our real world. A number of laboratories are working on the projection of animated holographic images, with remarkable results. Recently, researchers at the National Laboratory of Riso in Denmark have been able to produce a hologram in 5 billionths of a second with 20 three-dimensional images per second, a rate linked to the frequency of the lasers used. In about 10 years, it will be possible to achieve sequences at 24 images

---

[*] R. Brooks and P. Maes, eds., *Artificial Life IV: Proceedings of the Fourth International Workshop on the Synthesis and Simulation of Living Systems*, Cambridge: MIT Press, July 1994.

per second opening the way to true three-dimensional holographic color movies. Science fiction movies have already contained characters that communicated with the world through holographic projections, such as the small animated silhouette of the princess in *Star Wars* or the life-size form of Arnold Schwarzenegger in *Total Recall*. Progress in the three-dimensional projection of virtual clones will make it possible to have animated characters appear in our real world and interact with us; they represent the next generation of intelligent agents, the symbiotic population of virtual robots.

The worldwide network of the Internet is the beginning of the new collective cyberspace containing virtual clones, intelligent agents, and, undoubtedly, viruses and other electronic parasites that infect the networks. Virtual reality is creating a dematerialized world without biological cloning (which is bioethically unacceptable), without invasive prostheses to connect brains to each other and without a menagerie of robots living in our immediate environment—a world that exists somewhere between the imagination and reality, and that is likely to have a profound effect on our individual and collective actions.

The technical conditions for symbiosis between humans and the social macroorganism have been met. One of the fastest-growing areas of development, and one of the most significant for the future, involves the planetary brain, biotic interfaces, and cyberspace. That is why I have chosen this area as the model for examining the emergence of symbiotic humanity. Using the machines, the muscles, and the brains of human beings, an immense planetary being is gradually taking shape and coming to life: the cybiont.

4

The Everyday Life of the Cybiont

A PLANETARY SUPERORGANISM

Humanity has taken on an unprecedented challenge: to build a living organism from within—an organism possessing a higher level of organization than its own and one that is destined to become its symbiotic partner. No political theory, philosophy, or even religion has prepared us for this titanic task, which calls into question the sovereignty of humanity and the impact of human action on the world.

To try to imagine such a prospect and to visualize the probable next stage in the evolution of humanity, I have proposed the metaphor of the cybiont, a planetary macroorganism that is currently evolving. In many respects, the cybiont already exists in a primitive state and is living according to its own dynamics. The diverse forms of social organization, cities, communities, machines, transportation, and communications networks are its visible macrostructures, its vital organs and tissues. Gradually, this hybrid human tissue is spreading out over the surface of the planet, differentiating and reproducing itself in a way that is analogous to the proliferation of the cells of an embryo when a living organism is formed.

The metaphor of the cybiont is useful for thinking about the global nature of the phenomena with which we are dealing. Let us compare the Earth and the cybiont. The planet is a self-regulating cybernetic machine whose functioning is analogous to that of a living creature. This model (which James Lovelock called Gaia) brings together in a single unifying concept elements from a number of different disciplines. The cybiont is to the social macroorganism what Gaia is to the planetary ecosystem. But, in fact, like Gaia, the cybiont is made up of competing subsystems. The diversity of the world is such that it would be unrealistic to think in terms of the emergence of a *single* planetary macroorganism. From one end of the Earth to the other, nations and human communities live within different time frames even though they appear to be contemporary. Each, with its own culture, traditions, world view, and pace of technological and industrial progress, is unique. The concept of more or less advanced nations is based on economic criteria that cannot be applied to the whole of humanity. Therefore, many macroorganisms will constitute the subsystems of the cybiont, and even many cybionts living in different time frames. Perhaps the future will see them competing for survival or domination.

To put it simply, then, I see the cybiont as a single planetary organism, and, more specifically, as the most advanced form of a *planetary brain* now coming into being. There are many reasons for this, the first of which is the speed of its development. As a result of the coevolution of communications and data processing systems, we are witnessing an autocatalytic reaction leading to the self-selection of a whole series of elements connected by network. A fundamental symbionomic principle that we have already encountered is at work here. Second, the cybiont, which is partially dematerialized, is one of the most sedentary forms of organization achieved by the biosphere at this stage in its evolution; at the present time it has no need to move, since its life as a parasite of Gaia provides it with the energy needed for survival. Finally, the cybiont in its current form is capable of contracting time through the accumulation of a critical mass of information, and it is spreading over the whole planet by means of its communications networks. Its organizing influence and its role as a catalyst will be increasingly decisive. Thus, the cybiont is winning out over any other emerging form of macrolife.

Scientists, philosophers, science fiction writers, and political visionaries have spoken of the advent of planetary superorganisms and even described them, sometimes in great detail. It is a possibility that inevitably suggests itself if one takes a sufficiently distanced view on the evolution of humanity (and of its inventions, productions, and constructions) as a whole, although we may have reservations because of the disparities, inequalities, and unequal rates of develop-

ment of different societies in the world. The descriptions of such superorganisms are sometimes naive, utopian, or poetic, but they do
recognize the macroscopic phenomenon of which we are both witness and agent. One can refer to several approaches: the Noosphere
of the French Jesuit and philosopher Pierre Teilhard de Chardin, a
global sphere of all minds connected through communications networks; Jerome Clayton Glenn's worldwide "Conscious Technology";[*] Gregory Stock's "Metaman" concept; or the work undertaken
by Francis Heylighen and the Principia Cybernetica Web international research group on the computer-supported collaborative development of an evolutionary-systemic philosophy (Web site: *http:
//pespmc1.vub.ac.be/*). As a major application, the group is writing a
hypertext about the global brain created by the interconnection of
humans, computers, and networks.[†]

Without shying away from the use of analogies, which are often
creative, but at the same time being wary of latent anthropomorphism, which is always reductive, I would like to draw on everyday
language and images to describe the life of the cybiont. I see this as
a necessary step toward understanding the role of symbiotic humanity in the development of future forms of organization.

VITAL FUNCTIONS ON A GLOBAL SCALE

On the human scale, the life of the cybiont is not easily perceptible.
But the night-time view of a city from an airplane window can
sometimes suggest the vibrant pulsating life of a vast luminous cell
spread out below, while the incessant traffic of the city's highways—
white lights on one side, red on the other—calls up the image of
blood cells circulating along veins and arteries. From higher still,
satellite images give us the unforgettable and magnificent vision of
the blue planet, complete with signs of social life—megalopolises,
highway networks, industrial fumes. A single glance reveals various

---

[*] *Future Mind: Artificial Intelligence*, Washington, D.C.: Acropolis Books, 1989.
[†] F. Heylighen and J. Bollen, "The World-Wide Web as a Super-Brain: From Metaphor
to Model," in *Cybernetics and Systems '96*, R. Trappl, ed., Austrian Society for Cybernetics, 1996, pp. 917–922.

aspects of civilization: the orgiastic luminosity of the three megalopolises, eastern United States, western Europe, and Japan; the
streams of light of the great transportation routes, the highways of
northern Europe, the Trans-Siberian Railway, the Nile Valley; the
flames of gas flares in the oil fields, but also the lights of fishing boat
flotillas and the myriad forest and brush fires lit to clear land in developing countries.

These images are strong, but they are fleeting. From our usual
vantage point, things return to their fixed, human-centered shapes—
the cities, of course, which are the macroworld of the immediately
visible, but also the communications, transportation, railroad, and
electricity networks; large construction projects, bridges, dams, factories; and especially the infinite variety of landscapes shaped by human beings, who have lived in symbiosis with the land for millennia.
The macroworld of the invisible includes the economy, with its innumerable and simultaneous transactions, and radio and television
waves relayed by satellites weaving an immaterial web around the
planet. It is also the world of the international money markets, of underground or underwater oil pipelines, information superhighways,
computerized data banks, and the laws, codes, and temporal conven-
tions that control, regulate, and synchronize the multiplicity of activities of human societies.

Like any living organism, the cybiont provides for its major basic
functions: self-preservation, self-regulation, and self-repair. Using
people and machines, it feeds itself, converts energy, digests, and
eliminates its waste (still imperfectly). Its main foods are oil and carbohydrates. The former is used to run mechanical machines and,
through electricity, electronic machines; the latter, the product of
photosynthesis and agricultural production, feed biological machinery, human and animal. The cybiont also feeds on other forms of energy (nuclear power, biomass, and natural gas), but on the global
scale, oil and carbohydrates are its staple foods. Biological, mechanical, and electronic machines convert energy into useful work, maintaining the structures and functions of the cybiont and enabling it to
develop.

The vital tissues of the planetary macroorganism are differentiated, like those of a living organism. Cities, for example, have areas

that consist largely of housing. The rural areas of the world are dotted with farms, self-sufficient units that use the sun's energy and biomass for the survival and development of human beings and animals. The farm, in fact, is an advanced form of symbiosis between humans and nature. In urban areas, there are storage areas for food, oil, water, materials, equipment, information, and capital. The internal circulation of the cybiont resembles that of a living organism. The arteries, veins, and capillaries of transportation systems carry energy, materials, and information by air, water, rail, and road, and distribute them to every household. Each mobile machine involved in this circulation has its own specific characteristics and functions, like cells and blood corpuscles. People and goods circulate from country to country on an endless carrousel, while entire zones of the cybiont's tissues and organs repair, heal, and renew themselves.

The digestive system of the cybiont transforms complex materials into simple substances that can be used by its metabolism or stored for later consumption. The wastewater and garbage are taken away by the sewage system, collected by cleaning services, and eliminated, treated, and recycled by specialized units that fulfill the function of the kidneys or the liver in a multicellular organism. The digestive system of the cybiont does not yet function in symbiosis with Gaia: waste is "encysted" in dumps or piled up in the open air and allowed to pollute whole regions of the planet. The cybernetic loops of macroregulation are not yet closed, as they are in the natural ecosystem by the work of decomposer microorganisms.

The cybiont is made up of a multitude of nested defense mechanisms or systems, which maintain its structures and functions. The city is a protective system that insulates a human community from the outside and supports its cultural, political, industrial, and commercial exchanges. Originally, the walls of cities served to protect the inhabitants against invaders who came to plunder their crops and possessions. With energy distribution, waste collection, and communications technologies, houses themselves have now become microenvironments, their functions being regulated in symbiosis with humans. This type of symbiotic structure also extends to other controlled microenvironments such as those for work (office towers), commerce (superstores, shopping centers), recreation (indoor sports facilities, domed tourist centers), culture (museums, science centers), and travel (large airports). The army, police, and firefighters are the immune defenses that protect the social organism against threats and intruders.

The planetary communications systems connected to computers are the rudiments of the nervous system and brain of the cybiont.[*] Material and immaterial flows of data, regulatory instructions, conversations, images, and sounds circulate in an endless ballet, carried by wires, cables, optical fibers, electromagnetic waves, satellites, radio and television transmitters and receivers, computer screens, telephones, and news media. The networked functioning of human society has reached such a high level of complexity and is developing so fast that it has become a symbionomic phenomenon deserving special attention.

The nervous system and brain of the cybiont regulate the material systems of exchange and transportation that form the metabolism of the social organism and ensure its self-preservation. The linking of electronics and mechanics is a hybrid form of internal regulation of the flows of energy, information, and materials that are the major cycles of the relationship with Gaia, the global ecosystem. Macrointerfaces connect the individual human "neurons" to the major metabolic functions of the cybiont. They are connected to markets of goods and services, global airline reservation systems, and money markets through credit and debit cards and to satellite traffic-control systems, interpersonal computer communications networks, computerized polling, and economic and health indicators. The planetary eyes and ears of the audiovisual media and weather and other telemetric sensors are gradually becoming the true senses of the Earth.

The life of the cybiont is also evident, in a frenzied, accelerated form, in the ups and downs of the stock market and currency markets. The market is like a parallel supercomputer putting together the decisions and actions of multiple agents following simple rules— prices, rates, indexes. Thanks to computers, communications networks, and time zones, the stock market operates in real time almost

---

[*] See Joël de Rosnay, *Le Cerveau Planétaire*, Paris: Olivier Orban, 1986.

without stopping. Its fluctuations, as shown on graphs, are chaotic, almost biological, like the continuous measurements of vital signs such as pulse, rate of respiration, blood pressure, and hormone levels in the blood. When we observe the functioning of stock markets and world currency markets, we see that they constitute a living ecosystem. This regulatory macrointerface has its own "psychology." Commentators describe the moods of the stock market in human terms: it is depressed, euphoric, morose, feverish; it waits expectantly or anticipates events. These descriptions have become so commonplace that we forget their macroscopic nature. The stock market is nothing less than a directly perceptible sign of the life of the cybiont.

I could go on for pages and pages metaphorically relating the life of the cybiont to the life of a biological organism. That is not my purpose, since the limitations of such a description quickly become evident. My first concern is humanity, symbiotic humanity. How will human beings carry out their activities and express their freedom given the constraints of the cybiont? And how will humans benefit from the regulated, harmonious operation of the social macroorganism?

Two basic functions of the cybiont allow us to begin to answer these questions: *self-preservation* through the linking of ecology and economy and *self-perception* through the emergence of a collective intelligence and consciousness. It is in these two functions—one ecospheric, the other noospheric—that the symbiotic relationship between human beings (as creators and agents) and the cybiont is not only being born, but is developing and accelerating at this very moment.

GAIA AND THE DAISYWORLD

The idea that the ecosphere functions as a kind of living organism is not new. As early as 1795, James Hutton compared the planet to a superorganism. Vladimir Vernadsky invented the term *biosphere* to designate all living organisms and their networks of interactions. In 1969, James Lovelock put forward the Gaia hypothesis (named for the Greek goddess of the Earth) to designate the living planet, a controversial concept but a fruitful metaphor if we rid it of certain presuppositions.

Lovelock applies a systemic approach and cybernetics to the entire Earth ecosystem. To a systems theorist, there is nothing shocking in this, although it has led to some naive and extremely limited interpretations. There is a kind of "pantheism" to the idea of Gaia, a new ecological cult of the Earth goddess.

Lovelock's hypothesis is appealing. People accept it instinctively and often emotionally. The main criticisms that can be made of it are that it is intuitive and that it is based on a hodgepodge of writings by other authors. It does not readily lend itself to the traditional scientific approach of hypothesis, experiment, publication, peer review, and theory. Moreover, it is not subject to Karl Popper's criterion of falsifiability. Richard Dawkins rejects it because it considers only one entity, with no competition from other "Gaias" and thus no possibility of natural selection. But it can be argued that there are competing subsystems within Gaia, and that the mechanisms of selection can function internally. Moreover, as we will see, the Gaia metaphor is useful for its synthesis, its integration of various disciplines. Though controversial, it advances scientific thinking and brings together researchers from different disciplines.

Gaia is sick. Humanity is like a parasite that threatens its equilibrium. The greenhouse effect is Gaia's fever. The hole in the ozone layer is a cancer of Gaia's "skin." Acid rain, solid waste pollution, and water pollution are Gaia's digestive disorders. If, with Hutton and Lovelock, we look at Gaia's global functioning in terms of "geophysiology," we can treat these diseases with a "medicine" of the Earth. Ecology and environmental policies are thus connected in the same way as biology—the knowledge of living creatures—and medicine—the prevention, diagnosis, and treatment of disease.

In *The Macroscope*, I used a similar approach, describing the Earth as a cybernetic machine with homeostatic properties analogous to those of a living organism. I also described the origin of life on Earth as a biogeochemical phenomenon involving the major cycles of global regulation.

The planet indeed functions as a cybernetic machine: it regulates its own functions, it comprises nested communications networks based on the variety of living species it contains, it maintains balance and is goal-oriented. The ecosphere fulfills all the definitions and descriptions of complex systems and their dynamics: open systems, hierarchical levels of complexity, cybernetic regulatory loops, communications networks, variety of elements, autocatalytic and homeostatic mechanisms, evolution, competition of subsystems, and constant disappearance and renewal of elements and structures. Living organisms are complex, autonomous, self-regulating, evolutionary systems. Thus, Gaia's functioning can plausibly be compared to that of a living organism. This is a fruitful metaphor that allows us to integrate many scientific disciplines previously divided in their approaches to ecology: geochemistry, geology, geophysics, population biology, plant biology, genetics, biochemistry, oceanography, meteorology, and climatology. The Earth is not an inert mass of rock inhabited by living organisms unable to modify their environment. It has an anatomy and a physiology, and a birth, a metabolism, and an evolution. The biosphere and the ecosystem as a whole are connected by multiple regulatory loops and cycles that constitute an indivisible complex system. Living beings are thus able to manipulate their environment—in particular, the atmosphere—to establish climatic conditions favorable to their survival.

How does the Earth automatically maintain its average temperature? It is believed that the regulatory system functions like a thermostat. If this is the case, who set the equilibrium value? Without falling back on teleology or some larger "intention" or "plan," cybernetics and systems theory show how such a balance can be established through coevolution and cross-catalysis. A model, the Daisyworld, was described by Lovelock, who made it one of the foundations of the Gaia hypothesis.

The Daisyworld is an imaginary planet inhabited by two species of daisies, white ones and black ones. The planet is illuminated and heated by a star that we will call the sun. The white daisies reflect the sun's heat (as does snow), cooling the local surface of the planet. The black ones absorb heat, warming the ground locally. The simulation, easy to carry out on a microcomputer, starts with a low temperature. The black daisies, which absorb the heat of the sun better, survive, develop, and occupy a large area. As a result, the temperature of the soil increases, becoming more favorable to life. The black daisies reproduce at a high rate but cover too much area, and the temperature increases above a critical point; the black daisies die off en masse. But the white ones adapt, develop, and colonize large areas, reflecting the heat and cooling the planet again. The temperature drops—too much. The white daisies die and the black ones return in profusion. After a certain number of fluctuations, a "mosaic" of black and white areas begin to coexist and coevolve on the planet's surface. Individual daisies are born and die, but the two populations, through successive heating and cooling, maintain an average temperature favorable to the life of both species, and this temperature fluctuates around an optimal balance. No one set the temperature; it simply emerged—the result of the daisies' behavior and of their coevolution. Moreover, if the "sun" were to heat up abruptly, the system would adapt to the new conditions and reach a balance around a new average temperature. Unlike the world of the two daisy species, the Gaia model comprises myriad simultaneous interactions that create a network of multiple interdependencies. But the fundamental principle remains the same: the emergence of dynamic equilibrium values that are favorable to life and that are influenced by the living creatures themselves in coevolution with their environment.

ECOLOGY: THE ECONOMY OF NATURE

Such a simple, productive model is extremely important in the theory of symbionomic evolution, because it helps us understand the emergence in human society of quantitative or qualitative equilibrium values that regulate complex systems, such as those involving prices, markets, poll results, and the distribution of votes. How does the ecosystem work?

> The ecosystem is much more than merely the milieu in which one lives. In a way it is itself a living organism. Its giant cycles activate everything in the mineral world and the living world. Its biological power plants produce billions of tons of organic matter, matter that is stockpiled, distributed, consumed, recycled in the form of mineral elements, then reintroduced in the same factories, to be replenished with solar energy and to re-

turn through the cycles that maintain the life of every organization. *(The Macroscope, page 24, original edition)*

It is solar energy that fuels the cycles of the ecosystem. The energy transfer between a heat source (the sun) and a cold sink (deep space) produces work—the movements of the ocean currents, the winds of the atmosphere, the cycles of the biosphere, and the reproduction of living creatures.

The ecosystem consists of four interacting realms: water (the hydrosphere), air (the atmosphere), earth (the lithosphere), and life (the biosphere). The elements essential to life are successively used and recycled in the great cycles of carbon, nitrogen, sulphur, phosphorus, oxygen, and water. They circulate as gas molecules, soluble ions, crystals of mineral salts, or organic molecules among three great reservoirs—the atmosphere (and the hydrosphere), biomass, and ocean sediments—where they are stored for periods of time ranging from a minute to millions of years. These reservoirs act as "buffer memory," helping in the regulation of the overall mechanisms and the maintenance of homeostasis. Because they involve the combined action of atmospheric, geological, and biological cycles, the major cycles of maintenance of the ecosystem are called *biogeochemical* cycles.

In this cybernetic macromachine—or superorganism—the biosphere acts as a "heart," activating these biogeochemical cycles by means of two simple reactions, nitrogen fixation, or the conversion by leguminous plants of atmospheric nitrogen into ammonium ions (the raw material of amino acids and proteins), and the conversion of inorganic carbon (CO_2) into sugars. These two reactions, with the help, respectively, of the catalysts nitrogenase and chlorophyll, contribute to the formation of the terrestrial and aquatic biomass and the development of human life.

The economy of the biosphere is based on the relationship among *producers* (plants that carry out photosynthesis), *consumers* (animals that feed on living organisms and produce their energy through respiration), and *decomposers* (microorganisms that recycle by feeding on dead organisms or waste). Producers manufacture sugars and oxygen from water, light, and carbon dioxide. Animals use oxygen to burn sugars, produce biological energy, and return carbon dioxide, water, and mineral salts to plants. Decomposers recycle the essential elements of the biosphere. All these functions are regulated in relation to one another in a "market" of exchanges and transactions, the market of energy, information, and building materials. Ecology is therefore an *economy* of nature, just as the economy is an *ecology* of the social system.

THE ECONOMY: A LIVING ECOSYSTEM

Nobody invented the economy. It arose through autocatalysis from a set of networks of interactions and closed loops that is the market. The system grew more and more complex until it became our modern economy. Ecology and economy are the two complementary aspects— although still antagonistic today—of the same global system of survival, self-preservation, and development, an embryonic system of symbiosis between the ecosphere and the technosphere. The former involves the "natural" ecosystem, or Gaia; the latter, the "artificial" ecosystem created by humans, or the cybiont. The metabolism of the cybiont has developed within Gaia, draining energy and resources for its own benefit and endangering the future of the planet to which it owes its survival.

The economy has its origins in gift-giving, then bartering, and then the market. The economy can be defined as a communications system or a multiprocessor operating in parallel. The market allows many agents to make individual decisions simultaneously, comparing desired goods and services according to their estimated or barter value, or their posted price. They can then acquire them through exchange for other goods or services or for currency. The market originally grew out of individual actions in the form of barter in village squares, a type of exchange that made it possible to balance the flow of objects fabricated and products consumed. With the introduction of currency, the market then developed in a more dematerialized form. This lubricant or catalyst of the economy made it possible for work, exchanges, consumption, and savings to be spread out in space and time. An hour of work done in one place could be exchanged in another place, at another time, using money that was freshly earned or had been stored for a long time.

By "desynchronizing" and "delocalizing" exchanges, removing the constraints of time and place, money created explosive conditions for autocatalytic development. The set of networks of interconnected markets self-selected through the symbionomic process of lock-in, already discussed earlier. The introduction of electronic money, connecting credit cards to the banks' computers in global telematic networks, added another level of complexity and speed. The market is thus a self-regulating adaptive system. Prices are established at the point of convergence of scarcity and desire, serving as information for the regulation of the "ecosystem" of the economy. The economy as a whole may be regarded as the system of production and exchange of goods in order to satisfy the needs of human beings.

Reduced to its simplest elements, the economy functions like an ecosystem: a transfer of energy produces work, making the machine run. Five major areas interact: companies (production), households (consumption), administrations (government), financial organizations (banks), and the outside. As in the ecosystem, these areas serve as reservoirs, are linked by flows, and are regulated by cybernetic feedback loops. Behind the flows and loops are a myriad individual and collective decision-making centers. Consumers work in companies and are paid wages. In the general flux of currency, they buy goods and services on the market, or save by investing their wages in financial organizations. Companies receive money for their products and buy materials and know-how for production, or invest their reserves. Governments acquire goods and services from companies in the private and public sectors, borrow from financial organizations, and provide social benefits to households. Private individuals and companies pay various taxes to governments. The regulatory mechanisms are constantly modified by external factors such as trade balances, currency markets, foreign debt, interest rates of foreign central banks, and prices of energy and raw materials.

Economic and political leaders act on the regulatory mechanisms of the economy by means of various "valves": bank interest rates, currency exchange rates, inflation controls, wage negotiations, measures to encourage consumption, taxation, tax cuts, job creation measures, export promotion measures, and sales of military material and heavy engineering equipment. But the combined effects of their actions are not always those expected. The complexity of the system and the unpredictability of the behavior of economic actors often lead to unintended results that go against their policies. In addition, the indicators, signals, and "control panels" used [gross domestic product (GDP), stock exchange indexes, currency values, reserve ratios, unemployment statistics, purchasing power] do not take into account all the actors and regulators in the system; they provide a reductive view of the relationship between the two ecosystems.

One of the main challenges of the third millennium will be to bring together ecology and the economy in a creative, mutually beneficial relationship. To accomplish this, we will need to change our attitude from "every man for himself" to "all for one and one for all."

FROM EGOCITIZENS TO ECOCITIZENS

The economy can no longer be viewed in its traditional form as a closed, isolated system, but rather it must be seen as a system that is open to an environment on which it feeds. When the economic machine accelerates or races out of control, it requires more energy, materials, and information, and discharges more waste into the natural environment. In the beginning, the dissymmetry between the metabolism of Gaia and that of the emerging cybiont was such that the economy seemed able to use inexhaustible free resources and produce waste, with little impact on the environment. But the flows, reservoirs, and concentrations of the economic metabolism quickly became as large as those of the natural ecosystem, and it became clear that the ecosystem alone could not ensure the survival and development of human societies, with their agriculture and industries. A new balance between growth, development, and the depreciation of Earth capital became crucial. The modern view of the economy is thus that it is inseparable from its physical relationship with the ecosystem. The energy that is expended in producing work and the flow of waste that results from it have repercussions on the whole ecosphere. Our model of the economy is incomplete if it does not include an external source of energy and resources, and if it does not take into account the waste produced by the economic machinery. To bring it closer to the model of the ecosystem, recycling loops and the degradation of potential energy toward entropy are necessary.

In order to better link the economy and ecology, we also need to introduce the concept of *ecocapital*, a form of capital essential to the survival of the system, to supplement the three forms of capital in classical economic theory (land, labor, and the capital of machines and finance). Ecocapital has to be "depreciated," like any capital, and renewed through investment. Gaia's contribution has to be taken into account. It can be entered in the accounts in two ways: as renewable and nonrenewable production resources, or as "nature services" (removal and elimination of toxic waste, recycling, maintenance of survival conditions through climate control, protection against UV radiation, etc.). When ecocapital and nature services are introduced, it becomes clear that the Gaia-cybiont symbiotic relationship is a vital necessity for the future.

There are therefore two ecosystems, one natural, Gaia, and the other "artificial," the economy, the metabolism of the cybiont. The former is based on symbiotic, or mutually beneficial, relationships, using the income from ecocapital; the latter is based on the accelerated exploitation of resources and the irreversible depletion of ecocapital. The former functions on solar energy and its derived forms; the latter functions on energy from fossil fuels, where reserves are limited, or nuclear power, which in the long term poses a threat to the biosphere. The conflict between the two types of ecosystems is evident in cities, made infirm by their own parasitism and the self-centeredness of their inhabitants.

It is astonishing how long it took economists to become aware of the nature of the relationship between the natural ecosystem and the social ecosystem. The same major symbionomic principles are at work: metabolism of energy; self-preservation, competition or cooperation among species or companies, populations or nations; transmission of information; culture; competitive exclusion; flows; reservoirs; decisions; markets; exchanges. Technical and social evolution and the economic ecosystem are not a direct extension of Darwinian biological evolution; they are different in nature. Conscious

beings act at the nodes of networks, but the same symbionomic principles apply. This demonstrates the unity of nature and suggests avenues for building the future.

For real symbiosis to be possible, people must divert part of their
individualism into participation in a system that is larger than themselves and from which they can benefit. The traditional economic
system is founded on individual reward, and everything—education,
advertising, the idea of success, politics—is geared toward stimulating individualism and the achievement of personal goals. The modern economy has become a machine that produces egoists, or "egocitizens." Public works, economic growth, international communities,
national competitiveness in world markets, and patriotism all take
second place to individual needs, gratification, or rewards. Only war,
unfortunately, often transcends these egoistic, partisan interests. Neither an ecosystem nor symbiotic relationships can function without
a collective intelligence that arises from actions involving both individuals and the larger whole. A change from today's top-down approach of political or technocratic plans and programs to a bottom-
up approach based on different values and involving membership
organizations, community life, and participatory democracy would
be a good start toward creating a new sense of community. (This
question will be discussed in Part III.) We are now reaching the limits of "economism." We need new values and a new ecoethics to be
able to move beyond individualism to an organized community that
respects individual freedom and personal initiative. To make the
great transition from the pursuit of individual goals to the conscious
coordination of collective actions, we must stop being egocitizens
and become "ecocitizens." The symbiotic human being is an ecocitizen of the world.

How can ecology and the economy be coupled in a mutually
beneficial partnership? What would such a symbiotic relationship
between Gaia and the cybiont be like?

THE SYMBIOSIS OF GAIA AND THE CYBIONT

Writers have described planetary macroorganisms in two strikingly
different ways. Either they see the ecosphere as the only model of a

planetary organism, or they regard human society and its machines as a social meta-organism, almost independently of their relationship with the ecosphere. The approach I have chosen connects the two entities in a symbiotic partnership that is in coevolution but still at a primitive stage. The two worlds are in balance. Humanity and its artifacts are not merely a small part of the ecosystem, but rather an entity that, because of its rapid development, its uncontrolled population growth, its energy consumption, and its pollution, is in direct competition with the ecosystem. Since the mid-twentieth century, the human population has doubled, world economic production has quintupled, and the gap between rich and poor has widened. In 1960, 70 percent of global revenue went to the 20 percent of the population in the richest countries; today the figure is more than 80 percent. World production of biological energy through photosynthesis can theoretically reach 150 billion tons of organic matter a year. Human beings have already destroyed 12 percent of this potential and directly use 28 percent of it, leaving only 60 percent for the rest of the entire biosphere and its millions of animal and plant species. Our relationship with the ecosystem is parasitic; deforestation, acid rain, the greenhouse effect, the destruction of the ozone layer, water and air pollution, soil erosion, and the reduction of biodiversity are the measurable manifestations of this parasitism.

A parasite can certainly kill its host, and there are abundant examples of this in biology and medicine, from cancer to AIDS. But the collective human intelligence that is beginning to emerge can also invent adaptive solutions in symbiosis with Gaia. The major planetary cycles and the regulatory loops of ecology and the economy can be coupled as they are in living systems, in which the linking of a number of cyclical reactions is the principal condition for the maintenance of the structures and functions of cellular metabolism. The symbiotic relationship between the economy and ecology can provide a durable foundation for the self-preservation and coevolution of *both* Gaia *and* the cybiont. This, in essence, is the meaning of sustainable development; however, this important concept does not bring out the real complementarity between ecology and the economy. I therefore propose the concept of *regulated adaptive development*, which goes beyond mere "ecological" considerations and emphasizes the vital need to seek symbiotic solutions rather than continue our parasitism—doomed in the long run—or envisage a sterile coexistence of Gaia and the cybiont and take the risk that the human species will be eliminated as a result of the overall reactive "egoistic" rebalancing of the ecosystem.

There is great cause for concern in the situation that exists today. Cities are a typical example of the parasitic evolution between the human community and its environment. Although we are individually intelligent, we seem collectively incapable of quickly finding solutions to deal with the constraints created by our rapid growth.

Sensing the danger, however, people are beginning to get organized. International treaties have been signed banning the use of toxic substances. There are sensors in cities, at sea, and on satellites that measure pollution of various kinds. Citizens, informed by the media, can limit the use of their cars or their furnaces. The sum of the regulations, detection mechanisms, preventive measures, and individual actions constitutes a cybernetic macroregulation loop. In keeping with a symbionomic principle already encountered, the collective behavior of individuals acting simultaneously according to simple rules can solve global problems. The big issue is the establishment of these regulatory systems and the closing of the feedback loops. This will require strong motivation, as well as reinforcement and reward mechanisms. These mechanisms are common in the ecosystem, but we have great difficulty implementing them in the social system, where they come up against the unwieldiness of our economic, political, and industrial structures as well as the selfishness of the egocitizens, whose prime motivation is still the satisfaction of short-term individual goals. On the other hand, if synergies can be developed in general motivation and communities of interest, the system as a whole could evolve quickly to the desired balances, as the following example illustrates.

Let us imagine that the capital of the Earth is divided into shares held by the five billion Earth-dwellers. On the basis of regularly published information and indexes on the "health" of their shared capital, the shareholders have the power to enhance its value. If the carbon dioxide in the atmosphere increases, or if the pollution measured by satellites rises dangerously, the value of the shares drops, and the Earth capital depreciates. To avoid this and to increase the value of Earth capital, each shareholder can invest time, savings, or know-how. Through informed individual action, the shareholders can collectively influence the trends. The idea of preventing the depreciation of Earth capital, or ecocapital, has greater motivating potential than does environmental protection, which may sound elitist. As shown in the figure below, reinvestment may take place during consumption or recycling; the capital remains untouched, and only the income is used.

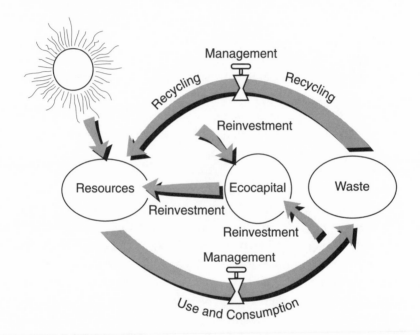

Of course, such a mechanism of share ownership in Earth capital is simplistic and utopian. However, it demonstrates the "virtuous circle" of macroregulation that could be established through the simultaneous decisions and actions of millions of individuals and brings out the advantages of a conscious symbiotic coupling of ecology and economy, of the metabolism of Gaia and that of the cybiont.

The Earth's metabolism fulfills the major functions of self-preservation: circulation and use of energy, production of goods, and recycling of materials. But information and networks also play a role, by fostering a collective consciousness. Cyberspace is the precursor of this new environment of dematerialized exchanges.

NAVIGATORS IN CYBERSPACE

The planetary brain of the cybiont is in the process of emerging. It functions—as we saw in the example of the Internet—through individual human "neurons" connected by computers and communications networks. The electronic highway provides the nerve pathways of the planetary nervous system, and personal computers, which are becoming more and more common and increasingly miniaturized, are the glial cells that allow the neurons to function and create interfaces. Through interconnected global networks—private, public, commercial, and military—local networks, and networks of networks, a collective brain is being created, a hybrid biological and electronic (and soon biotic) brain with a vastly greater processing capacity than that of our few billion neurons or our most powerful computers.

Human "neurons," electronic highways, computers, and megamemory are the building blocks of cyberspace or, better, "cyberspace-time," a new electronic environment for the collective thinking of the cybiont. Cyberspace-time is the virtual world that is emerging from the information exchanged by people on communications networks. It allows us to create infinite hypertextual and audio-visual environments that coevolve with the frequency and density of exchanges. The world of the Internet is part of cyberspace. It is creating the conditions for a new electronic citizenship; a new kind of relationship among human beings; new cultural, business, and research opportunities; and a new kind of competition. But cyberspace is still a jungle full of dangers in which it is easy to get lost, a digital wild west where bandits and villains roam at will. Cyberspace is a limitless, uncharted ocean into which we venture with rudimentary maps, without effective navigation tools, using a few procedures that are still very limited. We need to invent an *intellectual ergonomics* to help us enter and move around in this space of knowledge, creation, and recreation.

What are the basic rules of navigation in hyperspace and hypermedia? The rules of navigation at sea are well known. The navigator stays on a given course to reach port on schedule, taking into account constraints such as wind strength and direction, currents, reefs, and other boats, guiding the vessel by means of beacons and lighthouses and tools such as compass, sextant, charts, and even radar and sonar. In a car, we use maps and guidebooks, and we read the road signs. Similarly, in a book, we use running heads, page numbers, chapter titles, and the table of contents to orient ourselves. The analogies with the car and the book help clarify the scope of the cyberspace revolution. The book represents individual freedom of access to accumulated knowledge; the car, freedom of access to space. The computer, a means of "travel" in cyberspace, combines the freedom of the book with that of the car. It is an individual means of access and navigation in hypermedia, a connector, guide, chart, compass, radar, and sonar all in one.

But we need to look further at the "psychology" of the cybiont, which is still in its early stages. We are witnessing the beginning of what I call the *introsphere*, the result of the introspective awakening to consciousness of the "mind" of the collective brain. The time factor is not very important in the following description; predictions that extrapolate from linear patterns are very often wrong. Rather than predict when practices, tools, or procedures will be developed, I will describe the probable outcomes of coevolutionary processes as if they had already occurred. Here, then, in narrative form, is the innermost functioning of the interfaces between the cybiont and the "assisted" brain of symbiotic humanity.

VOYAGE TO THE HEART OF THE INTROSPHERE

Two of many possible worlds are opening to our exploration in the *introsphere*: a virtual world of synthesized spaces, communities, clones, and robots, accessed by means of the tools of virtual reality, and a real world of living biological beings connected by a dense network of computers that increases the intelligence of the organizations in which these beings live and work. These two worlds coexist in a complementary way in a variety of practices.

The interfaces connecting us to the cybiont are constantly being improved, and they are more and more like those in biological networks. We use hybrids of personal computers, telephones, and televisions that have been miniaturized and freed of the wires connecting them to the telephone network and power lines. They are mobile and portable, and their powerful batteries provide days of autonomy. We communicate with these machines by voice, in normal speech, with no need to pause between words. The machines speak to us in male or female voices that we select, and animated faces appear on the screen in two or three dimensions to personalize our relations with them. Sometimes little three-dimensional characters emerge from the screen, virtual holographic clones are projected by optical devices. The machines also understand messages handwritten, or even scribbled, on a flexible electronic pad resembling a sheet of paper. They recognize faces and facial expressions, gestures, and body movements and extract information from them to better understand us and talk with us. They can also pick up odors and use them as a source of information.

The portable versions of these powerful machines fit easily in a pocket, like a wallet. They communicate with us discreetly by speaking in our ear without wires, through induction or radio waves, or by displaying text and images on the virtual screen of lightweight glasses so that they appear to float in our field of vision. Virtual reality interfaces are simple and compact. Helmets have been replaced by three-dimensional glasses with wireless earphones. Feedback gloves have been replaced by sensors on the wrists or other parts of the body, which pick up bioelectric impulses from the nerves to the muscles. The feedback is transmitted by simple, lightweight systems. We can enter the virtual world at any time, thanks to intellectual ergonomics.

The networks are permanently connected to these prostheses. Powerful computers are thus accessible at any time, vastly increasing the processing capacity of personal computers. Networks of networks like the Internet are areas for advanced experimentation with the operation of the brain of the cybiont. The user interface of the Internet has been greatly improved. The browser's interfaces that were used to navigate from computer to computer throughout the world by clicking on icons or text have been replaced by the faces of intelligent agents or robots we talk to or present with images, text, or graphics. Digital radio, music, and films are available on the networks, as are interactive video for television, videoconferences, and telepresence, which is used for remote operations or manipulation in virtual reality. The "HomePage" explosion at the end of the 1990s is now relayed by the "HomeChannel" proliferation. Users can create, edit, and update their own video show and television broadcasts on their Web site with the help of special multimedia software. Manipulatable virtual spaces make meetings easy. They grew out of the work of researchers at the Xerox Palo Alto Research Center (PARC), who developed multiuser-domain object-oriented (MOO) programs that allow many remote users to interact in familiar spaces such as offices, cafeterias, or conference rooms with boards to write on. Following simple instructions, the users of these spaces establish audio and video contact, and act in real time on the same objects.

We can do laboratory research or consult huge virtual libraries in cyberspace, and when we do so, we feel as if we are moving physically in a lab or a library. For example, in the virtual library, we can look at a book by clicking on its cover; its type and color images are identical to those in a real book. The same is true of browsing in virtual supermarkets, shops, or catalogues, or manipulating molecules or moving around in extremely small spaces.

Interfacing with the networks of networks has been fundamentally changed by the widespread use of vocal commands, automatic connections with ubiquitous microphones, and intelligent agents. Just as many continued to use fountain pens in the era of the disposable pen, people will continue to use microcomputers. But microcomputers have become depersonalized, and they blend into the environment. Falling costs, increased power, and miniaturization have made them so common that a single office may have dozens of them, in the form of scratch pads, electronic badges, or intelligent "post-it notes." The computer no longer needs to be a nomad; it has become part of the environment, which the late Mark Weiser, director for research at Xerox PARC, called a "ubicomp." Ubiquitous and practically disposable, it communicates wirelessly, using radio or infrared connections, with networked computers and other "ubicomps" in its immediate environment. No need to log on to see if you have messages in your electronic mailbox; your intelligent agent notifies you, and reads them on request.

In large organizations, employees wear active badges that keep track of where they are, and cameras record the movements of people and documents. Procedures to respect individual privacy have been established and are continuously reviewed by the users. The whole organization thus assists in the memorization of facts, events, transactions, and meetings, facilitating the use, classification, and storage of this information. Computers record and summarize meetings, talks, and seminars and make the summaries available at any time on the network. Electronic scratch pads connected to video cameras allow you to jot down a sentence you've heard and click on it to access the digital sequence that corresponds to that precise sentence.

Methods and tools used to be aimed at increasing the efficiency and productivity of the individual. The purpose of today's communications and collective memory storage technology is to enhance the intelligence of the organization itself. The company is no longer a static information structure; it has become a dynamic communications ecosystem. According to John Seely Brown, director of Xerox PARC, it is a "refinery" of knowledge.

THE STRANGE POPULATION OF HYPERNETWORKS

The virtual worlds of cyberspace are populated by electronic beings that are essential to the real-time functioning of society. The most widespread of these are intelligent agents living in symbiosis with human beings. Agents are expert programs that have three characteristics. First of all, their programming is object-oriented, which gives them a great deal of flexibility to adapt to the missions assigned them. Second, they are extremely mobile in the networks, because they know all the connection and interface procedures. Third, they are parameterable, and can be given any form or style desired. Agents practice a variety of occupations; there are communications agents managing text and audiovisual electronic messaging, secretaries, librarians, consultants on purchasing or selling goods and services, managers of stock portfolios, clerks, messengers, and security officers. Like their "cousins," computer viruses, they move easily through the networks and mutate, recombine, and form subpopulations. They are personalized by their employers, and they are involved in a great many types of transactions.

Let us look at how an intelligent agent faxes a document requested by a correspondent. A call comes in on the digital videophone server at someone's home or office. The face of the person being called appears on the correspondent's screen, and a greeting is played: "I'm not in at the moment. My agent will field your request." The face of the agent in charge of messaging appears on the screen. A dialogue ensues concerning the document requested. The agent looks through the list of documents for which there is free access, identifies the document sought, and forwards it by fax or electronic transfer to the person making the request. If the request is particularly important or urgent, the agent informs its boss by portable telephone, pager, fax, or e-mail, selecting the appropriate means.

Another example is simultaneous translation. A person carries a powerful, miniaturized computer, with connections by hertzian modem to networked computers that specialize in the syntactic and semantic recognition of oral phrases and expressions. A microphone picks up the voice of the person's interlocutor. An agent establishes a link with the appropriate translation systems. The interlocutor's words are translated in real time, and the translated version, adjusted in volume and speed by the agent, is heard through miniature speakers placed in the ear.

Agents read all the interactive multimedia television programs; with thousands of channels available, it is impossible for the unassisted human brain to search the hundreds of pages of daily programming in entertainment, education, information, games, at-home shopping, sports, and financial transactions. Connected to the cable networks and the electronic highway, agents go directly to the source and extract the relevant information according to the interest profiles of their bosses, even adding some of their own suggestions. They thus help their bosses deal with information overload and info-pollution.

This reminds me of an anecdote. A few years ago, I went to great lengths to receive a personalized newspaper on my computer that was automatically printed every morning at breakfast time. All that was required was an initial connection to the various services available—news service, stock market index, weather forecast, etc.—and to link them together into the different sections of my newspaper. Each item of information was saved in a file and then printed. When I described this to a technophobic friend, he said he had the same service every morning, but with a human touch that was important to him. When I pressed him with questions about his hardware, his modem, his programs, he answered simply, "I have a chauffeur. Every morning when I get in the car, he gives me the information I need, with a little humor and personal opinion thrown in." This is a good lesson in pragmatism, but also a demonstration of the importance of personalization.

Agents can interact with each other to negotiate contracts, make appointments, and establish prices. Knowing their bosses' preferences and even some of their psychological characteristics, they search out partners in cyberspace for various types of needs, such as communications displays, photographs, documents, transparencies, or video clips, which can be screened individually or broadcast for teleconferences on multiple screens simultaneously. The agent organizes these in time and space, as requested. Instead of traditional, linear communication (X speaks, others listen; Y speaks; and so on), communication takes place simultaneously, with the participants displaying their messages in spaces that can be consulted in real time and in an order managed by the agents, as with the use of posters in the presentation of scientific papers.

BEYOND IMAGINATION: REAL VIRTUALITY

Intelligent agents manage interfaces by interconnecting all the existing networks, allowing people to access information and act in real time, as do the neurons of the brain. This new planetary neural hypernetwork functions chaotically, fluidly, and in a way that is constantly reconfigurable, in response to decisions made in parallel by hundreds of millions of interacting human agents and virtual robots. In this, it resembles the immune system, the hormonal system, and the nervous system, three interconnected networks that determine an organism's psycho-neuro-immunological behavior. Similarly, there are three main modes of human communication in networks: top-down, as in the mass media; bottom-up, as in social feedback; and transversal, as in interpersonal communication by telephone or communication among groups through interactive virtual communities. Their interconnection forms the basis for the psychology of the cybiont and contributes to its self-consciousness.

As a noninvasive interface, virtual reality is the ideal entry into cyberspace. It is an "introscope," a tool for exploring the "mind" of the cybiont. Freed from the material constraints of the body, we are able at will to explore dream—or nightmare—worlds inhabited by virtual clones and multifunctional software robots. Ubiquity, teleportation, telepresence, and cloning or duplication of the personality are all possible through the introscope. We can act on a time-sharing basis and take part in several simultaneous processes, entrusting time management to our agents, who act as impresarios or public relations officers. Working life and recreational activities weave in and out between the real world and the virtual world. Some people get lost in virtual reality; they are the new electronic addicts, cyberspace hobos living marginal lives in the infinity of hyperspace, electronic zombies eternally wandering in the limbo of virtuality. But others find a source of creative power in the pooling of brains assisted by systems of collective memory and time organization. Thanks to intelligent environments filled with computers and faithful agents, they succeed where individual brains previously failed. Symbiotic humanity, in partnership with the cybiont, has increased human creativity exponentially and made possible truly collective creativity.

We have reached a crucial stage: the emergence of a new space of imagination and waking dreams, the introsphere, the sphere of the virtual, manipulatable by the mind, by the senses, by actions. Its amplification of the powers of invention of symbiotic humanity further accelerates the symbionomic evolution toward higher levels of complexity and collective consciousness. This stage is so important that it must be examined in the context of symbionomic evolution.

Before the dawn of humanity, the "inventions" of life were the result of the interaction of DNA, living organisms metabolizing energy, and the environment. In biological evolution, every "idea" has to undergo full-scale testing in the form of a mutant species, one with new characteristics that might give it a competitive advantage. Through natural selection, the environment acts as a filter, eliminating the least fit "ideas" or "inventions." The transmission of the useful ones is linear and occurs only with the transition from one generation to another. This is why the overall process of biological evolution is so slow.

In intellectual evolution, where an invention is equivalent to a mutation, symbionomic evolution is considerably faster. Human beings can invent things without having to wait for the birth of a new generation to judge the results. Thanks to the relationship between the real world and the imaginary world, we can construct hypotheses and models and test them by reasoning or simulation, without necessarily having to translate them immediately into reality. We can think using symbols, analogies, metaphors, and inductive reasoning. Imagination acts as a random variety generator. DNA, once confined in the biological organism that ensures its survival, is now externalized in the form of plans, projects, diagrams, blueprints, patents, prototypes, guides, and electronic memory, making it easy to introduce changes, comparisons, or recombinations. Reality and imagination are the two complementary faces of invention and creativity. Hence there has been an extraordinary acceleration of technical and social evolution as compared with biological evolution.

With the introsphere and its connection to virtual reality, a new world has been created between reality and imagination (see the figure below).

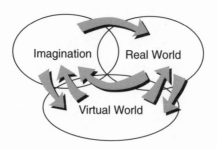

We can imagine complex objects and systems and their operation, build them, and test our hypotheses in the dematerialized world of the virtual. The introscope is an extraordinary catalyst for creativity. In addition, virtual space is accessible to other symbiotic intelligences that can select and eliminate or consolidate inventions, models, and constructions. The virtual world introduces a new dimension in the play of ideas, as money does in the economy. The unwieldiness of barter, as we saw, inhibited the flow of exchanges. Money acts as a lubricant in the economy, making time and space irrelevant. Dematerialized electronic money makes transactions and exchanges even more fluid and makes possible real-time management of economic and financial complexity. In the same way, the virtual world now complements the imaginary and real worlds, giving rise to an additional level of collective consciousness. These transitions happen in an accelerated time frame, particularly digital evolution, which is a self-catalytic process occurring much faster than technological or biological evolution.

But there is another crucial step to be taken in the relationship between the real, the imaginary, and the virtual worlds, an extraordinary threshold to be crossed: the direct connection of the brains of symbiotic humanity with the brain of the cybiont through a biotic interface.

Biotics is the marriage of biology and computer technology. Biosensors and transducers connected to the brain or other parts of the body relay to computers information that can trigger actions. A biotic interface between the brain and the virtual world will mark a new stage in the emergence of a collective consciousness, a meta-consciousness capable of outliving the individual consciousnesses that make it up. With the biotic interface, a true symbiosis will be established between humanity and planetary macroorganisms, of which the cybiont is a "thought model." Voice recognition, voice synthesis, and recognition of handwriting, facial expressions, and gestures are intermediate stages on the way to the ultimate interface between the human brain and the brain of the cybiont. The global neural hypernetwork will function and think using a new type of organization; it will be a hybrid planetary brain, both biological and biotic.

THE MIND OF THE CYBIONT

Gaia and the cybiont are partners in this symbiosis, the former with its primitive metabolism of self-preservation and development—the economy—and the latter with its embryonic planetary brain— the thinking network.

In living organisms, the use of energy is controlled by information. In the relationship between Gaia and the cybiont, we can conceive of the planetary brain gradually replacing the "natural" homeostasis of Gaia. Human beings could thus initiate the conscious macroregulation of economic flows and flows of energy, giving rise to the conditions for the dynamic stabilization of the environment. Some mechanisms that regulate flows of energy and materials by means of information have already been implemented: air traffic control using computers; the regulation of traffic flows on highways and in cities by means of intelligent tollbooths, systems to locate and guide cars using on-board terminals and relays, and satellite positioning; computer-monitored routing of parcels by the post office and other carriers; and electronic money, which combines the immateriality of electronics with the materiality of money, goods, and services and is already in widespread use. Unfortunately, there is no regulation of energy use at the point of consumption; electricity producers have no real conservation policies and actually even try to stimulate consumption.

The thinking network of interconnected brains, computers, and means of communication operates chaotically. Connections are created and then disappear. Groupings are formed, serve as dynamic memory, and combine with others. Some connections between nodes are strengthened, while others are weakened. Shapes emerge, associations of ideas, dynamic currents carrying messages, turbulence, stabilization, obliteration . . . the brain of the cybiont is fluid, in perpetual reconfiguration. In this, it resembles the immune system, which is a *mobile* brain, and the nervous system, which is operationally closed.

In 1949, in his book *The Organization of Behaviour,* Donald O. Hebb, a neurophysiologist at McGill University, in Montreal, proposed a revolutionary new theory of psychological behavior. According to this theory, the brain constantly reconfigures the synapses that transmit nerve impulses. Through the chemical action of activator or inhibitor hormones, the synapses are reprogrammed as a result of various stimuli. Through the successive stimulation of neural connections and pathways, whole areas made up of thousands of neurons are activated and connect so as to form subsets that store information through the reinforcement of impressions (shapes, colors, sounds, words). These subsets constitute dynamic networks of neuronal interactions, the brain's building blocks of information.

I propose to look at the formation and functioning of the brain of the cybiont in a similar way. Human beings, multiple agents in chaotic interaction, are the neurons of the hypernetwork. The links among them, occurring through computers (and even more directly through biotic interfaces), are giving rise to a conscious representation of the "mental" functioning of the cybiont, a global consciousness that is reflected in the introsphere. These links are reversible, and they can be reinforced or inhibited. Autocatalytic processes take place, leading to new concepts, solutions, or ideas. The Internet today abounds with examples of this.

In symbiotic humanity, each person functions as a node in this hypernetwork. Symbiotic humanity is both the totality of the network and one of its elements; it exists through the network, and the network exists only through it. Nodes and links are connected in an operation that, in turn, acts on each of them. The whole exists only through the conscious functioning of the parts, and each part is fed and vitalized, and has its intellectual potential amplified, by the functioning of the whole. Cities once provided the amplifying social network for people's physical, intellectual, and cultural capacities. Economic, sociological, and ecological constraints have now led us to seek other, complementary and dematerialized, networks in order to amplify our potentialities. The networks of networks that make up the electronic city offer a possible solution. The combination of individual brains, intelligent agents, and the mind of the cybiont is creating an informational ecosystem whose development now appears irreversible, giving rise to a collective intelligence, a consciousness that is increasingly becoming aware of itself.

The transition from the social being *Homo economicus* to symbiotic humanity presents obvious advantages, as with any symbiosis, but also new risks. Is this the kind of future we want? What are the advantages of the cybiont for humanity? How should we guide our evolution to reach this new stage?

At this point, it makes sense to try to determine rules for the complex systems of which we are both integral parts and responsible agents—rules that apply to traditional politics as well as to industry and the economy, and values and conduct that respect the community. I propose to develop such rules in the following chapters, which will deal first with managing complexity, then with the organization and production of the industries of the future, and finally with the individual and social values that are essential for the integration of all humans into a larger whole.

III

Wanting the Future

5

Managing Complexity

BACK TO EARTH: THE CHALLENGE OF A FRAGMENTED WORLD

As a symbiotic entity of a superior order, the cybiontic model illustrates the progressive transition of the human species toward ever more complex levels of organization. Signs of such an evolution can be found in political models of social organization. Communities, confederations, common markets, economic cooperation treaties, and supranational organizations are all steps on the road to creating a planetary macroorganism.

However, the febrile cybiont may seem like a parasitic outgrowth of the industrialized world, a cancer of developed societies, feeding on and draining away ever greater amounts of energy, information, and materials.

Parasite or symbiotic partner? Unique planetary life-form or macroorganism competing with others of its kind? I see the cybiont as a hypothetical model that can help shed light on the contemporary choices determining our future. It seems to me that the probable appearance during the next millenium of a planetary macroorganism superior to the human species has every chance of changing the relationship between humanity and itself and to its place in nature.

Almost worthy of science fiction, the sheer magnitude of this highly technological and futuristic vision might be shocking, even depressing, to some. An overly optimistic view of technological evolution might imply an image of a world that can find its own technological solutions to the great problems of humanity. Can a planetary brain made up of interconnected computers, an economic metabolism that benefits a fraction of the world's population, a growth that endangers the Earth's equilibrium, be considered the focal point for the evolution of the entire biosphere? Time for a reality check.

The everyday drama of our usual landscape is more familiar, of course. It is always more realistic to analyze the world from this point of view. Demographic growth, hunger, epidemics, wars, inequality, AIDS, drugs, urban overpopulation, the squandering of natural resources and food supplies, the extinction of species, environmental catastrophes . . . Our daily menu of world news does not help us develop a synthetic view or long-term prospect of possible avenues for technological and social evolution.

No solution will be found to the problems of equity and wealth redistribution, for instance, if we do not solve the question of demographic growth. There were one billion Earth dwellers when Napoleon became emperor in the early nineteenth century. Two billion around 1930. Three billion in 1960. Four billion in 1974. Five billion in 1987. Six billion in 1999. The planet's population will be somewhere between 8.5 and 12 billion in 2030. It will double within a single lifetime, whereas it took more than 10,000 lifetimes to reach the two billion mark.

Today, the world is divided among 5.5 billion individuals who belong to some 6000 different cultures. Can a mosaic of this kind contribute to the creation of a planetary macroorganism? Symbiosis seems unrealistic at a time when human and international relations are dominated by egoism, and our attention is entirely focused on satisfying basic needs, consuming the goods and services of the market economy, and, for the privileged few, accumulating yet more goods. This is how 20 percent of the world's population use 80 percent of the Earth's resources. How can we create salutary symbioses when poverty, inequality, despair, disease, violence, fundamentalism, intolerance, and attacks on individual rights are the rule rather than the exception? In a world of wrangling and merciless competition, is there room for cooperation, complementarity, solidarity? The world's life pulse is strictly synchronized by clock time. Yet, *many* worlds coexist, each in a separate time frame, enclosed within its own time bubble, and bearing its own particular time *density*.

We need only consider the relative global numbers for food supply and transportation to witness the profound level of disparity in all its brutality among the world's 6000 cultures. In simple terms, our world is divided into three demographic tiers or time frames: one billion people are destitute, four billion belong to the middle class, and one billion are privileged.

The billion most underprivileged human beings have no clean water and no electricity. The majority can neither read nor write. They owe their survival to the local biomass, which provides their main energy supply. They earn less than one dollar a day and gain in return only 1.4 percent of the Earth's riches. These billion people move about on foot. Six hundred million of them are on the threshold of chronic malnutrition, and 400 million are so undernourished that they are at risk for problems of growth, mental handicap, and premature death. One hundred million are homeless.

The world's middle class lives on the very edge of equilibrium. These three billion people travel by bicycle or bus, eat grain and leguminous plants that provide vegetable protein, drink barely clean water, and have milk for their children.

The richest billion human beings consume 66 percent of the world's food products, 70 percent of its energy supply, 75 percent of its metals, and 85 percent of its wood supply. They claim 90 percent of global research and development funds and 80 percent of education spending. This wasteful billion uses 10 times more steel than people in the third world; 12 times more petroleum; 15 times more paper; 18 times more chemical products; and 19 times more aluminium. Four hundred million of them drive cars and consequently create 14 percent of the world's carbon dioxide emissions. These billion meat eaters get 40 percent of their calories from animal fat. They eat three times more fat per person than the other four billion inhabitants of the globe. Their carnivorous bulimia gobbles up 40 percent of the world's harvested grain for use as cattle feed—it takes 5 kilograms of grain and the energy of 2 liters of fuel to produce a single kilogram of steak.

While 400 million men, women, and children around the world live below the threshold of survival, Americans spend $5 billion a year on weight-loss programs and diets. Children in the United

States get an average yearly allowance of $230, an amount considerably greater than the global income of the most underprivileged half-billion people. The gap between rich and poor is steadily growing, even in developed countries. As Mahatma Gandhi put it, "The rich must lead a simpler life so that the poor can simply live."

Such is the spectacle of our world—to take only two basic indicators, food supply and transportation. We are far from unity and solidarity. Under such circumstances, how can we successfully carry through the transitions that await us? The demographic transition toward equity. The economic transition toward using the Earth's income rather than its capital. The social transition toward a better redistribution of resources. The technological transition toward the use of environmentally friendly tools and machines. And the institutional transition toward a more stable equilibrium between national and international institutions.

A paradigm shift and a long-term vision of our own evolution can help us make these transitions successfully. The paradigm shift is already under way—witness the world view that has arisen from the ecological movement. A long-term vision that is no longer bound by sector-based and linear extrapolation will allow us to imagine the next step for the human race, in which the personal is enhanced while humanity is integrated into something greater than itself. Neither religious nor totalitarian, this natural artifice is organic, physical, and biological.

THE CYBIONT'S ADVANTAGES: THE ART OF SUBSUMPTION

To help our fractured world change and evolve in a way that respects humanity and human diversity, we need a global vision that integrates individual action into global behavior. To date, only religions and authoritarian political systems have been able to motivate, persuade, and pressure humans into moving in the promised or desired direction. With the discovery of the unitary principles of nature and the rules of symbionomic evolution, we now possess guidelines and beacons to guide us along this uncertain road. But nothing can be taken for granted, and progress is chaotic. We may fail at our attempt at symbiosis, or the cybiont may turn against us, becoming a cybernetic monster enslaving humans to its own purpose.

Still, the larger picture is becoming clearer—particularly, the gains to be made from a symbiotic relationship between human beings and the macroorganism. In such a relationship, the macroorganism would be answerable to humans, who would, in turn, be answerable to the macroorganism to an even greater extent than they are within the current framework of traditional "society." The relationship will require humanity and human organizations to renounce some of the sovereignty and control they hold over lower levels of organization. This is the cost of acquiring broader powers and means. And it involves applying the principle of *general subsumption* common to all hierarchical organizations, like those found in biology or ecology.

As part of a new approach that complements traditional hierarchical processes, it seems appropriate to revive a rarely used term—the verb "subsume." To subsume means to consider an individual object to be part of a larger whole (an individual within a species, a species within a genus, and so on). In Kantian terminology, to subsume means applying to sensory intuition the category of understanding that guarantees its unity.

In our understanding of organizations, we generally assume that orders must come "from above." Hierarchy involves a structure of command by which power is increasingly concentrated in fewer hands as we move up the ladder. The top of the pyramid is the preserve of the head of state or government. Power is not shared. Decisions cannot be made collectively.

The principle of subsumption involves reversing this form of hierarchy. In biology and ecology, lower levels of organization yield a share of their work to the higher level, but retain local control over certain functions, and retain their original structural integrity. Union differentiates. Rather than thinking we are enclosed within successive boxes in pyramidal structures, the subsumption principle allows us to think of ourselves as integrated, without loss of self, into something greater than ourselves. Each human stands at the tip of an infinite number of pyramids, which open out toward other organizational levels, and which ensure, through organized multiplicity, the functional coherence necessary to the community as a whole. Rather than depending on the single power of an elected intelligence, subsumption highlights the necessary emergence of a collective intelligence.

In other words, applying the idea of subsumption to society requires a common search for means that guarantee the unique character of individual action and freedoms, on a global scale and in the interest of all. Thus, the superior level can take charge of new global regulations without superceding those regulations that continue to work at the local level. By subsuming these kinds of functions, symbiotic humanity can acquire new technical, conceptual, and intellectual powers. Like a cell in the body, dependant and interdependant, but *autonomous* in its activity, symbiotic humanity will benefit from the cybiont's contributions while preserving its own autonomy.

Today's society already offers protection against chance and adversity. Thanks to individual financial contributions and to probability studies done on large groups of people, the citizens of developed countries are protected from risks of various kinds through life insurance or unemployment insurance, pension plans, social security, mutual insurance services, bank services, or goods and service distribution. On a more global scale, a planetary brain—whose complexity cannot be compared to that of our own brain—grants us the unmatched ability to solve problems and control, master, and regulate collective mechanisms. The exploration of the introsphere opens up new areas of knowledge and pleasure. Flow and force management within available macrosystems allows us to change our environment to suit our individual interests and improve our quality of life. Access to banks of infinite memory extends our learning possibilities and improves our capacity to follow multiple ecological and economic indicators in real time. It also encourages resource sharing and reduces inequality. Regulating energy consumption by sharing intelligence strengthens individual action without collective risk and maintains Gaia's equilibrium. Individual action is made more effective through better collective action against the potential negative repercussions of complex systems. And this makes possible the implementation of global cybernetic regulations that respect individual responsibilities.

GOVERNMENT, CYBERNETICS, CITIZENSHIP

Humanity is currently in the throes of a massive transition, progressively evolving out of individualism and into a consciously organized, living collectivity. The network's nodal points are individual humans, physically and intellectually nourished by the system as a whole. Since the very beginnings of society, all the great organizational systems of collective life have aspired to this. Codes, laws, and regulations constrain individuals, but liberate society as a whole. The fundamental shift here from the classical political viewpoint comes from nature; not *reducing* the workings of society through some positivist scientific view to a small number of simplifying mathematical laws; but rather *elevating* the intelligent conduct of these societies to a superior degree of thought and action through a creative compromise among natural laws, political action, and spiritual aspirations. Could the enlightening vision of a possible future help to unite religion, politics, and science, the three paths traditionally chosen by human beings on their lengthy quest for survival, knowledge, and action?

The transition from the social individual to the symbiotic human, consciously and naturally integrated within one or many suprasocietal macroorganisms, stands as one of the greatest challenges ever faced by humanity throughout its entire evolution. It is as crucial a stage as the transition from single-cell life to multicell integrated organisms. This stage is essential to the emergence of the planetary brain's global and introspective consciousness.

Our current social and political models will not see us through these stages. Democracy may seem like the least problematic way to foster individual freedom and strategic diversity. But its yield in human energy is extremely low. General regulations and local feedback loops essentially reinforce individualism and satisfy egocentric needs. The machinery distills or generates personalities and egos, but rarely becomes a network whose collective intelligence outshines the individual agents making it work. To ensure a successful transition, we need to break the chains of individualism and egocentricity that smother social solidarity. We need more *eco* and less *ego*. We need to get away from anthropocentrism (and even, sociocentrism) to make way for an *ecocentrism* that will benefit us all. The path is difficult, however, and our destination uncertain, given the current organization of the market economy, the profound inequity in the allocation of planetary resources, the lifestyle of privileged consumers, and humanity's habitual and halting response to all major change.

What does government mean in a symbionomic context? It is a steering mechanism that can run complex systems. The verb "govern" has its roots in the Latin *gubernare* (to steer) and the Greek *kubernetes* (a rudder). André-Marie Ampère called the science of government *cybernetics*, a term he coined in 1836. In 1948, the word was rediscovered by the American mathematician Norbert Wiener, who gave it its current definition as the science of regulation and communication in living organisms and machines. The (theoretical) role of government thus covers the implementation and use of mechanisms that run and regulate the dynamics of the complex systems that make up human social life. It is a form of government that respects human diversity and human freedom, and that gives everyone a chance to lead a meaningful life. But to be able to steer, you need a charted course, tools of measurement, instrument panels, and feedback from the environment on which you are acting. The short-term vision of traditional politics and existing vehicles of citizen participation (elections, votes) no longer provides effective complexity management.

We must therefore distance ourselves from political systems to consider the "world system" as a whole. We can take inspiration from descriptions of the cybiont's life to uncover the main lines of political action necessary for fostering the emergence of symbiotic humanity. This challenge is so complex that it stands beyond the management abilities of current government structures and operations.

REGULATING PLANETARY FLUX

One of the fundamental problems facing a cybernetic regulation system is how to use information to control flux. In a systemic model, the general dynamics of interaction between components depend on the interplay among reservoirs, outflow, and feedback loops. The intensity of the outflow is proportionate to the quantities held in the reservoirs. This is the case for electricity, for the energy created by a dam, and for the interest drawn from a capital source. Each potential (tension, gravity, concentration, monetary value) is coupled with a flow whose speed is proportionate to the force by which it is determined. It is expressed, like any outflow, as a quantity per unit of time: salaries as dollars per week, travel as people per hour, information as bits per second, car production as units per month. This hydraulic analogy helps to better illustrate the cybernetic control of system dynamics. Each flux is symbolically controlled by a "floodgate," which acts as a decision and action center. And in response to information received about reservoir levels and outflow, the levels can be regulated by opening or closing the floodgates.

What kinds of flows, floodgates, and reservoirs does a cybiontic system have? Imagine vast stocking areas strewn across a planet traversed by currents both visible and invisible. Arteries, veins, and paths of communication give physical form to the exchanges, while flows of information, capital, and finance remain unseen. There is a dreamlike quality to the magnificent, colorful atlas pages showing so many circuits encircling the Earth, the breadth of each line reflecting its level of flow. Here, we see the privileged connections being made between continental blocks, countries, and cities. The circulatory system is almost biological, an additional proof of the reality of cybiontic life: the flow of commercial products calculated in billions of tons annually and the monies flowing in return, the flow of finance (nearly $3000 billion every day), capital transfers, an energy network principally made up of petroleum (20 percent of the value of global trade); the flow of information (computer data, patents, news agencies), of raw materials, of food; the flow of car, plane, or computer parts to various global destinations for assembly. This dense trade network is evolving principally in the northern hemisphere, among the United States, western Europe, and Japan. Airline and maritime maps clearly show the Atlantic Ocean as the great crossroads of international trade, the "aorta" of the planetary organism. Rich countries import and export manufactured products; poor countries mainly export primary materials.

In addition to these visible and invisible flows, there are the great human migrations and the flows of illicit exchanges in the parallel economy, a parasite suffocating the cybiont. The great reservoirs of supply and demand determine the dynamics of global currents. Workers flow like sand out of huge low-income population reservoirs and into richer and less populated countries. Mexicans flow into the United States—during the last 20 years, seven million Mexicans have settled there, and 20 million more were expected at the beginning of the third millennium. Turks flow into the Netherlands, Algerians and Moroccans into France. The mediterranean countries from Morocco to Turkey have a population of 200 million, while central and western European countries have a population of 400 million. In a single generation, the former will reach 450 million and the latter 420 million. There is also the flow of tourists—mainly toward the Organization of Economic and Cultural Development (OECD) countries, which account for 90 percent of monies spent and 80 percent of revenues received from international tourism. The flow of refugees is constantly increasing, now at 15 million worldwide.

Then there are the mafia-controlled drug and arms networks, a metastasizing cancer eating away at the most fragile democracies. The great supply reservoirs are South America (Colombia, Peru, Bolivia) for cocaine; the Golden Triangle (Burma, Laos, Thailand) and the Golden Crescent (Pakistan, Afghanistan, Turkey) for poppies and heroin; and Hawaii, Jamaica, and Morocco for cannabis. The great demand reservoirs are the United States, western Europe, and Australia. Vast financial flows feed on these reservoirs: $50 billion a year. They resurface in money-laundering networks, in offshore societies, and tax havens. A grey belt surrounds the Earth from Switzerland to the Cayman Islands, from Hong Kong to Macao. Arms flow as well, often in the opposite direction from drugs. Arms account for close to $65 billion in annual trading and make their way from industrialized countries (the United States, France, Italy, Great Britain, Germany), from the CIS (Community of Independent States) , and from China, toward countries that are in permanent conflict (in the Middle East, Latin America, Africa, and Asia).

To this we must add the flow of third-world debt ($1500 billion), the financing for this debt ($400 billion a year), and global military expenses of about $1,000 billion a year. In other words, about $2 million every minute! The following comparative figures help put these abstract numbers into some perspective. For the price of a tank (or 35 seconds of military spending), you can build 1000 classrooms for 30,000 children. For the price of another tank, all these classrooms can be fully equipped. Half a day of military spending could finance the totality of the World Health Organization's program for the elimination of malaria. For the price of a fighter plane (or 12 minutes of military spending), you can build 40,000 village pharmacies. For the price of a destroyer, electricity can be supplied to 9 million people. A 10-year global program designed to satisfy the totality of the nutritional needs of developing countries and to eliminate world hunger would cost less than the amounts governments commit over a six-month period to arms development.[*]

The task ahead for democratic states is the global regulation of these flows to ensure a future for humanity. Yet, today's remedies are fragmented and uncoordinated: the rising and falling interest rates of central banks, fluctuations in exchange rates, restrictive laws regarding immigration or capital exports, international trade agreements (GATT, NAFTA); help for developing countries, debt swapping, International Monetary Fund (IMF) and World Bank loans, the war on drugs, the surveillance of money-laundering networks. These sometimes spectacular measures are mostly ineffective because genuine cooperation rarely wins out over egocentric pursuits and because the world lacks an overall long-term vision.

The implementation of effective global regulations based on current methods and power structures has been made impossible by the almost inextricable interdependency of nations and the interconnectedness of different circuits and networks. Even with the help of the best experts, government heads cannot solve the major problems of society, which, in turn, have become so many sets of alternatives: full employment or unemployment, peace or violence, the destruction of our ecosystem or sustainable development, the sharing of resources or the accelerated enrichment of a tiny fraction of hu-

---

[*] These figures are drawn from *The Gaia Peace Atlas* by Franck Barnaby, Pan Books, London, 1988.

manity, and so on. The systematic use of cartesian analysis and of rationality derived from nineteenth-century mathematical and physical laws no longer suffices. We lack the general goals that can excite and be understood by all. How does one steer without bearings?

The situation is more complex still. In addition to these interdependant flows, there is the phenomenon of fragmentation, which requires other forms of regulation, checks, and balances. The response to globalization tends to be atomization. Principles of self-organization seem to be giving way to the forces of self-disorganization—or perhaps to new levels of reorganization. Despite efforts to establish international cooperation, centrifugal movements are growing in Europe, Africa, and the CIS. On the one hand, community, federal, and confederal entities are attempting to reconstitute themselves, sometimes through agreements and treaties that excite little interest because they are written by experts far removed from the citizens concerned. On the other hand, entire countries are splitting apart, being cut up, succumbing to civil war, and new blocs are fighting or separating over irreconcilable religous, ethnic, economic, cultural, or linguistic ideas. A kind of biological phenomenon is at work: the more structures and functions an organism assumes, the more it becomes differentiated into specialized organs and tissues. It seems that nations respond to similar principles. By the middle of the twenty-first century, the world may well have close to 500 nations, a reflection of the desire for differentiation in response to globalization and interdependency. Nations resist the spreading values of civilization, which are necessarily all-absorbing and homogenizing, by protecting their cultural values, which are necessarily differentiating. To exist, they must differentiate themselves from others and preserve their originality. The erosion of national sovereignty, the globalization of the economy, the development of communications networks all incite a defensive reflex. The fear of homogenization spawns a feverish attempt to protect territory and traditional language, usage, and customs, all of which enable nations to maintain their cultural identity. But the fear of the outside world can also lead to nationalist isolation or to religious fundamentalism, permeating the political system and hindering the democratic process.

Europe is currently contending with both these trends. To the east, centrifugal forces are threatening peace. To the west, no political or economic movement has yet succeeded in creating enough cohesion to be able to construct a citizens' Europe. Europeans must respond to the Babel of communications and the threat of cultural homogenization posed by imported television. And they can, by reversing the proposition (as in the example of the prince and his two sons in Chapter 1), notably by *standardizing* means of communication and preserving *cultural diversity*. More than expert treaties or subsidiary rights, Europeans expect ever-increasing channels of communications, the growth of material and nonmaterial networks, and the widespread implementation of a truly European television that is culture-specific but translated into many languages. They hope for education facilities, universally recognized diplomas, cooperation on subjects concerning health, the environment, developing countries, and respect for other cultures. They also want strategies that emerge from the grassroots rather than from eurocratic summits and network organization and interactive multiplicity at every level to help collective intelligence emerge in a way that respects diversity. To date, however, humanity's greatest adventures have been motivated by fear, constraints, blind faith, or even power, pleasure, and individual enjoyment. Why not turn to intelligence instead? Is this too utopian an expectation?

ON THE EDGE OF CHAOS: DEMOCRACY, DICTATORSHIP, ANARCHY

Since the beginnings of civilization, the conduct of human affairs has oscillated between three types of regimes: dictatorship and anarchy have ruled each of the two poles, with democracy lying somewhere in between (see the figure below).

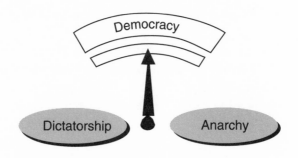

The centralizing authoritarianism of a totalitarian dictatorship (be it right wing or left wing) deprives human beings of their individual freedom. The state claims the privilege of complete freedom of action, its policies being guided by an ideology that is imposed and unchecked. The structural rigidity and necessarily rigorous order hinder the dynamic of growth and diminish the ability to adapt to change.

In an anarchic system, the priority given to individual freedom becomes excessive and thus hinders the capacity for collective and effective action. The result is that organizations are unable to face internal and external problems or to distribute resources fairly.

In a democracy, citizens elect representatives who enact laws to regulate the functioning of society. Democratic control is, in theory, exercised through elections, the interplay and alternation of political parties, the pressure of public opinion, the contributions of the media and of opinion polls.

From the proposed symbionomic perspective, dictatorship, anarchy, and democracy express three different ways of cybernetically regulating the dynamics of social systems. Only democracy respects human freedom and the responsibilities of individual and collective action. Together, these three forms of social organization reflect the dynamic described earlier (see Chapter 1) between order, disorder, and complexity (see the figure below).

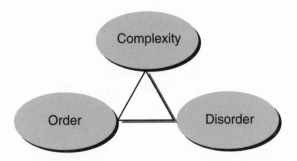

Totalitarianism imposes a rigid and structured order, most notably through its military and bureaucracy, which smothers and constrains individual initiative.

Anarchy is a kind of disorder and turbulence, which lacks the rules and constraints that tend to ensure self-organization and generate intelligent collective behavior, so that the actions of network-based agents become mutually inhibiting.

Democracy is a form of social organization that generates increasing complexity while encouraging responsibility and individual action. The role of a democratic government is to maintain the social system within the narrow margin between anarchy and excessive order so as to foster creativity, social innovation, thus making evolution, self-organization, and comanagement more complex.

The pioneers of chaos theory anticipated this constraint on the management of complex systems—the need to maintain the system "on the edge of chaos" so that complexity and collective intelligence could emerge (see Chapter 1). It is a narrow zone, perpetually dissolving and being created anew, traversed by multiple currents and conflicting forces, agitated by the constant renewal of its components. It is here that creative fluctuations, the seeds of change, are formed. Symbionomic evolution feeds on these processes, and we must know them to better use them. From this angle, a (cybernetic) government becomes a mediator, a catalyst, a scout. It delegates, arbitrates, and generates initiatives. No longer a hierarchical source of authoritarian constraint claiming complete omnipotence, it is rather a regulating body that can preserve and promote diversity, respect freedom, and anticipate and respond to change.

The current system of democratic government has engendered a severe crisis of legitimacy. The problems at stake are so complex that voters no longer believe any traditionally formed political party can reasonably solve them. Moreover, voters believe that questions more directly related to the life of the citizen (education, health, the environment, culture, leisure, community life, associations, neighborhood councils, local energy production, communications networks, lifestyles) should not come under the direct influence and control of the state. This gap has resulted in a crisis in political leadership, which is magnified by a conflict between short- and long-term interests, or "short time" and "long time." In short time, the news media push for immediate and spectacular results for the benefit of an audience that is conditioned and programmed to forget. The major shifts in the evolution of humanity, on the other hand, can only be achieved with the participation of all over the long run—in long time, a time scale that exceeds the length of a political mandate.

GOVERNANCE: BETWEEN DETERMINISM AND FREEDOM

The massive transition brought to light by the crisis in political leadership involves a transfer of power from government to governance. *Governance* is defined as the adaptive and network-based comanagement of all government action, or the ability of governing bodies to control, direct, and orient the populations for which they are responsible. Governance means that the power of political governments, which is concentrated in precise fields of jurisdiction, is shared with all human organizations cooperating at various levels in the main sectors of public life. Hierarchical, centralized authority thus complements the networks of interdependent levels of governance. Those closest to the problems respond to them with the knowledge of familiarity, while broader, more centralized guidelines are defined to preserve the collective interest. Thus, the work of the rank and file is linked to the necessary guidelines and regulations that come from the top. This is a concrete demonstration of the principle of subsumption, which underlies planetary symbiosis.

Already made necessary by the political crisis in leadership, the transition from government to governance would seem even more urgent because of the progressive erosion of national sovereignty. Undermined from within by local and regional constraints, challenged from the outside by international, transnational, and supranational demands, and short-circuited by the growth of global interpersonal real-time communications networks, national sovereignty must relinquish some of its prerogatives and restrict its autonomy to specific actions whose legitimacy is recognized by the community as a whole.

In their perpetual search for the most effective modes of action, the governments of democratic countries unknowingly rediscover the principles of symbionomic evolution, principles that oscillate among law and order, anarchy, chaos, and turbulence, authoritarian and lax regimes. The oscillation leads to periods of decadence, of technocratic simplification, or to the necessary comanagement of complexity.

Numerous forms of participatory social dynamics management have been explored or outlined throughout the long and difficult transition from classical government to governance. Self-management, democratic planning, citizen participation in public life, and popular referenda are steps along the way. To help foster the conditions for a balanced global and symbiotic relationship between the economy and ecology, Gro Harlem Bruntland put forward the notion of "sustainable development." I suggest we replace this term with another, *regulated adaptive development*, since it brings out more clearly the cybernetic nature of governance (see later). Here, transverse management and catalyzing structures are put in place to respond to the new requirements of complexity management. Because of corporate and political unwieldiness, these essential aspects of participatory management are much more slowly applied to the affairs of the state. Greater openness can also have negative repercussions. Everyone always expects more from the state. But it is never enough, and a vicious circle begins, which only leads to diminishing returns. Giving more means collecting more, so that levies, contributions, and taxes must be increased to pay for a lifestyle beyond our means. This, in turn, leads to new conflicts over the state's omnipresence and its nit-picking control.

The principal issue raised several times in this book seems to me more than ever to be that of creating a balance between the natural constraints of self-organization and the exercise of individual and collective human responsibility. The "great laws of nature" have always worried politicians and sociologists. If everything is predetermined, is there room for individual freedom? This traditional philosophical question dates back to the Stoics, but knowledge of symbionomic principles and the practice of social symbiosis can offer the beginnings of an answer.

The concrete case of the electronic superhighways of the future illustrates the relationship between top-down political decision making and the spontaneous self-organization of users. A study might recommend that information highways rely on fiber optics and a wide bandwidth transmission and interconnection mode (asynchronous transfer mode or ATM). The cost would come to hundreds of billions of dollars over 20 years. A new network would thus be added to existing ones, without any real understanding of the market or of the programs needed. And investments would be locked in for several years. But we might try another quasi-biological approach, which takes its cue from the development of the brain. First, the interconnection between existing networks (telephone, cable, digital networks, cellular radio communications, wave frequency television, and satellite networks) must be maximally promoted. The investment required would be much less than for the "fiber optic" approach. Second, a policy for the interconnection of small (even individual) units must be systematically enacted (lowered rates, flat-rate billing based on information flow rather than on online hours, reduced modem prices). Thus, a hypernetwork would slowly evolve through use, bringing us closer to the electronic highways of the future. The hypernetwork would generate new applications and prompt the requisite increase in bandwidth. Finally, existing networks would be entirely opened up to international networks by adapting billing systems. As with the biological formation of a neural network, the very operation of the system will lead to an internal mechanism of Darwinian selection, eliminating redundant links and reinforcing more relevant ones. The network would be built and developed from within, and would not require massive investment at the start. This example illustrates two approaches. The first is traditional, the second symbionomic. The best way lies somewhere in between the two, since we need both centralized decision making and local user initiative.

Beyond the old relationship between centralized planning and self-management, we now need to establish some kind of conversation between government and governance; between hierarchical centralized authority and decentralized participatory democratic behavior. To maintain the fragile equilibrium between ossified order and sterile turbulence in this narrow transition zone "on the edge of chaos," humans must relinquish part of their individualism and allow it to be subsumed into something greater that will offer them freedom and more power.

The basic rules of future governance depend on the combination of two elements: individual action and social feedback.

HUMANITY: INDIVIDUAL GENIUS, COLLECTIVE IDIOCY

Whether as producers or consumers, men and women interact as agents in a variety of ways within communications networks that are governed by simple rules: laws, codes, constraints, prices, advances, and promotions. Unlike insect societies, which rely on the development of a collective intelligence, humanity appears less able to solve complex problems collectively than individually or in small groups. A model for human society, however, will evidently not be found among ant colonies, whose individual members lack insight, breadth, and freedom. The rules of cybernetics and self-regulation must not hinder free will. They must be adapted to allow for freedom, autonomy, power struggles, conflicts, and even deviance and folly, all of which reflect the conscious expression of responsibility, ways of being, and decision making. But the chaotic action of myriad individuals—buyers, sellers, decision makers, voters, or users—does not necessarily lead to the emergence of a real collective intelligence. Public opinion, of course, can pressure governments. Growth, competition, or (in times of conflict) mobilization against an invader can certainly become collective forces that can bring about change. But these forces generally lead to change or evolution that is more sudden than desired.

Given a minimum amount of reflection, however, the solutions to our major problems seem obvious. Cars pollute cities, so let's encourage the use of electric-powered public transit, pedestrian areas, and cycling. Millions of people are dying of hunger, so let's mobilize resources to share our overabundant food supplies. Each year, tens of thousands of people die on roads, so let's make the necessary collective efforts to minimize this slaughter. Fossil fuels pollute and are becoming scarce, while nuclear energy is dangerous over the long term, so let's make it a priority to combine renewable sources of energy and make engines more efficient. I could go on, but it seems almost naive to state the obvious when we know that nothing can realistically be done about any of it, at least within a reasonable time frame. Why? Because we are too egocentric, individualistic, possessive, hedonistic, and intelligent. Our education, our economy, our industrial growth, and our international competitiveness are entirely based on developing and encouraging personal intelligence, consumption, ownership, and the accumulation of goods.

While ants might be said to behave like individual idiots and collective geniuses, humans behave rather like *individual geniuses* and *collective idiots*.

It is time we subsumed some of this individualism into something greater. The mere suggestion is often enough to incite protesting voices, decrying the loss of individual freedom—a privilege whose sacrosanct status undermines our collective well-being. How do we find a balance between individual freedom, respect for simple rules, and the exercise of collective intelligence? Only an established symbiosis can provide an answer to this question, which is why it is so important to consciously implement symbionomic mechanisms that allow us to evolve in this direction.

We already gladly accept numerous constraints. We elect representatives to enact laws and regulations that, in a way, restrict our freedom. As a collectivity, however, we all benefit. Such is the case with the criminal code, tax laws, the highway code, even the Declaration of Human Rights, the Ten Commandments, national constitutions, treaties between countries, the statutes of a company, the internal regulations of an association, or the clauses of a contract. In return, we get insurance, security, pensions, retirement, guarantees, job security, social benefits, etc. Infractions are punished with fines, the removal of rights, or imprisonment. The motivation needed to ensure compliance is sustained by fear—in certain countries, by the fear of retaliation that can include death. The complexity of the "system" makes it seem an impersonal, cold, and distant monster, a machine that crushes individuality and freedom. Hence the cheating, resourcefulness, and corruption that are bred by badly managed systems and practices.

Without some kind of motivation, there is no effective collective action. In our day, the prime movers are fear, money, power, pleasure, and tributes. Fear and pleasure are the oldest forms of inducement in history. Punishment and reward are the golden rules of training. But there are other ways to motivate that include combining different approaches.

Constraints, information, rewards, and fiscal incentives can all be used to encourage better waste management. Simulation studies and field work both show that constraints alone are not enough, nor is information or education. Maximum effectiveness is obtained through a combination of methods: explanatory information and feedback, education programs on the use of different recycling options, and rewards for recycling. This kind of approach can be applied to numerous fields for which intelligence and collective discipline are necessary: carpooling, noise reduction, or a more reasonable use of energy.

Let us take another example, a street intersection. Drivers can be compelled to respect traffic lights and offenders can be prosecuted. Individual participation is minimal—simply obeying the traffic signals. But another approach would be to create a traffic circle, so that a form of collective intelligence contributes to regulating the traffic. Designers must make sure here that sight lines and signals are clear, and that rules are kept simple. Drivers need to look at several access points, evaluate the speed of cars entering the priority zone, and control their own speed around the circle. Thus, if multiple agents acting in parallel can respect a simple set of rules, a *collective* behavior that enhances *individual* security can emerge.

Effective cooperation between people is possible without being enforced by a central authority. Individuals here must privilege personal interest in a reciprocal fashion, so that symbiotic relationships can be established. This is what game theory expert Robert Axelrod has demonstrated through computer simulation. Essentially, this type of cooperation is not developed by isolated individuals, but rather by small groups whose cooperation is reciprocal, even if their exchanges represent only a small part of their general interaction.

PARTICIPATORY DEMOCRACY AND SOCIAL FEEDBACK

These forms of coordinated collective action and cooperation are obviously impossible without the real-time feedback of information. Measuring the effects of one's actions and comparing them to the actions of others is essential. At the national and community levels, I call this information loop *social feedback*. I described its advantages and disadvantages in *The Macroscope*. In 1975, however, technical systems for mass communications were poorly developed. Today, new communications and data processing tools and systems allow information in organizations to rise from the bottom up.

Current forms of social feedback are limited. Voting only provides a rudimentary expression of voters' choices, but the rise of the media has created varied and indirect feedback possibilities. On camera, a street demonstration gathers an emotional potency that can become highly influential. Media, street, emotion, and the forces of amplification fold together into an expanding and sometimes vicious spiral—a spiral used, unfortunately, by international terrorism. Forms of popular expression in the streets or in stadiums are limited to mass gatherings (demonstrations, concerts, sporting events, religious gatherings, pilgrimages). Signs of unity are just as rudimentary (clothing, ornaments, slogans, banners, stadium chants, the use of lighters at concerts, or even ecoactivist human chains).

Opinion polls are another, more subtle, form of feedback. Published by the media, they act as regulating mechanisms, reflecting society back to itself, readjusting, readapting, reconverting. Their indirect influence is considerable in democracies where opposition and majority hover around 50 percent and where elections are played out on a few percentage points. The market is another form of real-time social feedback. Publicity, word of mouth, product boycotts, and the innumerable decisions made by buyers and sellers all act as regulators whose effects are hard to predict, since actions are chaotic, simultaneous, and often irrational.

In the coming years, growing electronic interactivity will increase the role of these social feedback loops. Already, the telephone and the Internet are frequently used during radio or television programs to send personalized information to central control booths. But the great global interpersonal computer communications networks offer new and worrisome possibilities. Internet pioneers are proposing to develop "electronic assemblies" that would allow citizens to vote on a variety of subjects day and night. In his electoral platform, the American millionaire and ex-presidential candidate Ross Perot promised to install an electronic "voting box" in every American household.

This type of global social feedback seems to me to be particularly dangerous. The need for instant social feedback to issues raised in society can result in trend setting or else create fleeting or irrational fads that are rapidly made obsolete. This sort of social "short circuiting" does not allow for the natural response time that is inherent in social systems. It belongs to the emotional short term fostered by the media, and lacks any real capacity to build over the long term. This is why intermediaries (local councellors, deputies, leaders, members of parliament) are indispensable to the control of information flow; they create a cushioning effect, softening societal oscillations and diminishing the effects of media amplification. All forms of social feedback must therefore take into account the hierarchy that allows intermediaries and representative organizations to fulfill their roles as cogs in the machine. The friction, filtering, delays, and constraints of the social system indirectly ensure its protection. They help to level out the magnitude of the oscillations, reducing interference, and revealing over the long term the deeper trends from which policies can be developed.

Social feedback is being progressively implemented within specific "niches": television shows, major polls, games, contests, computer networks. Some systems developed for more limited environments are already in place. Businesses make use of instantaneous voting mechanisms, whose real-time curves, tables, and graphs help to break down voting tendencies, and whose color animations are made generally accessible on public screens. A number of public venues equipped with this kind of system can accommodate up to a thousand participants.

One of the most astonishing applications of real-time collective participation is "Cinematrix," a feedback technique developed by Rachel Carpenter in the United States. Participants sit in an auditorium large enough to seat thousands and equipped with a massive screen. Each participant is given a spoon-shaped manual reflector, one side of which is red, the other green. Video cameras pick up the selected color, reflected off the devices, and transmit it to a computer. At the start of the experiment, the host draws a rectangle on the screen. He asks the thousands of audience participants to randomly place themselves within the rectangle (by flashing red) or outside of it (by flashing green). In an instant, the rectangle becomes red. The two halves of the auditorium are then asked to play a game of tennis. The ball on the screen is sent back and forth by raising (green) or lowering (red) each of the two rackets. The correct speed of the rackets' manipulation is determined by the correct number of red or green voters. Visual coordination is essential to the players on both sides to anticipate the direction and speed of the ball and correctly position their own racket. In a final game, a multicolored cube rotates on the screen. Players are asked to stop it when they see its blue side appear, by slowing the rotating cube down (red) or speeding it up (green). If the blue side goes by too fast, the players must make it turn backwards, a maneuver requiring delicate collective coordination, with the correct proportion of red votes to green. Thousands of people are able to perform this task perfectly and efficiently with no help beyond the real-time on-screen visualization of their movements.

I have chosen this example to illustrate one of the fundamental principles of network interaction: complex problems can be collectively solved by thousands of individual agents acting in parallel if they follow certain simple rules. This form of social feedback can be translated into electronic communications systems displaying instant results. With the interconnection of interpersonal computer networks, hundreds of millions of *surfacing* bits of information will play an increasingly important role in regulating the cybiont's major metabolic functions. While large public demonstrations might suggest that the masses do not necessarily display a high level of collective intelligence, social feedback systems can help to develop a collective intelligence that is *superior* to that of isolated individuals.

In symbionomic terms, coordinating individual action through social feedback becomes one of the basic elements of the cybiont's intelligent behavior. Its brain function involves a myriad chaotic actions, microdecisions, readjustments, and the multilevel regulation of its human neurons, all magnified by the mirror of the media or differentiated through specific connections. Such interactions within the nodes and links of the hypernetwork are one of the keys of symbiosis and of the progressive emergence of symbiotic humanity. But for us to benefit from both individual action and social feedback, a new category of political leader will have to emerge in the coming years.

THE NEW POLITICAL LEADERS

It is common practice in democratic politics for opinion polls to fulfill the function of social feedback. Through the media, they introduce new forms of collective action into society and disturb the reasoned conduct of its complex systems. In a world of inequality, of divergent evolutionary time frames, of varying behavior and culture, governance must make it possible for societies to evolve in ways that respect diversity and liberty. The shape of the human social organization of the future can offer an elucidating retroprospective on our present choices.

The new constraints have inspired leaders to adapt their ways of exercising public responsibility. The notion of the "great helmsman" (an implicit reference to the *cybernetic* nature of government), steering his country (the ship) through dangerous waters, and reaching his destination in firm control of the helm, has had its day. The helmsman has given way to the "surfer," riding the wave of public opinion, progressing, wave upon wave, from media event to consensual decision making. Carefully balanced on the wave, neither too far forward (for fear of taking a nosedive), nor too far back (of missing the crest), the surfer-politician seeks to create events that supply the political machine's necessary powering fuel. As Henry Kissinger once said, "not only do you need to surf the wave of events, you also have to create the wave itself." Serious crises often catch up with politicians. All their skill (and that of their advisers) must be focused on responding to these crises so they can bounce back with even greater force.

The surfer's balancing act in the midst of such instability is driven by a perpetual flight forward. Its subtlety is given strength by the practice and experience of managing complexity. New roles that are common to politics and business are beginning to emerge: the mediator, the communicator, the catalyst. Mediation involves detecting the seeds of change and working with them rather than imposing them. Communication involves grasping the major trends of society and knowing how to synthesize them into motivating principles for the actors concerned. Catalytic action involves creating structural and functional conditions that foster change through a subtle balance of various methods. A combination of action, mediation, communication, and catalysis can lead to important change within a framework of clearly expressed and widely accepted objectives. This is where the importance of social feedback is most evident. Cybernetic loops set up at the various network nodes and links, and on multiple levels of the organizational hierarchy, provide the information and regulatory elements. Politicians cannot direct, change, or impose at every stage. The "government" must allow for change by creating empowering conditions that make possible, with a minimal expenditure of energy and information, the effective management of a complex social system. It must rely on a form of social acupuncture rather than on aggressive remedies—a form of political judo or martial arts that throws the opponent off. Working in symbiosis with a multitude of individual responsibilities, the government must shed some of its outdated prerogatives (authority, strength, hierarchy) to focus on those that will ensure lasting cohesion, general motivation, and appropriate preparation for the major collective decisions.

These are the principles on which network governance and the intelligent coordination of international action can rest. National sovereignty, hierarchical power structures, and cartesian-based responses have come up against the brick wall of complexity, and can no longer solve the major problems of our world. Given the erosion of national sovereignty, an acknowledgment of skills and diversity, an openness to other approaches must count among the new values of governance. Piloting and catalysis are the keywords for this new political stance. Mediators, catalysts, communicators, and even "surfers," make up a new generation of leaders who will bring new solutions to the present crisis in political leadership . . . insofar as they can master the great leviathan of the media.

THE DANGERS OF MEDIA IMMUNITY

Adapted to the demands of symbionomic evolution, this new political stance can be challenged or inhibited by the negative effects of excessive media coverage. In democratic countries, opinion polls and television have provided initial attempts at social feedback, but in the short and medium term, the system can lead to dangerous excess. As an emotional mirror to society, television magnifies the excessive individualization of behavior. In the virtual case given here, we see how the omnipresence of the media helps to create a special form of public protection, or *media immunity*, for public figures.

Let us take the case of a politician who is in the limelight. Given current media conditions, he can rise to power quickly insofar as he is able to fulfill three conditions. First, he must be a good communicator. Second, he must be able to draw to himself several networks of influence. Third, he must occupy a political niche giving him the potential power to transfer votes to and from the major parties at play. These are the conditions outlined earlier for self-selection through amplification and for "locking-in" a desired sector (see Chapter 1). The convergence and association of networks of influence have been essential to traditional political power. Convergence reinforces power, and the numerous "niches" exploited in this way are enhanced by the catalyzing effect of the individual positioned at the center of the geometrical form created at the centerpoint of all the interconnections. Those whose livelihood depends on these niches, who profit from their expansion, have every interest in reinforcing the influence and power of the principal catalyst, so that mechanisms of competitive exclusion are gradually implemented, as with any biological system that competes with others.

The public constitutes a new and important niche through which direct and short-term *media suffrage* replaces universal suffrage. When the media focus is negative, the emerging profusion of multiple opinions creates a kind of permanent debate that indirectly protects the person in conflict with the political community, with the media, with the justice system, etc. Discussion and public debate only help to reinforce the existing defenses of the person under attack, so that a form of media immunity, a superior form of parliamentary or diplomatic immunity, is gradually established.

Television creates strange relationships. We think we know the people we see, but none of them recognizes us. We think we can see into the secret life, the mood swings, or deep convictions of a television host or political figure, but in reality we do not see beyond the surface. Moreover, if a public figure can communicate a concrete theme with emotion, we identify with both the message and the messenger. The regular television presence of a personality evokes in us a reflex of connection and protectiveness, much like the feelings we have toward a family member or close friend. Everyone has a personal opinion about public figures in the hot seat. When these opinions come into open conflict, they reinforce the grid of immunity. Politicians will hesitate before taking a decision. Journalists will ask fewer questions. Judges will be more careful. Clothed with such media immunity, able communicators can enter the free and infinite space of virtual politics. Their names will garner votes and will carry increasing weight on the political scene. Their participation in political demonstrations will attract crowds, despite the fact that the relevance of their political ideas—measured solely by the yardstick of the crowd—has become confused with the very event their presence has generated.

Media immunity is doubly problematic. It flouts republican law and promotes virtual politics, a politics based on the illusion of appearances rather than on the substance of existence. It can also create terrifying backlashes when public opinion abruptly turns on a former political darling.

I have offered this example to illustrate the role and influence of multiple agents acting within nested networks and receiving similar types of information through the mass media. The emergence of media immunity is also related to collective amplification mechanisms. The effects of self-selection and competitive exclusion created by media immunity lead to a runaway phenomenon well known in cybernetics. The system slips out of the bounds of its regulatory loops, and the ensuing negative repercussions jeopardize its overall stability. Subject as they are to the effects of political media magnification, our societies face the very real danger in the near future of the rise to power of opportunistic leaders who take advantage of every flaw in the system, and who scorn the values, morals, and ethics on which democracy is based. A better understanding of these mechanisms can help prevent such an outcome.

THE LIMITS OF ECONOMISM

The new "cybernetic" politics, or governance, will promote the development of the major managing priorities of symbionomic evolution. These include a long-term vision, great rallying objectives, a new economic science, education and awareness campaigns, and social feedback mechanisms to cultivate a collective intelligence. The long-term vision must anticipate the consequences of the next step in the evolution of the human species: the creation of a new form of global organization, partially described by the cybiontic model. The transition from the individual to a multiperson hypernetwork will be as critical historically as the passage from single-cell to multicell organisms.

Economic science, the secular arm of traditional politics, will have to give way to a kind of meta-economics, integrating the traditional economy and ecology in a tight symbiosis. Also called *ecological economics*, it will have to recognize the ecosystemic properties of the economy.

Economic science defines and implements the principal guidelines that fuel the production machine and theoretically ensure the sharing of wealth. We now know its limitations. In a system originally conceived as separate from the environment, the economy is functioning as a closed circuit. It has become disconnected from the ecosystem. Even its control panel instruments no longer conform. The gross national product (GNP) must begin to take into account the vast sums drawn on the ecocapital and the irreparable damage done to the ecosystem. A balanced gauge should lead to a corrected indicator—a GNP from which we would deduct social costs, environmental protection, and military expenses. The net national product (NNP) would thus become the clearest indicator of value-added ecocapital and of developing human resources.

It is evident that classical economic science cannot solve the unemployment problem. An economic system based on mass production, work contracts, consumer spending, and growth is a paralyzed system. It only takes into account the market value of goods, services, and people. We do not lack activities to help develop and build the social macroorganism. In its current rigid framework, however, classical economic science does not know how to transform activities into jobs. For that, it would need to take into account nonmarket activities. These are based on the exchange of other values indispensable to the maintenance and growth of societies, and include mutual education, solidarity, social aid, shared knowledge, and voluntarism as an investment in ecocapital. Thus, economic science must also recognize that—no less than material needs—spiritual, social, emotional, and artistic needs must be fulfilled.

Inspired by ecological concerns, numerous proposals have been put forward to reformulate classical economic science. Ecological economics, or "eco-economics," relies on balancing economic flux and seeking out ways to preserve the ecosystem when developing economic resources. Another, radically liberal, approach is evolving in the United States—"bionomics." Modeled on the natural laws of biology and ecology, and recognizing the general principles of self-organization and interdependence within exchange networks, bionomics nonetheless draws on the principles of laissez faire. The rules of self-organization only apply if they are free from centralized control. Some even advocate the total absence of control from the top to allow systems to develop a complexity that will ensure the emergence of new properties.

Because the economy is an ecosystem created by humanity, symbionic principles apply. But human beings have consciousness, free will, and responsibility. They can plan, make reasoned or nonreasoned choices, and define the conditions of their own evolution. It is thus essential that the constraints of self-organization be balanced by the guiding will of social evolution. Choices should be made according to a system of values. Ideology, in the best sense of the word, should be a driving force of action. Cybernetic governance should be founded on top-down and bottom-up modes of regulation. Competing ideas are essential to the achievement of optimal governance. Thus, an ecology of ideas should be created, a cognitive environment within which the great themes that drive the world compete and work together. Bionomics and the advanced anarchy of the new American laissez faire fail to see the contribution made by the healthy competition of ideas to the regulation and running of major social systems.

Even the famous concept of "sustainable development" can have negative repercussions. It can lock economic development and environmental protection in a futile conflict. These proposals appear mutually exclusive. Can growth pay for *additional* environmental *costs?* Does protecting the environment necessitate *limiting* growth? Economic logic appears, at the present time, to be winning out over ecological logic. We are heading toward a system in which ecological costs are gradually being taken over by the traditional economy—a trend which could lead to the "commodification" of natural goods. Putting a price on everything—a dolphin, a cubic meter of air, a forest—giving free rein to the regulatory mechanisms of the market, taxing the consumption of natural resources or the emission of pollutants can have equally formidable negative repercussions. If we push this reasoning further and assess the price of "natural services" (like the cleansing effect of photosynthesis in the air and water or of bacteria in the ground), we essentially create the right to pollute in regions of the world where natural services are still highly effective and thus less expensive than are the environmental technologies of developed countries.

Some of these approaches reflect a general movement toward a hard-line "economism" that rests entirely on the logic of the market economy. What right does economism have to impose its logic on society? As we saw earlier, economic science has cut itself off from nature, placing the inputs (nonrenewable natural resources) and outputs (waste) of economic machinery outside its sphere of action. Since resources are considered infinitely abundant and waste not to have any market value, these inputs and outputs have simply never been taken into account.

Predating the logic of the human economy, however, the coevolutionary logic of the natural bioeconomy has allowed the Earth to preserve its evolving ecosystems. The coevolution of ecosystems has a billion species of animals and plants interlinked through the major biogeochemical cycles, and is made up of a whole set of subtle and time-honored regulations that influence the collectivity of biospheric elements within their fragile networks.

TOWARD REGULATED ADAPTIVE DEVELOPMENT

The logic of "economism" and the "commodification" of natural goods can be countered by a global approach of ecosystemic management, with humanity and Gaia as symbiotic partners. This form of management relies on the regulating and self-organizational mechanisms that I attempt to outline in this book and that I group together under the rubric of symbionomic evolution. It is this new vision and complementary path that we must now reconcile with the economy. The new approach will help bring together the two domains of ecology and the economy, which stem from different cultures but are equally essential to the future of the planet and humanity.

From the point of view of long-term macroregulation, I suggest we replace the term "sustainable development" with "regulated adaptive development." It seems to me that the latter expression has the advantage of linking the notions of adaptation and self-regulation to the development of human societies in the larger context of the biosphere.

Like any cybernetic system, self-regulating development and measured growth require sensors, communications networks, systems of amplification, and feedback loops at a variety of levels. All participants in global regulation must be informed at their level of skill or specialization of the effects of their local actions. This allows them to make choices, make decisions, and correct problems in an interactive and participatory manner. In countries where pollution levels are published daily by the media, for instance, citizens are encouraged to take initiative in limiting automotive traffic or the levels to which they heat their homes and offices.

Market and fiscal regulations have proven effective, of course, and it would be foolish to try to abolish them. Without the implementation of global plans, however, their effects can only be felt in the short term. On the other hand, for self-regulating mechanisms to be effective, the implemented measures must be complementary. The interdependency of factors plays a fundamental role in sustaining dynamic equilibria and navigating complex systems over time. This is why regulated adaptive development must rely on a *policy mix*, including prices, taxes, regulations, source and feedback information, education about planetary ecocitizenship, and inducements.

Above all, self-regulation requires the involvement of the ecocitizen. When multiplied by millions, even billions, an individual adjustment in the consumption of energy, goods, or services has a powerful global effect. Hence the almost organic importance of widespread awareness campaigns to provide a foundation for social feedback. The ecocitizen will also have to join forces with the more traditional consumer associations, labor unions, lobbies, and non-government organizations.

To ensure a successful transition, individual, political, economic, and industrial regulatory action will need a unifying element, a set of shared values, that is, an ethics of the environment, or ecoethics, "regulating" and setting limits to prevent the economistic stance from getting out of hand. Bioethics has already established the necessity for sanctuaries that are free of market values—such as the human body. An ecoethics can help prevent our slipping into the total commodification of natural goods by clarifying the current confusion between use value and exchange value, and restoring to the word "value" its full significance. The notion of regulated adaptive development can help bypass the apparently insurmountable dualism between economic development and environmental protection.

However, the accelerated development of industrialized societies, subject as they are to the values of the market economy, jeopardizes global equilibrium. We are witnessing a Darwinian evolutionary mechanism on a global scale—the self-selection of the most advanced nations. One of the fundamental rules of symbionomics is the selection of an evolving population through autocatalysis and competitive exclusion. The process is occurring before our very eyes. Competitive exclusion (economic, technical, and cultural marginalization) is occurring at the very heart of the nation, between cities and their suburbs, between the rich and the poor. On a global scale, this can be seen in the ever-increasing gulf between the privileged and the underprivileged. Autocatalysis generates different time densities. Despite our apparent contemporaneity, we all remain isolated in our individual time capsules. This is *fractal time*, separating us from one another and encouraging us in our attempts to conquer time. The competitive exclusion of the underprivileged is one of the most serious threats to humanity ever encountered in its history. We are heading toward a world made up of varying evolutionary speeds, in which individuals grow (or stagnate) in their own time bubble, with each bubble becoming increasingly incompatible with its neighbors. Some have already adapted, encouraged by the existing diversity among cultures and peoples. "After all, why not give way to the natural laws of competition between peoples? And may the best competitor win."

The alternative to competitive exclusion is sharing and solidarity. Human values are shared values. The transition toward the next step in the global organization of humanity requires everyone's cooperation, while maintaining behavioral diversity and the expression of free choice. This is one of the most important collective decisions that humanity will have to make as it heads toward global economic and ecological symbiosis.

PRIORITIES FOR THE FUTURE

Given the parameters of adaptive development and anticipating the objectives of governance, I outline here a number of priorities for the future. Some may appear utopian to us today, but in my mind it is essential that they be implemented in the third millenium.

Support demographic transition. With the transition already under way, the world's population should stabilize at about 11 billion around the year 2100. To help this transition along, the status of women should be given greater value, the use of contraceptives should be made more widespread, and countries with high birth rates should be encouraged to bring their rates down to 3.2 children per family.

Reduce and convert military spending. Current military spending totals $900 billion annually and consumes a huge portion of human, scientific, technical, economic, and natural resources. These funds should be gradually reoriented toward education, health, and the environment—part of the challenge we will face when restructuring governments in the new century.

Ensure a balanced energy policy. Doing so will create a healthy metabolism for the cybiont and support its symbiotic relationship with Gaia. This policy should respect local responsibilities in the production and distribution of energy, and should involve financial savings, control, rational use, efficiency, and the use of renewable resources.

Implement a symbiotic economy to ensure self-regulated adaptive development. Replace the GDP with new indicators that take into account the damages done to the environment and to human resources. Redistribute resources, reduce inequalities, and reinvent work.

Control global environmental effects. Reduce CFC (Chlorofluorocarbons) and carbon dioxide emissions. Control the desertification of land. Regulate the climate and the environment in an intelligent way through the macroregulation of major cycles and functions. Respect ecoethics, that is, an environmental ethics that defines limits for human action. Restore an ecological agriculture. Reduce the massive industrialization of agriculture through modularized production. Reduce deforestation. Revitalize landscapes.

Enhance the status of women. Restore a healthy balance between masculine and feminine values to ensure the controlled adaptive development of human societies, industries, and economies. Harmonize responsibilities within society. Give greater value to the family-based, educational, and care-giving tasks usually carried out by women.

Ensure basic health for all. The World Health Organization's goal for the year 2000 is to reduce the rate of infant mortality to 50 for every 1000 births, and to ensure each child achieves a normal weight and has access to clean drinking water. The cost of primary care is $50 billion a year; clean water and sanitation will require an additional $30 billion.

Ensure basic education for all. Today, 105 million children do not have access to schooling. There are 900 million illiterate people in the world. UNESCO estimates that by the year 2000, it will cost at least $5 billion annually to educate the world's children.

Promote progressive and adapted technologies. Put an end to gigantic installations controlled by the few, to heavy technologies that have a massive environmental impact, and to techniques that pose a long-term threat to the biosphere. Foster technologies that are adapted to social needs.

Find a compromise between real and virtual traffic. Promote networks and modes of interpersonal communications, information highways, and informational democracy. Slow the expansion of mass transportation, particularly the growth of air transportation, truck transportation, anarchic highway construction, and the proliferation of traffic arteries that destroy landscapes and urban life.

Launch major urban projects. Progressively eliminate cars powered by internal combustion engines; promote nonpolluting and quiet means of transportation; reconfigure public transportation. Rehabilitate neighborhoods; foster associative lifestyles and the desire to take responsibility at the local level.

Balance civilizational and cultural values. Implement governance and social feedback mechanisms. Improve the symbiosis between humanity and society through the complementarity of top-down (hierarchical), bottom-up (participatory), and transverse (interactive) approaches. Preserve diversity. Respect justice and the rule of law. Respect and value senior citizens. Promote planetary ecocitizenship, bioethics, infoethics, and ecoethics.

Such priorities cannot be implemented without close cooperation among governance, the new economy, and industry. We must thus devise new organizational models that are better adapted to the production and distribution of tomorrow's goods and services.

6

Creating the Industries of the Third Millennium

THE BUSINESSES AND ORGANIZATIONS OF THE FUTURE

To prepare for the symbiotic societies and businesses of the future, political leaders and CEOs, the "managers of complexity," will need new, shared rules of organization and management—rules for piloting, catalysis, and communication and for accelerated evolutionary development. Hence the need for a macroscopic vision of industry and business and of what they produce.

Industry is a macromachine. It provides the goods and services needed by human societies and produces the world of tomorrow. Business, understood in the broadest sense of the term, will be called on to make an important transition: from the era of mass production and the market economy to the era of knowledge societies, based on information and communication. This is a profound paradigm shift that will affect every aspect of business.

The transition from agriculture to industry resulted in huge migrations of workers into cities. The transition from manufacturing industry to service industry led to an enormous increase in the number of white collar workers. The computerization of society is changing the situation once again, causing an unprecedented increase in the productivity and power of the human brain and making necessary massive readjustments in the economy and the job market. The first transition took millennia; the second, three centuries; the third will take a few decades. It is during this period of time—barely a generation—that the industry of tomorrow will have to be built so as to ensure the vital functions of the coming planetary superorganism. And hence the need to consider possible forms of organization for the future.

The structure of a traditional business, based on nineteenth-century knowledge and experience, is centralized, hierarchical, Taylorized, and specialized. The business of the twenty-first century will have to be based on sharing and be adaptable, mobile, and light. It will not only have to produce, distribute, and create wealth, but, more important, to anticipate and adapt. The image of the traditional business was the clock, with its cogwheels and control mechanisms. That of the business of the future will be the biological cell networked in an integrated organism.

From the symbionomic perspective I am proposing, a business is an evolutionary superorganism analogous to a living system. It is a hybrid system, both biological and artificial, human and mechanical, evolving within its own constraints and in its own spaces. Its operation is based on symbiotic relationships at various levels, among people, machines, and organizations. Thanks to this structure, the business acts as a transformer, a catalyst, and an amplifier. It transforms flows of money, energy, matter, and information into value-added goods and services and into new flows of money. It catalyzes processes of production, exchange, and distribution. It amplifies human action and enhances human powers through its hierarchical structure, distribution of tasks, and communication among levels of operation. In symbiosis with the "business" macroorganism, human beings can thus convert energy, time, information, and financial resources into action, know-how, and added value.

Four fundamental reasons justify the need for new forms of organization in business. The first concerns the outdated linearity of traditional approaches. Our organizations are, for the most part, still hierarchical and sequential in nature. Orders come from the top down, and operations are carried out in sequences, particularly in heavy industry. In the information and communications industries, parallelism in tasks is more widespread, but sequential organization remains strongly rooted. This is no doubt due to the fact that we have great difficulty thinking in terms of parallels and circular causality. Our thinking and even our ways of communicating are sequential and linear. However, many operations in nature are carried out using "parallel processors." This is the case, as we have seen, for an ant colony and for biological evolution; in both cases, information is processed by large numbers of autonomous agents. The sequential, linear approach is no longer suited to complex situations; only parallelism will allow for systems to evolve at digital speed.

The second reason for new forms of organization is the need for structures to adapt quickly. The complexity of organizations inhibits in-depth change. Inertia and conservatism (homeostasis) strongly resist any changes in structures or functions. Since the elements are interlocked at many levels, the alteration of one part, one cog, leads necessarily to the reorganization of the whole—which is costly in energy, time, and information. This is why most organizations prefer to grow rather than to change; they merge or absorb each other, but they have great difficulty reorganizing in depth.

The third reason new forms of organization are needed is related to the development of human resources. People who work in companies ask for remuneration and participation in forms other than salaries: considerations, motivation, participation, profit-sharing, appreciation, professional development.

The fourth reason follows from the merging of three formerly separate fields, mechanics, biology, and computer science. Three complementary concepts of the business of the future, three steps in the coevolution of humans, machines, and the environment, are now converging toward a common approach that is characteristic of biology and computers: configuration in networks. Business can no longer remain disconnected from the networks that nourish it. Just as a living organism cannot survive in isolation, the modern company must be permanently connected to financial, information, and distribution networks. In the future, these vital connections will become even stronger, profoundly changing the nature, structure, and functions of business.

The reconfiguration of companies is an attempt to respond to these new needs, requirements, and constraints. I will consider three forms of organization, each representing a way of adapting to the conditions of the environment.

The *mechanical* model, based on physics, leads to a pyramid structure, hierarchical control, and the separation of tasks. The organization is regulated in terms of linear time. Its method of management is programming and quantitative control.

The *biological* model, which is more recent, favors organization in networks. Its method of management is piloting rather than direct control or detailed programming of tasks. Its time frame is nonlinear; it expands or contracts according to the phases of a company's life, that is, periods of intense activity or of restabilization.

The *chaotic* model is suited to the complexity of the environment. Its organization is fractal (divided into many autonomous units) and its method of management is catalytic, creating the conditions for effective action. The organization is based on a densely connected network of agents performing specific tasks in parallel, with a knowledge of the objectives and general rules. The agents receive information (feedback) through immediate observation of the effects of their actions on the environment (products, markets, reactions of customers). The company functions in real time. Figure 9 summarizes the three types of organization:

Model	Organization	Management	Control
Mechanical	Pyramidal	Programming	Hierarchical
Biological	Reticulate	Piloting	Interactive
Chaotic	Fractal	Catalysis	Autonomous

Current efforts to reconfigure companies are directed toward the readjustment of structures, functions, and processes in response to new challenges related to the transitions between the mechanical, biological, and chaotic paradigms.

THE INTELLIGENT COMPANY, THE VIRTUAL COMPANY

In most companies, there is a balance among the three types of organization. Some large international corporations are organized in a pyramidal, polycellular, reticulate way. But the companies best suited to surviving and thriving in the world of networks and dealing with the constraints of complexity and acceleration are hybrids of the mechanical and biological models. In certain fields, such as communications, computers, and telecommunications, the biological and chaotic models dominate.

The hybrid companies that will have the best chance of surviving and developing in the age of networks will be intelligent companies. Intelligent people have the capacity to think abstractly, prioritize, and solve problems. They use logical reasoning, deductive and inductive. They have the ability to synthesize, answer quickly, and correct their mistakes. They can adapt to varied situations, and demonstrate high principles and open-mindedness. Intelligent companies share some of these qualities, which are manifested in their overall behavior: speed of action, adaptability to changing conditions, operational flexibility, skill in relationships, dynamism, intuition, openness, imagination, innovation. An unsophisticated company, on the other hand, is slow, heavy, defensive, overprotective, and unwieldy. It has no overall vision or plan, and lacks imagination and the capacity to innovate.

Since the intelligence of the company is based partly on the wise use and rapid circulation of information, sensory systems that inform the company of changes or innovations occurring in its environment are very important. The "sensory" company can set up systems for gathering and evaluating information on new technologies, competition, and markets. It is able to organize and implement an effective system for monitoring technology and competition.

But with networks and the widespread use of computers, the intelligence of companies will take another decisive step forward, becoming integrated into their very structure. Computer technology will be decentralized, becoming part of the background, with all kinds of miniature computers, communication boards, screens, and communicating badges to help teams create intelligent interfaces among their members.

Personal computing has, until now, focused essentially on increasing the capacities of the individual brain. Now it will also focus on increasing the collective intelligence of the organization as a superorganism equipped with a decentralized brain. The people working in these communicating offices, these information-processing macromachines, will truly be in a symbiotic relationship with their environment; they will be the neurons of the superorganism. This emergent nervous system of the company will create a new kind of ergonomics: intellectual or cognitive ergonomics. Rather than merely adapting buttons, levers, knobs, steering wheels, or seats to the human body, it will be possible to interface brains with the transducers, sensors, and "ubicomps" that inhabit the environment. This intellectual ergonomics will further accentuate the symbiotic nature of the relationship between human beings and the environments in which they work and create.

The increasing reticulation of society will lead to the gradual decentralization of certain types of companies. The virtual company is nothing other than an intelligent polycellular network whose nodes are reduced to the minimum of their active, effective critical mass. It is located in many places, each one of which is a cell made up of a small group of people performing certain specific functions and subcontracting those functions that are beyond their means. Decentralization in functional modules reduces fixed costs. Certain virtual companies function with only a hundred people. They are connected by networks to other independent companies with which they work on certain tasks (assembly, accounting, advertising, marketing) and for certain periods of time. In this way, they are able to accomplish the same amount of work as companies with thousands of employees, whose action is limited by unwieldy hierarchical structures.

As an example, Cisco Systems sells about 80 percent of the routers and other types of networking systems that power the Internet; 55 percent of incoming orders go through the company without being handled by anyone. Through an extranet with its suppliers and subcontractors and extranet links with its customers, Cisco manages a continuous flow of information, orders, materials, and spare parts or components, permitting a constant adaptation to supply and demand. This process is called *dynamic trade*: 80 percent of the company's sales come from the Web with more than $15 million of equipment sold per day. And 80 percent of customer and partner queries are answered online. Although sales are now six times their 1994 level, technical support staff has only doubled since then. Cisco Systems is saving more than $500 million a year using the

Web. The company is a model of a virtual enterprise, with highly personalized contacts and relations with its customers and partners.

The virtual company is symbiotic. The company and its symbiotic partners work in close cooperation, with a common interest and optimizing their resources. The simplest form of virtual company is a single person associated with intelligent logistics, the prostheses of the brain. The personal computing power available today can transform an individual into a microcompany, a cell and basic node in a network that encompasses the world. A growing number of people in the computer generation (those who grew up tapping on the keyboards of PCs or Macintoshes) are choosing to leave big companies and set up on their own in a variety of fields. A single person with logistical support is equivalent to a company with five or six employees; word processing, document management, communication by fax and e-mail, accounting, production (audiovisual, graphic, design, publishing, decoration), promotion, advertising, and sales are all handled with a computer that serves at various times as a communications device, a printing press, a photo processor, and an audiovisual cassette maker. The computer replaces secretaries, filing clerks, bookkeepers, graphic designers, and telephone operators. The widespread use of such processes and practices will increase unemployment in some sectors and create employment in others. It will cause problems in the transfer and creation of jobs in a society that is poorly prepared, but will mark a significant step in the transition to the age of networks.

In the new services of the quaternary sector—education, communications, consulting, and planning for the future—small teams assisted by computers and telecommunications devices will have as great an international impact as some large companies once had. Personalized computing and networks increase the power of the individual in relation to large organizations. With the power of the Internet a person can create a *one-person multinational company*.

NETWORKED RESEARCH AND FRACTAL PRODUCTION

The networked structure, parallel operations, and chaotic behavior of the new forms of organization are radically changing the major functions of the symbiotic company. To illustrate this, I have chosen examples from research and production. Multinational corporations with hundreds of thousands of employees, such as those in the chemical and pharmaceutical industries, have armies of researchers that usually operate according to the traditional mechanical model, which is hierarchical, linear, and sequential. Research projects follow certain channels, like bundles of unconnected fibers running side by side. The project is first reviewed by evaluation and monitoring committees. If accepted, it receives initial funding and then continues on, under the auspices of a department or laboratory, to discovery, patenting, and, possibly, industrial application. But this process is inefficient and expensive. The traditional stages are followed in sequence—basic research, applied research, research and development, industrial applications—like a river running from its source to its mouth. Even the vocabulary used reflects this approach; research is said to be the "source" of industrial applications, its primary cause.

But the limits of this type of organization quickly become apparent. It is difficult for the generals to make their platoons of researchers communicate with one other as a way to foster the cross-fertilization of ideas. Basic and applied research scientists do not share the same "culture"; they connect only randomly through chance encounters or when someone happens to read something in a journal. Moreover, it is difficult to stop projects, and this inevitably leads to diminishing returns. New ideas become increasingly difficult to get accepted, since this involves going all the way up the decision-making hierarchy. The system is self-limiting.

Another way would be to organize teams along the model of neural networks. Each researcher is closely connected to the others by various technical and human means. The system functions through catalysis. Ideas are discussed and tested against real problems. Basic and applied research coexist in a multidimensional matrix. Rather than imagining the usual bundle of projects running side by side, we should visualize research spatially as a sphere (see the figure at the top of the next page).

The volume of the sphere increases with new knowledge from basic research, but it also contains many other spheres of know-how. Data banks of experimental and practical knowledge constitute the

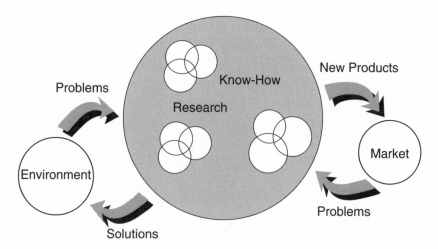

knowledge-capital of the company and its future potential. Confronted with problems that come from outside (new markets, the environment), the network reorganizes itself by *recombining* its know-how; it restructures itself using its memory and its experience. The launching of new projects and the elimination of others is much more balanced. As research on learning, particularly in children, has shown, the brain does not develop simply by accumulating new knowledge; it must also manage and organize what it already knows. A significant part of its activity consists of managing the interconnections of its knowledge. In a symbiotic, communicating structure, a neural network of researchers constantly recombines what it already knows in order to find solutions to the problems that arise.

Industrial mass production took a giant leap forward with the introduction of the assembly line, in which products at various stages of manufacture or assembly are conveyed from one workstation to another so that people or robots can perform specific tasks on them. Instead of one worker needing to have all the knowledge required to assemble a complex object piece by piece, the elements are presented in succession to a number of specialized agents. The assembly line thus changes training time into Taylorist space.

This ordered, hierarchical, programmed form of production will gradually be replaced in some industries (as we are already seeing) by the chaotic model and fractal organization. Chaos does not at first glance seem very compatible with the strict organization of an assembly line, but it should be noted that order can emerge from chaos as long as the system can be maintained in that critical transition phase—at the edge of chaos—between inflexible rigidity and sterile turbulence, the critical phase that gives rise to creativity, innovation, and complexification. The fractalization of an organization abolishes the linearity of its operations and creates feedback loops at every level (see the figure below).*

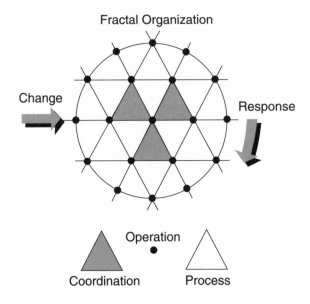

A fractal factory is one in which all the agents involved in the production or assembly of an object are organized in autonomous but interdependent modules. Some agents act upstream (planning, design, computer-aided design), others downstream (packaging, promotion, marketing), but the team functions as a unit in which the individual agents can work at their own pace according to the constraints of their planning—chaotically—as long as they observe the prescribed time limit. Moreover, some agents are interchangeable and multipurpose, which increases the flexibility of the operations. Motivation and participation are high in a fractal structure because it is a microcosm of the factory; micro reflects macro. Since the

---

*Adapted from: Norman Myers, *The Gaia Atlas of Future Worlds*, London, Robertson McCarta, 1990, p.66.

teams are linked in a network, the whole is a living capital of shared knowledge, organized hierarchically as in hypertext, with each item of knowledge or practice leading to another, thanks to a human or electronic link. In this way, the workshop, the factory, or the company as a whole, like a living organism, adapts to the chaos of the surrounding world. Rather than isolating itself behind rigid structures, the fractal factory coordinates flows, functions, and regulations, harmonizing them in relation to external constraints.

The chaotic model and fractal organization will be necessary in any type of dematerialized, decentralized production, such as that already being done in cyberspace. This is the case for creators of audiovisual programs (graphic designers, producers of synthesized images, writers, musicians, creators of special effects), who work in teams that are physically separated in a delocalized virtual electronic studio; organized in modules connected by electronic networks, they transfer their work in accordance with the organization's overall plan. This type of arrangement is the dematerialized equivalent of computer-integrated production in a factory based on the principles of just-in-time, zero stock, and zero defects. Computer-integrated creation follows similar principles. In the future, these information factories (multimedia or unimedia) will clone themselves according to the chaotic model and fractal organization, and contribute to educational, media, and artistic creation.

These new forms of organization of production and research will enable business to adapt to the constraints of evolution. Special attention will have to be paid to valuable human capital. Beyond the customary management of human resources, new bonds will have to be formed between people and companies, bonds based on respect for individual approaches and their enhancement through various levels of training. One means of achieving this is better management of information, time, and personal energy, basic flows that determine people's performance in their job functions and that, when well managed, add meaning to their lives and improve their symbiotic relationship with the company.

At the same time, the company will have to have a long-term strategy, breaking with the traditional approach based on extrapolation, and opening up to systemic planning that integrates many evolutionary currents into one comprehensive vision illuminating the future.

A CRYSTAL BALL: SYSTEMIC PLANNING FOR THE FUTURE

Our traditional way of looking at the future, by extrapolating and projecting from the present, demands dates and timetables. When we talk about a future technology, for example, everyone asks when it will be available. The approach I have adopted, without entirely avoiding references to the future, puts the emphasis, instead, on the convergence of trends and the probability of general models. One such model is the cybiont, a hypothetical yet probable model for the organization of (some) human societies, particularly given the progress in communications technology.

So many different methods are available for describing possible futures, and they all have some merit: scenario writing (the construction of plausible accounts of conflict situations), the Delphi method (questioning experts about the probability of some technical or social change), discovery matrices (combining several hypotheses), linear extrapolation (extending evolutionary trends), and simulation (creating computer models and studying the effects of particular parameter changes). By putting together just the right mixture of these ingredients, forecasters and futurologists are helping us to invent the future. Although they are far from infallible, some of them have built international reputations. Herman Kahn, John Naisbitt, Alvin Tofler, and Faith Popcorn, in the United States, and Jacques Lesourne, Thierry Gaudin, and Hugues de Jouvenel, in France, all use their own individual approaches. These approaches include consumer behavior patterns (Popcorn), media analysis (Naisbitt), scenarios of technical and political subjects (Tofler), and utopias that are achievable within a century (Gaudin).

I use a complementary method focusing on the current convergence of strong trends and their fusion during the next millennium. This requires a background in various areas: biology, computer science, communications, and systems theory. The dates of particular innovations are of secondary importance, but the feedback effect—in the long term—of potential models resulting from these trends is a powerful catalyst that will enable us to better decipher the future and act on the present. This is an approach that may be described as *retroprospective*: the construction of a scenario of the future so as to better identify factors in the present that will bring about that future. The scenario is modified in an iterative process based on precise information on the trends, which are themselves reinforced by the scenario. I call this method systemic planning for the future through the evaluation of trends and the validation of scenarios.

The first step is active technological monitoring. The data collected serve as the basis for the creation of an initial scenario describing events occurring, for example, in the next 10 years. The second step (undertaken in the present) is the "retroprospective" selection of strong trends converging toward the situation described in the initial scenario. The relationship between the trends selected and the scenario is tested for pertinence, resulting in the possible modification of the scenario and the creation of a second version incorporating the selected and pertinent facts. The third step is a new retroprospective validation of the trends, which further refines the second scenario, making it more pertinent. Through this interactive process of analysis, combination, and validation of trends, it becomes possible to predict situations, products, or services resulting from the convergence of several sectors—a result that is difficult to obtain by simple extrapolation from established trends. Thus the cybiontic model (or scenario), considered as a possible stage in the organization of human societies—accelerated by the communications explosion—sheds light *back* on some of the choices of the present day.

I have been using this method for many years to try to decipher the currents that are shaping our future. It is clearly the basis of this book and, in particular, of the following reflections on new fields for possible industrial developments in the context of symbionomic evolution. Two sectors seem to me representative of this evolution: the industries of the immaterial, in particular the information industries, with their economic and social spin-offs, and the new industries of matter, micro-, nano-, and macroengineering.

THE INDUSTRIES OF THE IMMATERIAL

We regularly hear the terms "communications revolution" and "information explosion" used to describe the amazing *media morphosis* we are now experiencing as we become an information society. We are in the process of building a vast information infrastructure from within, analogous to neurons interconnecting and building the infrasturcture of the brain. I described the broad outlines of this transformation in Part I, and I would now like to examine further some of the challenges and dangers it poses. I am doing so on the basis of two major and, in my opinion, irreversible trends: the worldwide expansion of the Internet and the introduction into the home of interactive multimedia television, which I prefer to call self-service information unimedia—a new type of digital television resulting from the merger of the Internet and television.

High-speed Internet videoservers will use parallel computers and will provide multimedia services (movies, educational programs, e-commerce, video games, information, weather reports). Users will be billed through a personal digitally coded meter or a smart card with an intelligent remote control connected to a "home server." These services already exist in part; some are in the testing stages. They no longer have anything to do with TV as we know it—no channels or programs or the ritual of the nightly news, but, instead, a huge audiovisual bookstore, a global hypertext accessible through this universal unimedia connector that the computer has, quite unexpectedly, become.

The merging of these self-service unimedia with the computerized interpersonal communications networks is natural. The Internet, the network of networks, brings together 20 million users in 146 countries. The cable companies and the operators of large commercial telecommunications networks are all linking up with the Internet. Television, teleconferencing, Web TV, "push media," interactive video, multimedia e-mail, virtual laboratories and studios, digital radio and downloadable music, remote manipulation of instruments, video games, virtual communities . . . we can no longer keep track of all the dematerialized human activities appearing in cyberspace for the purpose of creation, pleasure, knowledge, or work.

The introsphere, the cybiont's mind, is gradually being created beyond the bounds of the noosphere. New hopes, new constraints, and new dangers will arise with this information ecosystem. A virtuous circle is being established, leading to the autocatalysis and self-selection of the technological and economic sectors that will experience strong growth over the next 20 years. Once again, the sym-bionomic laws of organization will apply.

The user friendliness and power of personal microcomputers are bringing multimedia to the general public, and the images, sound, and video that are available are increasing the demand for informa-tion and education. The CD-ROM and the DVD (digital video disk) seem like the ideal interactive media, extensions of the book. The demand for computers with CD-ROM or DVD readers is growing, reinforcing the interest of educational and game software producers in creating new programs. At the same time, the connectivity of mi-crocomputers is improving and modems are falling in price and in-creasing in speed, making them more attractive to people who want to get connected. The number of people on the networks is climb-ing, attracting even more, which has an impact on the prices and performance of the hardware and software. A whole series of niches are forming, developing, and thriving through this amplification effect, which is then reinforced through cross-catalysis. The lock-in mechanism comes into play and becomes stronger. An autocatalytic loop is in place: the whole sector with its interconnections self-selects and inevitably emerges (see the figure below).

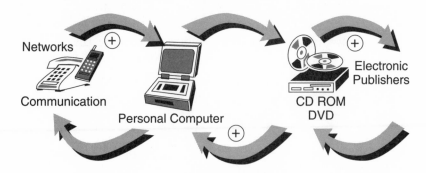

As shown in the figure, each element is the catalyst for another through the action of reinforcement loops (+).

TELE-ACTIVITIES AND TELE-EDUCATION

Two sectors developing quickly are: tele-activities and personalized tele-education. Tele-activities include, but are not restricted to, telecommuting, which is a far too narrow vision of this emerging sector. According to the most widespread view, telecommuting means working at home rather than going to the office, an arrangement that is accepted and recognized by an increasing number of companies. In 1998, 10 million Americans—approximately 4 or 5 percent of the workforce—defined themselves as "telecommuters" or "teleworkers." By 2001 nearly 8 percent of the workforce will be composed of telecommuters. It is clear that not all types of jobs can be performed remotely, but those that involve the dematerialized world of cyberspace and unimedia are incresingly being affected by telecommuting. New niches are being created, accelerating the growth of traditional sectors such as publishing, the press, and education. The development of networks, integrated hardware (videostations), and software for tele-activities (connection software) will amplify these trends. Some new characteristics will arise from the spread of tele-activities, among them personalization, demonopolization, a reduction in the use of certain forms of transportation, and real-time social feedback.

Personalization: Personalized computer power is reinforcing the autonomy and independence of "knowledge workers," new nodes in the planetary neural networks. The individual has become the basic "entrepreneurial" cell of the global system of production and creation. A person with a computer and communications logistics now has a capacity for influence and action equivalent to that of a centralized company of the Taylorist period. With a few clicks of the mouse, he or she can travel in space and time, saving energy and money, expanding his or her networks, and responding quickly to clients' requests.

Demonopolization: The pyramidal structure for the distribution and dissemination of cultural, educational, and informational goods and services has turned us into passive recipients. We live and work in societies of distribution and dissemination. Large public and private enterprises, often seeking to monopolize, are involved in every aspect of our lives. The distribution of food products, gasoline, information, and manufactured goods everywhere involves pyramids with the consumers at the base. Information moves downward, but does not easily move upward, and it is practically obligatory for any creator to go through producers, sponsors, partners, financiers, publishers—that is, the top of the pyramid—in order to be distributed to a wide audience. Television and radio companies, publishers of books and music, and film producers have until now held monopolies that could not be circumvented by any creator who wished to become known and have his or her work disseminated. Mass production and distribution require centralized means. This is the case for the publication of a book, the broadcasting of a television show, the production of a recording, or any creative activity requiring mass distribution. This is why writers, artists, directors, and programmers have always encountered selection, filtering, and support systems, power relationships and leverage on the difficult road to the eventual recognition of their talent.

All this is changing with the extension and development of the multimedia hypernetworks of interpersonal communication. Today anyone can produce, create, compose, present, and distribute his or her own products, becoming a vendor in the new market of cyberspace. With electronic money and promotion on the networks, many new markets are being created. When hypernetworks like the Internet provide widespread transmission of animated images and sound, the market for paid tele-activities will take off. There are already Internet television networks, or Web TV, that distribute videos made by private individuals. So-called amateur productions (films, books, recordings, and software) will gradually become more professional and they will be directly available on the networks. From a society of pyramidal distribution, we are moving to a reticulate society of real-time creation and integration. The result will be that monopolies will gradually be circumvented, short-circuited by transversal relationships among producers, vendors, and purchasers. Certain dinosaurs of television, radio, and publishing are threatened with extinction by the transversality of the networks, and it is time they realized it. The transversal and reciprocal relationship among creators will undermine the established powers. The ability to evaluate, select, and distribute on a mass scale will no longer be a privilege reserved for the few. Collective creation will be freed from the narrow framework that now confines it. Symbiotic culture will be able to express itself in all its chaotic turbulence. The new general culture, as we will see, will be a fractal culture of reconstruction.

Transportation: The old utopian idea of using electronic communication to reduce the need for physical displacement is on the way to becoming a reality. Of course, people are gregarious, social animals, and will always feel a physical and psychological need for the real presence of their fellow workers. The body is not virtual but material, and situated in space and time. However, environmental constraints will reinforce the need to reduce "automobility," and now advances in computerized interpersonal telecommunications technology and the lowering of its costs make this possible. During the Gulf War, when under the threat of terrorism, or following earthquakes in California, thousands of professionals whose daily commutes were suddenly impeded discovered the advantages of telecommuting using videoconferencing and network connections. The market for this kind of technology is developing at an ever-increasing pace. Admittedly, these forms of communication do not replace the multidimensionality of human relationships, but they are perfectly suitable for many work and recreational activities. The development of tele-activities is one long-term means of controlling the proliferation of cars in our cities and the dangerous increase in air traffic above them.

Social feedback: The hypernetworks provide the means for general participatory feedback. Through constant mutual consultation on subjects related to everyday life, associations, professional activities, and decisions affecting the future, network users will have a continual and precisely nuanced say. This is necessary for the co-management and copiloting of the complex systems they are part of (associations, clubs, companies, cities, regions). Strict rules for the use and control of this form of real-time participatory feedback will have to be implemented in order to prevent dangerous negative effects.

Widely available personalized tele-education is another aspect of the information and knowledge society. Industry hesitated a long time before investing in educational technology. Some companies went into it too early and failed dramatically. Today, thanks to the synergy between technological progress, economic opportunity, and consumer information—the catalytic alchemy characteristic of any mechanism of social natural selection—this sector is really taking off.

Personalized education is coming into the home primarily through the Internet and CD-ROMs for young people. Children who are accustomed to the interactivity of video games prepare their parents for educational and game software. Since CD-ROMs are an extension of the familiar audio CD, they are reassuring to consumers. This type of localized interactivity prepares people for, or else supplements, tele-educational interactivity developing on the Internet. In addition to the educational software designed for children, even very young children ("totware"), that is currently driving the market, programs are being developed for personalized training in business and for the use of families at home. The strong growth sectors will be audiovisual encyclopedias, simulation programs, and health programs. Encyclopedias on CD-ROM or accessible in real time on networks are one of the engines of growth in tele-education. With powerful simulation programs, such as the now-classic SimCity and SimLife, educational game software is reaching both parents and children. Simulation programs on subjects such as economics, chemistry, ecology, and biology will set new standards for educational simulation games in coming years. Cybermedicine is already widely available on CD and the Internet; there is a growing demand for interactive medical consultations, with anatomical cross sections and descriptions of treatments and operations.

Tele-education on CD and the Internet will destabilize the traditional school. The conflict between the short term (news, film or video clips, zapping, interactive games) and long term (education, training, evolution, reflection) will be exacerbated. The analytical, linear, sequential, subject-oriented world of the school will increasingly be confronted with the emotional, global world of interactive television and the Internet. We should not try to compensate for the gap between these two worlds by filling the school with the latest educational and communications technology. We need, rather, to find a balance between short and long term by adapting educational methods and tools. A *re-engineering* of the classroom will be necessary, no less than for the company. Unless the schools adopt such an approach, they are in danger of becoming nothing more than babysitting services, with the real education taking place elsewhere, through the networks and electronic unimedia.

THE ECONOMY OF NETWORKS: PIRACY AND ENCRYPTION

Without the market and the economy, there is no place for industry. However, the economy and the very specific new markets that are being established on the networks are creating new niches for complexity and development. I will first consider the effects of the reproduction, amplification, and acceleration of information in the new economy of cyberspace. Then I will look at the new rules of markets.

The paradox of the information society is the nature of information itself. Unlike energy, which is destroyed through use (leading to increased entropy, the "used" form of energy, which cannot produce work), information is amplified and self-catalyzes when used. Another paradox is that information societies are societies of *reproduction*, in which everything exists to facilitate reproduction: fax machines, photocopiers, laser printers, computer programs for copying material on hard or floppy disk, electronic messaging, still cameras, camcorders, scanners, and audio and video cassettes. Our society of electronic text, image, and sound is a macrocopying machine. Yet at the same time, this seemingly natural action is repressed. Under totalitarian regimes, directories, tape recorders, and camcorders are prohibited. Even in democratic countries, citizens' band radios, modems, and portable telephones have for a long time been, and still are, heavily regulated, undoubtedly because being connected is in a sense equivalent to copying or reproducing material outside of hierarchical control.

Through copyright, royalties, and licences, we set up barriers (which are justified in an economy of *things*) against pirating and unauthorized photocopying. But in a *dematerialized* economy, it is hardly possible to resist the pressure to reproduce material. Like viruses, ideas are infectious; they spread like epidemics, and it is through copying that people become "contaminated." Every living thing in nature seeks to reproduce itself. Information, too, seeks only to be reproduced, yet we make this duplication illegal. Plagiarism, which disregards the moral rights of authors (let alone their financial rights), is unacceptable of course, but the functioning of the introsphere may well be based precisely on the unrestricted reproduction of information. In the new information ecology, reproduction is the rule—as it is in biological evolution. Without reproduction, there is no mixing of genes—or of ideas—and no generation of variety or new species, no evolution.

The solution of the future is to liberate the reproduction of information by using personal encryption. Once reserved for embassy cipher clerks and the military, encryption technology is now available to the general public. Smart cards, passwords, television decoders, and encrypted telephone lines are all common. They are the precursors of the generalized use of coding. A further step will be the adaptation of military technology for personal computers. Encryption software for the general public—like PGP (Pretty Good Privacy)—is already widely used. A huge market will develop for this technology, since it makes it possible to reproduce information while complying with the rules of trade, the basis of the economy, and the rules of privacy, the cornerstone of diversity.

Encrypted information will arrive in homes via information highways or on CD-ROMs. The cost will be based neither on the duration of use nor on the number of bits of information, but on the *use* made of the information. Information cannot be used unless it is decrypted, so each decryption will generate a small fee. Thus, users will pay only for what they actually consume. With encryption, the home *information meter*, like the gas or electricity meter, will become a reality.

Software creators will draw on the methods used to protect the copyright of songwriters and music composers. Recordings are provided freely to radio stations, but a fee is paid when the station broadcasts a particular piece of music, and this is monitored statistically. The same principle can be adapted to the sale of software. A computer connected to the networks could copy all desired programs; it would be analogous to a radio station with only one listener. Each use of the software would generate a fee, with encryption technology being used to protect confidentiality and access to personal accounts. Thus, users would not pay for the object (the diskette), but only for the use of the program on it, which could be copied any number of times, generating further fees.

The law of *increasing* returns is the rule in the economy of networks. Cyberspace is a form of information *capital* that bears *interest* in the form of information. The more it is used, the greater the value of this capital and the more interest it bears. Cyberspace is growing in complexity and value from within. (I will show here how this is transforming our very concept of time.) The law of increasing returns leads to the lock-in effect discussed earlier, which is the basis of all mechanisms of self-selection through autocatalysis or cross-catalysis. The success of fax machines and modems is based on the same logic: a single device has no value, since there is nobody else to communicate with, but when there are two, ten, a hundred, a thousand, a million, each additional one increases the value of all the others. Thanks to the logic of networks, the same snowball effect will undoubtedly occur with videophones for the general public, leading to a similar explosive growth.

TO LEARN IS TO ELIMINATE

But the logic of networks also has negative effects. The multiplication of connections can lead to infopollution and a reduction in the capacity for creativity and adaptability of the network as a whole. Already, many electronic messaging systems produce information that is more polluting than pertinent. "Overconnected" professionals receive hundreds of messages a day. Advertising by fax clogs the terminals of companies, leading to a waste of time and therefore a loss of efficiency.

However, the economy of networks can also achieve optimum functioning. Each percentage in the number of additional users increases the information capital of the whole network in a nonlinear way. An increase of 2 percent in the number of users can mean a 10 percent increase in traffic, since each user increases the number of links and therefore the flow of information. The question is at what number of connections per node will a network stabilize and find a creative zone that fosters its harmonious development? Studies on biodiversity show that below a certain threshold of variety (number of species in existence), an ecosystem stagnates. Above a certain level, productivity is reduced; too much variety leads to diminishing returns. Similarly, experiments on the origin of life show that a variety of molecules in interaction quickly generates combinations that serve as building blocks for more complex molecules. If there is too little variety, the structures break up and disappear. If the variety is too great, energy is lost in infinite combinations.

The logic of networks is interconnection ad infinitum. Placed in a culture, neurons want only to connect. Telephones catalyze even more telephones, and modems, more modems. Pushed to the extreme, however, this "connectivist" logic can lead to a system whose sole justification is communication for the sake of communication. What is required is a regulator to control this propensity and maintain the creativity and adaptability of the network at an optimal level. In biology, such regulation is provided by the molecular coding of information. Cells recognize each other by specific signals displayed on the surface of their membranes. The highest variety of signals is produced by molecules called glycoproteins, which offer an infinite variety of combinations and thus provide a vast array of connections between cells while protecting and maintaining their specific characteristics. Other molecules, like nucleic acids, can also recognize highly specific sequences, which prompts them to hybridize, or stick together, strand by strand. The cells of the immune system rely upon molecular coding to recognize the diversity of the organism and then to detect and destroy molecules that are foreign to it. Thus, the molecular coding of information ensures operational diversity and, at the same time, regulates that diversity by allowing cells to recognize each other and either stick together or destroy invading cells. An analogous logic of coding is used to create natural antivirus defenses for computer systems.

We see another parallel in brain development. When a child is learning, certain connections between synapses in his or her brain are selectively stabilized. After a phase of expanding and redundant connections, priority circuits form between neurons. Through interaction with the environment, the biochemical "welds" linking certain circuits are reinforced and stabilized. Following a process of internal Darwinian selection, the other connections degenerate and disappear. Thus, as Jean-Pierre Changeux has pointed out, to learn is to *eliminate.* This symbionomic law is essential in the development of the cybiont's planetary brain.

In the age of the portable telephone and electronic telephone directory, the great temptation exists to get an unlisted number. Similarly, personal encryption will reduce systematic interconnectivity. Human intelligence is seeking ways to slow down the globalization of interconnections. Fear of cultural homogenization through networks has prompted people to fight for their language (a form of protective encryption of diversity), to create "cultural exemptions," and to protect traditions, territories, and religious practices. Displacing the "melting pot" so dear to the Americans, certain communities are beginning to prefer (and insist on) the "salad bowl" with each leaf in its place and a common seasoning to amplify the synergy of the flavors. A dynamic equilibrium obviously must be found between connectionism and isolationism, between the uncontrolled lowering of cultural barriers and the withdrawal into a dangerous and sterile nationalism. But paradoxically, in a hypercommunicating world like that of biology or networks, it is coding that protects difference.

Computer simulation makes it possible to identify the symbionomic laws of equilibrium between connectivity and the maintenance of diversity. Once again, the macroscope enables us to see the fundamental relationship between order, complexity, and chaos. Too large a number of connections leads to chaotic, turbulent, anarchic, sterile functioning; the system is blocked, as if "deafened" by the "noise" it generates. Conversely, too small a number of connections produces a rigid, inflexible system that is incapable of adapting to change. Between the two, there is a transition phase, an optimal zone "at the edge of chaos" that favors adaptability and creativity, as shown in the figure below.

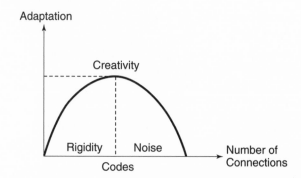

Specific coding acts as a regulator to maintain the system in this zone. This *infostat* (like a thermostat) prevents runaway reactions that would lead to a blockage of functions or infinite complication. This figure should be compared with those on pages 159 and 160, which show how the rules, codes, and laws of democracy act as regulators to maintain diversity with equality and to foster creativity and adaptability. In anarchic or totalitarian systems, the absence or the excess of codes, and the plethora or the lack of personal freedoms, impedes evolution toward a harmonious complexity of structures and functions; the processes of symbiosis between the individual and society are unable to get under way.

THE NEW MARKETS OF CYBERSPACE

The economy of networks gives rise to new forms of market. In its traditional form, a market is a space of evaluations, exchanges, and transactions that obey simple rules. In this space, multiple agents work in parallel. They have indirect information on the effects of the transactions that take place in the market. A *transaction* is the process in which currency is exchanged for a good or service. The price established between the vendor and the purchaser is the basis of the regulatory mechanisms since it is both value and information. A market thus behaves like a massively parallel computer capable of processing and integrating large volumes of information simultaneously. The chaotic and unpredictable behavior of agents leads to the emergence, at higher levels, of a dynamic stability that prevents overly abrupt variations. A regulated free market has capacities for adaptation much superior to those of a hierarchical system controlled from the top.

A particularly interesting experiment carried out by researchers at Xerox brings out the difference between the two. The objective of the experiment was to optimize the use of the computers at the research center. Depending on the types of tasks and their frequency and complexity, certain computers were busier than others. To distribute the work in a harmonious way, the researchers initially designed a "big central regulator" that assigned to the various projects whatever free time and space were available on the machines. Unfortunately, this "big regulator" required extremely complex programs to manage the scheduling, which used a great deal of the machines' time. The researchers then tried a completely decentralized "internal market" system. A "budget" was attached to each task. The computers that had free time posted a processing "price," which depended on how busy they were. And the various computers were assigned tasks through electronic tendering and transactions between the machines, with each computer seeking to maximize its revenue. The project managers automatically managed their budgets by optimizing the time (and cost) of processing in relation to the priority placed on each task. The system worked perfectly, in a decentralized way and with very little computing time required for coordination. The market found its own equilibrium.

The functioning of such a market is analogous to the process by which bees inform their hive of a new source of pollen (as we saw in Chapter 1). By means of information transmitted through their dances, the bees modify the probability of the exploitation of one source relative to another. The number of "undecided" bees diminishes, while that of bees "convinced" of the quality of the new source increases, leading more bees to go to the new source.

A similar phenomenon can be found in a mass market such as the car market. Each undecided person who is convinced by a relative or friend, or by advertising, of the merits of a certain make of car shifts the balance of probability of purchase toward that make, thus gradually increasing the flow of buyers. Obviously, other effects come into play in the opposite direction, making the establishment of equilibrium more complex. But the figure on p. 26 showing the structure of the bees' collective decision-making mechanism as a parallel microprocessor, can be applied to the evolution of the market for two competing makes of cars.

In the examples described, the information possessed by the agents (producers, distributors, vendors, purchasers) is *indirect*. The effects of the transactions (or of their absence, in the case of a product boycott) are only measured afterwards. With the spread of telecommunications networks, self-service unimedia information outlets, and electronic money, there will be a constant, *direct*, massive return of information. This type of real-time social feedback from the market will transform the very foundations of the economy and create new negative effects. This is already the case for daily stock trading on the Internet or commercial offers of goods and services with no fixed price.

REVERSE MARKETING AND SELECTIVE MARKETING

Two aspects of the new markets, both of which emerge from the logic of networks, merit consideration from a symbionomic point of view: reverse marketing and computerized selective marketing. What I call reverse marketing belongs to a new form of market created by a *reversal* of the traditional arrow that goes from producers' offers to consumers' demand. Today, producers mass produce goods for mass consumption. These products are stored in zones of exchanges and transactions (wholesalers, stores, markets, department stores) to which buyers go to get the products of their choice, with only a very small proportion of purchases being made by e-commerce. Companies spend substantial amounts of money on market research, advertising, and marketing to gain market share, but they have only a small amount of statistical information on potential buyers and growth of market shares over a relatively long term.

All this changes with real-time feedback, for example, by means of interactive multimedia television. The arrow is reversed, going *from* demand *to* supply. The wishes of buyers are expressed in a continuous flow and in detail: which colors, which shapes, which functions. Buyers vote constantly on the Internet through remote controls, personal computers, television sets, and intelligent telephones located in their homes. Using this direct information, producers can regulate their stocks more precisely and adjust their production for maximum benefit, particularly because of the flexibility of automation.

Reverse marketing will lead to an explosion of diversity in some sectors and increased conformity in others. An infinity of market niches will be created, each reflecting the desires and needs of a

small number of consumers. The mass market will become a personalized market to an extent never before seen. The information feedback loop between the consumer's purchase, the ordering of materials by the producer, and the manufacturing of the product will be
tightened, and companies will be able to respond in a few weeks, or
even a few days, to sudden consumer fads for fabrics, clothing, or
personalized cars. The connection of reverse marketing networks
(providing information feedback) and flexible factories (using
computer-integrated production systems) brings out the quasi-
biological nature of this mechanism: a supply that continually adapts
to the demand.

Another development—one that represents a dangerous step toward the invasion of privacy—is computerized selective marketing
(database marketing), in which companies use all the information
they can get concerning the behavior and interests of consumers.
The massive use of computers makes it possible to recreate the old-
fashioned neighborhood store in which buyers and sellers have
known each other for years. Each current or potential customer receives promotional information that is personalized (according to
income, age, occupation, habits, hobbies). Niche marketing is facil-
itated by the use of parallel computers that can process large
amounts of information very quickly, neural networks that build
models of buyers' behavior according to their previous transactions
and create data banks that make it possible for them to index and
cross-reference information on millions of people.

All consumer transactions, choices, and preferences, and all actions related to credit card purchases are recorded on computer, as is
the information in coupons, questionnaires, guarantee forms, or
product surveys they fill out, calls they make to a toll-free number,
and programs they select on interactive television. For example,
companies will keep an electronic trail of stores where individual
consumers shop, the films they see, their favorite restaurants, where
they travel, the airlines they use, and the economic and climatic conditions where they live. Information of this nature from a number of
associated companies is compiled in computers and used to prepare
promotional activities that can target even a *single* person—the basis
of "one-to-one marketing."

The trend appears very difficult to reverse. Nearly 60 percent of large American companies maintain such networks and databases, and the information in them is commonly shared among banks, credit card companies, large retail outlets, automobile manufacturers, and agrifood companies. In France this practice is controlled by a regulatory commission. But some European credit card holders are "on file" in U.S. computers that provide data for selective promotional campaigns. It is becoming increasingly difficult to control this phenomenon, which arises from network globalization and from the growth of the planetary brain. One possible solution, as suggested by John Hagel, is to create a new kind of intermediary between customers and producers: "infomediaries."[*] They will protect the consumer from invasion of privacy and provide producers with authorized and highly personalized lists of potential customers' demands.

THE PARASITIC ECONOMY, BIG BROTHER, AND ELECTRONIC DRUGS

Electronic money is responsible for another negative effect of network logic: a parasitic electronic economy, a parallel economy that will shake the very foundations of the traditional economy. Encrypted electronic money eliminates the need for a wallet stuffed with banknotes. Unlimited sums can be deposited in bank accounts anywhere in the world, which makes money laundering much easier. Already, organized crime and traffickers in all kinds of goods are using international telematics networks (including the Internet), cellular telephones, pagers, and electronic money to evade the control of governments. Companies and individuals will even issue private electronic money, competing with the central banks of states. Counterfeiting banknotes will no longer be necessary. With the appropriate software, private individuals will be able to carry out financial operations and transactions once reserved for specialized agencies and professionals as easily as they use a spreadsheet. What impact will these millions of autonomous financial agents have—agents

---

[*] John Hagel and Marc Singer, *Net Worth*, Cambridge: Harvard Business School Press, 1999.

who, thanks to electronic networks, can constantly take part in the major financial transactions of stock exchanges or currency markets, and thus amplify the action of a few clever raiders or insiders? The stock exchange information available on the Internet has already caused some stock prices to rise or fall dramatically. Daily trading through millions of online traders can transform the stock market into a virtual casino.

The combined effects of the big global networks, electronic money, and dematerialized products that can be downloaded at home (software, images, sound, videos) will abolish the borders, barriers, quotas, and protectionist national policies set up for a material economy, an economy of things. I regularly buy products I have seen advertised on international satellite networks or offered in electronic catalogues on the networks. I pay for the product by electronic transfer, and my purchase is downloaded in compressed form or delivered to my home through some routing center located on the other side of the world. Virtual stores are being created, and they will proliferate for the simple reason that they have no stock, pay no direct costs for premises, have no advertising expenses, and employ little staff. They have a further great advantage over traditional stores: they are able very quickly to meet demand and adapt to the market. With the downloading of high-value-added dematerialized products and with payment in encrypted electronic money, we are entering the age of commercial cyberspace.

There are new dangers associated with the operation, even at a still-rudimentary level, of the cybiont's planetary brain: cyberspace infopollution and congestion, stifling cybernauts with complex practices and instructions, and widening the gap between the "inforich" and "infopoor."

There are other, even more disturbing, dangers. The main one is the invasion of privacy, as we saw in the case of computerized selective marketing. The more complex the networks become, the easier it is to find information on people, and even to steal or pirate it. The Internet is already a hideout for a new generation of "electronic highway robbers" who steal passwords, break into e-mail, blackmail users, and divert funds. With ubiquitous miniaturized electronic technology, it becomes easy to spy on your neighbors or employees.

The specter of Big Brother looms over the international electronic networks. A conversation between two cellular phones, a call for a taxi, a withdrawal from an ATM, the purchase of a gift, a lunch in a restaurant, the rental of a car, the electronic payment of a highway toll, or the purchase of gasoline—all these everyday actions are now dated, located, and stored in computer memories and can be used to retrace a person's actions at a particular time.

The fragility of these networks, precisely because of their complexity, also presents the possibility of danger. Computer viruses are a good illustration, as are breakdowns and crashes of these ultra-sophisticated systems. The computer programs that control the piloting of modern airplanes or the electronic switchboards of international telephone lines are so complex that it is practically impossible to foresee every eventuality, or—more disturbing still—to maintain them in perfect working order.

There is also the danger of people becoming isolated in their own "electronic bubbles" in front of their computer monitors or television sets, receiving information by satellite or interactive cable networks, living by e-commerce, meeting by teleconference, and having cybersex!

Finally, another danger is of a sort of electronic drug addiction, a risk of people escaping into new types of artificial paradise, which we see foreshadowed in young people's passion for video games. This danger already exists. We know that a drug is characterized by three properties: dependence (irresistible need), habituation (need to increase dosage), and withdrawal (physiological effects of deprivation). To some extent television fulfils these criteria, and millions of viewers have become dependent on it. Stronger and stronger doses of emotion are needed to "sell" a repetitive news item. Deprivation of the familiar daily ritual of watching televised images—such as those on the news—leads to withdrawal and insecurity. The Internet is another type of electronic drug. Its users experience need, habituation, and withdrawal. Some Internet addicts spend 15 hours a day on the Net! How will we react to the spread of virtual communities, dematerialized travel in time and space, the exploration of cyberspace, and immersion in the introsphere, the shared sphere of emotions, feelings, abstractions, and unlimited imagination? And how will we be able to control the sale and the effects of future electronic drugs that will be downloadable from any point in the world and distributed directly to the brain through bioelectronic interfaces?

THE INDUSTRIES OF THE INVISIBLE

The information industry is the foundation of a dematerialized economy. But the processing of materials will remain one of the basic tasks of industry in the future. Mechanics, biology, chemistry, and microelectronics will change profoundly in two ways: the merging of these fields and the increasingly refined control of the organization of atoms and molecules for the manufacture of a vast variety of materials and micromachines.

Engineering had its greatest successes at the beginning of the twentieth century, with the application of the laws of physics to the processing of materials and the construction of complex structures and machines. Gustave Eiffel and Isambard Kingdom Brunel were the heroes of that era, which saw the construction of suspension bridges of great technical daring, giant steamships, towers reaching toward the skies, locomotives, and the first airplanes. The engineering of the twenty-first century will focus on the infinitely small and the infinitely complex: processing atoms, building microstructures, assembling biological and mechatronic micromachines; establishing procedures for managing and controlling the complex systems in which human beings act; setting in motion macroregulatory processes on a planetary scale. Its field will extend from nanoengineering (a nanometer is a billionth of a meter) to macroengineering, including, of course, microengineering, which has undergone major expansion at the end of the twentieth century with biotechnology and microelectronics.

Molecular biology paved the way, and genetic engineering followed. Biologists have developed an extraordinary array of tools to manipulate living matter and reprogram cells (which I described in detail in *L'aventure du vivant*), and discussed briefly in the preceding chapters): copying machines (PCR: polymerase chain reactions), scissors, glues, transporters, drills, probes, programmed molecular machines, catalytic antibodies (abzymes), and RNA enzymes (ribozymes). Biotechnology is a form of microengineering. Bacteria are miniature factories that are reprogrammed by means of molecular codes, which engineers are able to modify at will and which the bacteria can interpret. The process is analogous to computer programming; a single computer can carry out different tasks with simple changes in the program. These new tools of biotechnology, to which we must add computers, are the basis of the expansion of bioindustry.

In its progress toward the infinitely small, microelectronics has almost gotten down to the microscopic dimensions of biological viruses (which are smaller than bacteria!). The goal of computer scientists is to create structures with features about 0.1 micrometer (100 nanometers) in thickness in order to concentrate tens of millions of transistors in a square millimeter. We are now reaching the physical limits of this type of circuit, although this concentration is low compared to that attained through biological compaction. The main techniques used in making microelectronic circuits are based on photoengraving, which involves *removing* matter, whereas biology proceeds by *adding* elements through the self-organization of matter from the bottom up, building increasingly complex structures, from a fertilized egg to an organism of trillions of cells, or a tree 100 yards high. The world of biology provides a permanent showcase of models of molecular machines that nanoengineers can draw on.

One example of such molecular machinery is the "nose" of the coliform bacterium, a common and usually harmless microbe that is able to recognize "smells." The bacterium looks like a tiny bag 1 micrometer (a thousandth of a millimeter) long. Within it are various molecules, including proteins and the long DNA molecule that carries the genetic code. It swims around in its environment by means of flagella that undulate like the tails of spermatozoa. It has a sensory system that enables it to detect the molecules it feeds on, to move toward areas where these molecules are most densely concentrated, and to flee harmful substances. The bacterium has approximately 3000 chemical receptors grouped at the front of the cell, which measure the concentrations of molecules as it moves, and which send chemical signals to the molecular engines, causing the flagella to accelerate, slow down, or change the direction of movement. Thus, the microbe is able to "smell" nourishment and steer toward it, which it does at a speed of 10 to 20 micrometers a second. A kind of conveyor belt continuously captures the food molecules and crams them into the cell, like a boiler being stoked with shovels full of coal. So we see that the bacterium travels by means of flagella, miniature oars moved by molecular microengines, that it detects molecules by means of microsensors, and that it steers by means of a guidance system based on the concentrations of those molecules—a series of mechanisms from which molecular engineers can draw inspiration.

THE RISE OF NANOTECHNOLOGY

The idea of copying biology to build nanomachines goes back to the late 1950s. At a convention of the American Physical Society on December 29, 1959, scientists gathered in the big auditorium at Caltech could not believe their ears. The future Nobel laureate for physics, Richard Feynman, had just declared, "What would happen if we could arrange the atoms one by one the way we want them? . . . it would have an enormous number of technical applications. . . . For instance, the wires [would] be 10 or 100 atoms in diameter, and the circuits . . . a few thousand angstroms across." Feynman was right. He died in 1988, and thus was not able to fully take part in the development of nanotechnology, a strategic industrial sector in which international corporations have invested hundreds of millions of dollars.

Eric Drexler, president of the Foresight Institute, is another pioneer and catalyst in the development of nanotechnology. His first contribution, which attracted a good deal of attention, was an article on molecular engineering published in September 1981 in the *Proceedings of the National Academy of Science*. He was then 26 years old. A controversial figure in the world of physics and chemistry, Drexler nevertheless played an important role in making scientists and business leaders aware of the importance of nanoengineering.

The objective of nanotechnology is to manufacture—atom by atom—machines, circuits, and networks that can function on a molecular scale, and to have these machines, in turn, produce others like themselves, eventually leading to materials and systems that function on a human scale. This technology is based on a whole toolkit of instruments developed in the last 15 years, among them the scanning tunneling microscope (STM) and the scanning force microscope for observing and manipulating individual atoms—the lathes, drills, and milling machines of the nanoworld. In 1990, Don Eigler of IBM astounded the world by using the STM to write the logo of his company in letters 5 nanometers high, using 35 xenon atoms deposited on a nickel surface. If they were as big as the capital letters of this text, a human hair would be 55 yards in diameter. Other tools that have been developed include laser "pliers" to grip and move molecules, laser "cameras" to take snapshots of the movement of atoms, and traps to collect atoms and sort them into small packets, as well as the biotechnology tools for cutting, copying, gluing, sorting, locating, and reprogramming molecules.

Using these tools, nanoengineers have already made wires, tubes, molecular "velcro," switches, microengines, microgears, ball bearings, shuttles that move on a wire, rotors, cubes composed of DNA, double helixes, thin coatings consisting of superimposed plates a single molecule thick—a whole Meccano set of parts that can be assembled into more complex structures.

These engineers and architects of the infinitely small have also defined the conditions for the self-assembly of the parts and structures, the holy grail of nanotechnology. Their objective is to "grow" the machines and circuits of tomorrow. After all, the life of the giant redwood, an immense solar collector, begins with the chemical program of a molecule of DNA. In addition to the chemical program, energy (from the sun), basic materials (carbon dioxide, water, mineral salts), and molecular machines (enzymes) are also required to build this immense structure in space and through time. The leaf is a self-assembled photovoltaic cell. Using their know-how on the chemical and biotechnological manipulation of atoms and molecules, nanoengineers hope to produce self-assembled structures as complex as a tree.

Each type of molecular machine used by nature will be copied, modified, improved, reinvented: first, assemblers and disassemblers to speed up the assembly and disassembly of complex molecules;

then, sensors, effectors, and nanocomputers to control the manufacturing process; and then, motors, conveyor belts, automatic sorters,
and micropumps. Nanorobots will be created, machine tools for
manufacturing larger microrobots that can perform molecular repair
tasks, for example, within the human body: unblocking, stitching,
cleaning, destroying, or reporting danger. These microrobots will also
be able to act in colonies or swarms, like ants or bees, to build macrostructures directly usable by people. Computers and computer-
aided design (CAD) will be widely used to design new models and
define the stages of their assembly, as they are today in the automobile or aeronautics industry. Key achievements have already been
made in this direction. At Xerox PARC, Ralph Merkle has designed
models of micromachines on computer. Julius Rebeck, at MIT, has
synthesized molecules that have the capacity for spontaneous self-
replication. Francis Garnier, of France's National Scientific Research
Centre, has developed plastic transistors on flexible sheets. Jean-
Marie Lehn of the Collège de France, a Nobel laureate and pioneer
in supramolecular chemistry, has created molecular wire in which
the current can be turned on and off by means of a molecule-switch
that allows a flow of electrons to pass when lighted with UV radiation and that stops the flow when it is lighted with infrared. Laboratories working in these fields are proliferating around the world. The
United States and Japan have invested massive amounts in development and production centers that use nanotechnology or molecular
electronics. One of the key areas is represented by research on mi-
croelectromechanical systems (MEMs). At the Massachusetts Institute of Technology, a team headed by Robert Langer has developed
a "smart pill" based on a tiny chip equipped with sensors and able to
deliver drugs at regular doses and time intervals. Microlabs, or "labs
on a chip" with 80-micrometer capillaries, picoliter volumes, nano-
liter-persecond-flows, 100-millisecond separations, and 500,000
tests of new molecules per day, are also under development or in
production and will revolutionize pharmaceutical drug research and
medical and hospital biochemical tests.

The material industry of the future is thus being created from
the fusion of four sectors described at various points in this book:
biotechnology, artificial life (or neobiology), molecular electronics

(and biotics), and nanotechnology. An extension of the chemical and microelectronic industries, the rational manipulation of materials, a cross-disciplinary field, will involve health, computer science, robotics, communications, agrifood, mining, the production and distribution of energy. It will pave the way, among other things, for biorobots and biocomputers, neobiological hybrid machines necessary for the functioning of the industries of the future and basic components of the cybiont.

THE TRIUMPH OF THE MULTIPLE: PARALLELISM AND THE "VELCRO EFFECT"

Another major trend in the industry of the future will be the systematic implementation of parallel processes at all levels of organization. Our centralized, Taylorized, linear, sequential view of industrial production has hindered operational parallelism—partly because parallel processes lend themselves less readily to rigorous control than the traditional pyramidal hierarchical organization. However, the vast majority of metabolic processes and information processing that take place in nature are parallel, as we saw with the ants and bees. The same type of organization exists in many animal societies. The systems of spontaneous exchanges that are the basis of the self-preservation and self-replication of human societies—such as the market or, more generally, the economy—are massively parallel. The future belongs to parallelism and the multiple. This means human beings will have to partially abandon a certain type of control over their own creations. Three examples from the future illustrate this development: parallel computers, combinatorial chemistry, and swarms of microrobots.

Parallel computers will gradually replace sequential computers. Interconnected multiprocessors are being built on the model of neural networks; they can recognize shapes, faces, handwriting, and voices. Data banks on parallel computers will provide hundreds of thousands of people simultaneously with video films, games, or news clips on demand.

Molecular electronics will favor the development of cellular automata, which operate in parallel. John von Neumann, the inventor of the modern computer, envisaged two modes of information processing: sequential processing and the cellular automaton. Advances in electronics favored the former. The creation of biochips and biocomputers will now develop along the lines of cellular automata, bringing computer science closer to biology. Programming will no longer be rigorously controlled by humans, but will in large part consist of self-programming by means of genetic algorithms. Like biological evolution, these programs will proceed through successive mutations, selection, and trial and error, and they will solve problems so complex that they are now beyond the abilities of human beings. This is the case for programs consisting of millions of lines of code that are used in real-time operations in communications or aeronautics. The parallel computers of the future will handle the maintenance, operation, and adaptation of these hypercomplex programs. Not a single programmer will know or understand how the machine finds the solutions, or even know how the programs work. But parallelism and artificial evolution will guarantee the dynamic stability of systems on which the lives of millions of people may depend. The human-computer symbiosis will lead to a copiloting of complexity.

Parallelism will also dominate in chemistry. Today in the pharmaceutical industry, it takes 10,000 molecules, synthesized, analyzed, tested, and selected, to finally produce a single one that is developed and put on the market. Operations are sequential, communications between sectors are uncertain, and research and development can often take as long as 10 years. Combinatorial chemistry will revolutionize this process. As opposed to traditional chemistry, synthesis is carried out in parallel, simultaneously producing billions of *different* molecules. This is done using chemical chips created by means of techniques similar to those for making electronic chips.

Let us imagine we are looking for an M molecule that is able to bind strongly with L molecules to inhibit a particular biochemical reaction, and that thus may be used as a drug. We start by attaching to the surface of chemical chips a first generation of molecules (for example, peptides, which are combinations of amino acids, or fragments of the nucleic acids DNA and RNA). The surface now resembles a grid, with each little square easily identified. By successively applying masks to protect certain reactive chemical groupings, we selectively add new "building blocks" to the existing molecules, thus gradually creating an entire population of billions of *different* M molecules, grouped in families and zones. It now becomes possible to *simultaneously* test the capacity of the *whole* population of these molecules to form bonds with the L molecules. To do this, we dissolve them in a liquid we "pour" over the surface of the chemical chips. Each one of these test molecules is marked with a chemical "label" readable by laser. It is thus easy to locate the square in which L has bonded and to multiply the M molecule to which it bonded.

The parallelism of combinatorial chemistry has led to an extraordinary saving of time—it may take a few days, as opposed to years, to find a molecule of interest for pharmaceutical purposes. Stephen Fodor, the founder of Affymax, a biotech company, pioneered this technology, and some 15 other high-tech companies were formed to apply it. Certain major chemical and pharmaceutical companies will have to either adapt to it or go out of business, because parallel synthesis, with its savings in time and costs, will quickly take over the field.

Biologists also use parallelism in molecular evolution in the test tube in order to find molecules with certain specific properties. (An example of this was described on page 62, in Chapter 2.) This approach is based on principles analogous to those of Darwinian biological evolution and those used in genetic algorithms. Like combinatorial chemistry, it will necessitate an in-depth reorganization of traditional chemical and biological companies.

Colonies of microrobots are another example of parallel operation. Rodney Brooks's insectlike creatures are the ancestors of future miniaturized mobile robots. These new generations of robots will arise from the convergence of molecular electronics, biotechnology, and biotics technologies, and they will represent a major step forward in artificial life or neobiology. Populations of microrobots, each performing a simple, limited task but communicating with the others—just as ants do—will carry out tasks involving pollution cleanup, collection, extraction, construction, assembly, and disassembly. NASA even envisages sending swarms of microrobots to Mars.

In biology and ecology, parallelism is the rule, for both forces and information. Cooperative effects are based on multitudes of connections that are individually weak but whose synergy is strong. This is the case of the hydrogen bonds that hold the double helix of DNA or the structure of proteins in place. In an everyday context, velcro is an example of a bond with a weak local effect and a powerful overall result; at the level of the individual fibers clinging to each other, the force involved is negligible, but when it is applied over the length of a whole strip, the resulting force can support the weight of an adult. The "velcro effect" illustrates the cohesion a society needs for its overall functioning: a multitude of individual actions in parallel.

In a centralized, sequential, Taylorist mode of functioning, the tendency toward operational parallelism will be reinforced, posing problems concerning the relationship with the institutional monopolies of energy production, financial management, and communications, with each one seeking to maintain its centralized control. The "parallelizing" of society can already be seen in the desire for autonomy in communication, with the proliferation of individual satellite dishes, personal cellular telephones, communicating microcomputers, and hypernetworks, and in the area of renewable energy, with solar panels, wind generators, and other decentralized systems of energy production. The parallelizing of the production and information networks of society is one of the essential factors in the emergence of symbiotic humanity.

MACROPROJECTS AND MACROREGULATION

Another major avenue for the industries of the future is macroengineering. The regulation of any cybernetic system is based on the action of positive and negative feedback loops, which ensures dynamic stability and development. Unlike biology and ecology, which are governed by regulatory principles, industrial societies function in "open loops," without macroregulation. Production and consumption are carried out sequentially, which results in waste that accumulates in the environment. Ecological pressure in recent years has gradually forced the adoption of recycling, closing the loops, but while it is gaining ground, recycling is still used only in a limited number of industrial sectors.

The industry of the future will have to function like an ecosystem. Industrial ecology is not only "ecoindustry," a token of the industry's concern for environmental protection. Nor is it "green" products or the partial recycling of waste. It is the complete *reengineering* of industrial processes, from the regulation of flows of energy, raw materials, and products to the rational reuse of discharges. Industrial ecology must recognize the biological nature of the cybiont's planetary metabolism. It will have to rediscover and observe the rules of the food chains of ecosystems: the products and wastes of some are the raw materials of others. Everything is reused or recycled—closing the global cybernetic macroloops, the biogeochemical cycles, that are the basis of Gaia's functioning.

Industrial ecology is at the basis of what I called ecoengineering more than 20 years ago in *The Macroscope* (Chapter 3, p. 166 original edition):

> Ecoengineering, with the help of new methods like energy analysis, will enable men for the first time to control consciously the energy circuits of the ecosystem for the good of man and nature.
>
> Like doctors or surgeons working in the very interior of the organism, we shall be able to reestablish the great feedback loops of reward and reinforcement on which the "economy" of nature is built. We shall have to close in, reconnect, and even "naturalize" the chains and networks of the socioeconomic system (such as those that eliminate wastes and produce food).

The great challenge for industrial ecology or ecoengineering is to close the loops left open by our system of production and our economic system, to establish the macroregulation required by the cybiont's metabolism in order to enable human societies to reach a new stage in the symbiotic relationship. Industrial ecology, based on the principles of biology, will give rise to a *demanufacturing* industry as important as the traditional manufacturing industry. From the automobile to aeronautics, from construction and public works to power plants, from the agrifood industry to electronics, all products and structures that are manufactured will be designed from the start to be easily dismantled and recycled.

Ecoengineering and macroregulation are opening up other sectors to the industries of tomorrow. A better knowledge of Gaia's functioning will allow macroengineers to act on some of its major metabolic cycles to produce energy or modify the climate. Photosynthesis and albedo are two mechanisms Gaia uses to regulate its temperature. *Albedo* is the reflection of solar radiation by the clouds, snow-covered areas, and pale-colored surfaces of the planet. The forests act as thermostats, absorbing heat from the sun and producing water vapor. Photosynthetic algae living on the surface of the oceans also play a regulatory role. Human beings will act on these mechanisms in order to amplify their effects. They will be able to act rationally to control the climate. Today's steps to reduce the greenhouse effect or the growth of the hole in the ozone layer are the beginning of macroregulation on a planetary scale. But these are actions with statistical effects, and not rational interventions like those in bioengineering, for example. More directly, macroregulation will involve action on the forests (protection, reforestation), seeding of certain ocean zones with phytoplankton, changing the distribution of agricultural areas (light and dark surfaces), installation of reflective surfaces in the deserts, and the construction of huge "power plantations" for the production of solar energy.

The domestication of photosynthesis will be a key stake in the new millennium. The transition to solar energy will be a determining factor in the success of the symbiosis between individuals and society and between Gaia and the cybiont. Life faced a comparable challenge when a symbiotic relationship was established between primitive living things feeding on organic materials in their environment and those able to produce their own substance through photosynthesis. That symbiotic relationship is the basis of the complementary relationship that exists today between animals and plants. The transition to solar energy is of a similar nature, only, this time, the entire human species and the whole biosphere are involved. This transition will mark our passage from a *Promethean* civilization that draws on its ecocapital of nonrenewable resources or makes short-term profit from antinature forms of energy to a *Gaian* civilization that lives in symbiosis with its environment.

The domestication of photosynthesis involves the production of biomass or new materials as well as energy production using appropriate technology. Considerable progress has been made in these areas in the past 25 years, both in the theory of the fundamental mechanisms of photosynthesis and in the practical development of high-output photovoltaic cells and flexible solar collectors using photosynthetic pigments. There will be more rapid development of the solar sector, which comprises the five forms of direct or derived solar energy (photovoltaic cells, heat collectors, wind, biomass, and hydroelectricity). The solar industry, in the broad sense, will be one of the engines of economic development in the first half of the twenty-first century. But this development will require new types of organization of the production and consumption of energy—decentralized, parallel, reticulate structures suited to the symbiotic nature of the relationship between individuals and society. These *heliostructures* will compete with the existing infrastructure and the centralized power of the producers and distributors of oil and electricity.

Solar macroprojets will emerge: vast areas covered with solar panels and collectors in desert regions or on floating islands in the ocean, with facilities to produce hydrogen from the electricity, using electrolysis, and to liquefy this hydrogen for transportation and distribution to consumers (car engines, local power plants for the production of electricity using fuel cells); wind farms generating megawatts of power on platforms at sea; local urban plants for generating both electricity and hot water. Also, solar tiles will be used in buildings and flexible solar blinds on windows. All these installations reduce harmful gas emissions, increase energy efficiency, and empower users.

Ecoengineering macroprojets will include the installation of measuring and monitoring devices on satellites, the "senses" of the Earth, a development that has already begun. In its symbiotic coevolution with Gaia, the cybiont is gradually acquiring sensory devices, basic sensors for planetary macroregulation. But, just as the development of bioengineering required the application of bioethics to limit the dangers of practices contrary to the good of the human species, in the same way the development of ecoengineering will have to rely on ecoethics to reduce the risks of uncontrolled manipulation of the ecosystem.

It may be useful to look at some of the technological innovations that are likely to appear in the course of the next century. To demonstrate their potential impact, here is a series of imaginary news flashes from the future.

THE INNOVATIONS OF THE NEXT CENTURY: NEWS FLASHES FROM THE FUTURE

Paris. March 14, 2001. 5:45 P.M. AFP. Old Master Paintings on Flat Screens for the Home. Today the Artronics Gallery is celebrating the installation of its 50th digital painting. Developed for exhibition in businesses and private homes, these digitized versions of works by Impressionist or contemporary painters are displayed in their original colors on plasma screens that can be hung on the wall. At a press conference, Sandrine Koffler, president of Artronics, announced the signing of a contract with the AGE Insurance group to supply the offices of more than 2000 of its subsidiaries with these electronic paintings. The Japanese-made flat screens measure up to 6 feet diagonally. Subscribers select the paintings displayed by means of a computerized control unit, and the compressed digital images are transmitted through the WorldCom ATM network. In the past month, Artronics has provided its customers with a Matisse exhibition, a selection of works from the Hermitage museum in Saint Petersburg, and drawings and paintings by Paolo Uccello. But the legal battle over the right to digitize and disseminate some of these works is still ongoing.

New York. June 12, 2001. 4:17 P.M. Reuters. Antinoise Walkman. No more need for earplugs and double-glazed insulating windows. Personal antinoise devices that are as easy to use as a walkman are the latest rage. These devices create a sound wave that cancels out ambient noise, producing silence. You just select the frequencies of the sounds you want to eliminate in order to "teach" them to the device. Various sounds can be stored in its memory—a dog's bark, scales played on a piano, jackhammers, airplanes, snoring, etc. The power of the new electronic chips enables real-time processing and elimination of unwanted noise. Following advertising campaigns on interactive multimedia television, American and Japanese versions of the device (NCT's Noise Buster and Fujitsu's SoundCracker), which have different types of applications, are in hot competition. There are also compact models to eliminate traffic noise heard in bedrooms, miniaturized portable models with earphones, and models for use in cars or airplanes, which will allow travelers to listen to Mozart in digital quality without being disturbed by engine noise.

Paris. May 16, 2002. 6:55 P.M. AFP. Portable Videophone. The major international telecommunications companies have reached an agreement on the Sony UnitCom standard, which allows data from telephones, videophones, and computers to be transmitted to personal digital assistants in fractally compressed form. Videophonic communications can be transmitted from anywhere in the world on the global satellite network. The UnitCom incorporates a video recorder and camera using electronic chips, with no moving parts, to record and transmit video messages.

Paris. November 28, 2003. 2:20 P.M. AFP. Cybermedicine on Trial in France. France's College of Physicians and Order of Pharmacists met in Paris yesterday and instituted proceedings in the court of The Hague against the American company CyberDoc of Atlanta for the illegal practice of medicine. This fast-growing company, which now counts nearly a million subscribers throughout the world, provides information, telediagnoses, and medical assistance on its TransNet network, all accessible on the high-speed Internet 2. Using a computer television or personal multimedia computer, subscribers can get answers to spoken questions by interactive videocommunication. Home testing devices in the form of miniterminals are sold by the Interbiotech Corporation, a subsidiary of CyberDoc; they make it possible to receive real-time diagnoses based on a drop of blood, an electrocardiogram, or a retinal examination.

Boston. January 3, 2004. 8:12 A.M. UPI. Personalized Electronic Newspaper. The Electronic Data Corporation has announced the launch of the *Personal Daily Planet,* a personalized newspaper available on the global telematics networks. The newspaper is compiled by virtual agents, which select the items from the major newspapers and magazines according to subscribers' registered interest profiles, format them, and prepare them for transmission. The electronic newspaper is available in video or audio form.

London. March 12, 2004. 4:46 P.M. UPI. Electronic Drug Traffickers Arrested. Police this morning arrested 14 members of an international network of traffickers in laser minidisks containing programs that stimulate areas of the brain. Used with biofeedback devices connected to the brain by means of patches applied to the temples, these programs activate the pleasure, visual, auditory, and olfactory centers to produce animated shapes and colors, sounds, sensations, and emotions. Their effects are so powerful that users of the electronic drugs soon become addicted and stop eating. Hundreds of thousands of young Europeans could be affected by this new scourge.

Berlin. July 15, 2004. 6:15 P.M. UPI. Active Buildings for Energy Autonomy. Berlin's new neighborhoods are now energy autonomous. Their architects have used "active" construction technology, whereby the buildings produce and regulate the energy they consume. The basic needs of the buildings are supplied through a combination of modules: steam and electricity are produced by the incineration of household garbage; solar collectors are located on the roofs and walls; boilers use biomass; and invisible wind turbines are built into the taller buildings. The energy consumption of these buildings has been substantially reduced through the use of computer technology that rationalizes energy use (heating, air conditioning, heat recovery from the facades). The efficiency of these autonomous units can reach as high as 90 percent, compared to 35 percent for energy generated in traditional power plants outside cities and carried over long distances.

Zurich. March 18, 2005. 9:28 A.M. SwissTech. Wireless Devices Corner Market. There are fewer and fewer cables and wires on the electronic equipment at this year's International ElectroMedia Fair in Zurich, confirming the trend of recent years. Personal computers, modems, lamps, lasers, copiers, and television sets now operate without wires, using induction, microwaves, infrared, or hertzian waves to exchange information or recharge their batteries.

New York. April 15, 2005. 2:45 P.M. Reuters. Videophone Answering Machine. AT&T has announced the introduction of an intelligent videophone answering machine. The miniature answering machine, which is connected to the digital networks, displays a *virtual clone* of the person being called on the caller's screen. A voice-recognition system and integrated *neural network* enable it to understand voice instructions. The clone has a real-time conversation with the caller. Intelligent agents residing in the software of the answering machine can be asked to perform tasks such as retrieving documents and sending electronic messages, digital videos, or color faxes to callers.

Paris. October 10, 2008. 8:36 A.M. AFP. Peugeot Introduces Hybrid Car. A car with an electric engine will be presented at the next International Car Show. This nonpolluting vehicle runs on an electric motor supplied by a gas turbine. Sodium-sulphur batteries are used for city driving. The vehicle's maximum highway speed is 100 miles per hour. And it can go as far as 400 miles between fill-ups. Peugeot announced that the next model will be powered by a fuel cell.

Paris. September 8, 2009. 5:30 A.M. AFP. Flexible Plastic Battery Introduced. The EuroSaxt Corporation, a subsidiary of CGE, has announced that it will soon introduce a long-life battery called the Hydronic, which uses metal hydrides. Developed in cooperation with the American company Ovonics, the battery can be fully recharged in 5 minutes and provides power for 12 to 38 hours, depending on the model. The battery has a miniature version (the size of a keyboard key) for portable computers and telephones and a "HiPack" version (the size of a book) for electric cars. The Hydronic battery provides the power to travel 150 miles at 80 miles per hour.

Osaka. February 18, 2012. 8:41 P.M. Japan News. Electronic Paper Screen. In a development that may revolutionize computer communication, a consortium made up of the Japanese companies Canon, Fujitsu, and Ricoh has introduced a flexible flat computer screen that looks like an ordinary pad of paper. You can write on the screen with a special stylus, and it also displays information from a miniature computer contained in the pad's binding. You can also dictate your text into it by means of a voice-recognition system. This revolutionary screen is based on a discovery by a team from France's National Scientific Research Center, which in 1994 developed plastic transistors that were produced using printing technology.

Los Angeles. February 7, 2014. 2:45 P.M. UPI. Stirling Engines in Desert. An engine invented in 1816 by Father Robert Stirling is producing electricity for the California network at an efficiency of 36 percent. Giant parabolic dishes that follow the movement of the Sun concentrate energy at a specific point on each of the 82 Stirling engines assembled in the Mojave desert. If this first solar power plant is a success, dozens of others will be built in the American deserts. It is estimated that a desert area of 100 square miles would be sufficient to produce electricity for the entire United States.

Boston. September 24, 2014. 5:24 P.M. Reuters. 3-D Holographic Projection. Holographic theater can now be found in the homes of several thousand Americans taking part in a field test. Using three-dimensional color holoprojection technology developed by MIT's Media Lab, viewers can watch life-size characters, reproduced in excellent graphic quality, moving around in the middle of their living rooms. The same type of projection will also be used for teleportation and ubiquity. Ubiquitel booths will allow people to teleport themselves by creating digital virtual clones that can be compressed and sent over the electronic highways at high speed, and then reconstituted in three dimensions. This will allow a person, for example, to give lectures in three places thousands of miles apart at the same time.

Stockholm. October 4, 2019. 9:32 A.M. Swenska Newstliet. Personal Health Monitoring Devices. Sweden's minister of health today announced that some 14 million personal health monitoring devices (PHMDs) are now in use worldwide. Produced using technology developed at Upsalla University and licensed to 22 international pharmaceutical companies, PHMDs are worn on the wrist or waist, in contact with the skin. Their enzyme biosensors monitor major health parameters and the data are transmitted by hertzian modem to medical diagnostic centers. Patients can also connect by videophone to interactive videoservers that prescribe treatments and transmit additional information.

Tokyo. November 21, 2026. 10:22 A.M. AFP. Thought Transmission Between Computer and Human Brain. The ATR Corporation has developed the cyber helmet, a system of direct transmission of information between the brain and the computer. Using the "silent speech" technology developed in the 1990s by Fujitsu, the cyber helmet displays images directly from the brain on a screen and transmits computer-generated images and sounds to the brain by stimulating the visual and auditory centers.

Paris. October 26, 2032. 11:23 A.M. AFP. Car-Free Paris. An entire week of festivities and events will mark the end of renovations in the center of Paris and the elimination of the last private automobiles from its streets. This culmination of an ambitious urban redevelopment program, launched after the 2017 referendum, was announced by Paris mayor François Darouin. Public transportation includes buses with quiet, nonpolluting, hybrid (turbine and electric) engines. They are equipped to receive information, which they then transmit to passengers. Minibus-taxis carrying small groups of passengers are guided by computer according to riders' requests transmitted from mobile or stationary communications terminals. Fast subways intersect the city, along with underground expressways for heavy trucks and cars with internal combustion engines. All types of private cars, electric or not, must pay high taxes, set according to their surface area occupied, in order to circulate in the city center. Most streets of the inner city are reserved for pedestrians, bicycles, and electric bicycles. The number of parks, markets, squares, playgrounds, and recreational spaces has mushroomed over the last 15 years.

Paris. December 3, 2038. 7:02 P.M. Reuters. Sea and Desert Solar Power Plants. SolarMer, successor to France's former Atomic Energy Commissariat, yesterday inaugurated two solar power plants for the production of hydrogen for motor vehicles. The two production facilities were built in cooperation with the Japanese Sumimoto group and the Chinese AquaCell corporation. One of the plants consists of hundreds of thousands of flexible solar panels floating on pontoons in the Pacific Ocean. Located near the atoll of Uanagunu in the Tuamotu archipelago, this artificial island is 3.5 miles in diameter. Computers keep the panels facing toward the Sun at all times. This facility produces 940 megawatts—as much as a nuclear power plant of the 1990s. The energy is used for the electrolysis of water and the production of hydrogen, which is liquefied and carried by pipeline or ship to plants that produce and refill cartridges based on carbon nanotubes for hydrogen-powered cars. A similar, but smaller, station (1.5 miles in diameter) in the Sahara desert has also been inaugurated. SolarMer estimates that by 2050 there will be some 30 marine and desert solar stations producing 36 gigawatts of energy.

Tokyo. December 2, 2058. 7:42 A.M. Japan TechNet. Agricultural Biorobots Sent to Farms. The world's first agricultural microrobots have been mass produced by programmed nanomachines, the TransTech-Net information hypernetwork announced today. The microrobots, developed by an American-Japanese consortium including two European companies, are the size of crayfish, and they are designed to work in swarms of 20,000, collecting pharmaceutical substances produced by genetically modified plants in fields that are difficult to access. One of the most interesting things about these microrobots is how they are produced. They are assembled from biological materials, mainly chitin (which forms the carapaces of insects) and lignin (from trees)—two particularly strong molecules. Molecular nanomachines (automatic assemblers, amplifiers, and sorters) first built a number of modules, which then self-organized into the basic components. Macroassemblers carried out the final phases of assembly, including the molecular electronics, sensors, microengines, and organs of movement and collection. The manufacturers' only fear is that these robots will invent their own form of sexuality and reproduce beyond the control of their creators!

These few scenarios of the future provide a glimpse of a brave new world, the world that science and technology have in store for us. However, what is important for symbiotic humanity is not merely technological development, but the amplification of human potential. To build the future, we will now have to rely on new values that transcend traditional politics and economics, values of culture and education, and feminine values that will help us embark on a new age of individual and collective creation.

7

Culture and Values for a New World

BUILDING A WORLD WITH FEMININE VALUES

The world is not built solely on economic values; human, moral, and spiritual values play a fundamental role. Symbiotic humanity will arise from a respect for shared values. However, today's prevailing values divide people rather than unite them. The main factor in economic and social development is competition, a value that is justified in the context of Darwinian evolution and the struggle for survival but that does not provide an adequate basis for the next stage of human evolution.

For millennia, human subsistence depended on the domestication of solar energy through agriculture. This stage in social evolution favored values of a symbiotic nature: complementarity, equilibrium, the frugal use of resources. The period of economic and industrial conquest of the last few centuries, based on the accelerated exploitation of fossil fuels, favored "masculine" values: competition, conquest, domination, and growth. The transition now embarked upon by humanity—the postindustrial or bioecological organization of an information and communications society—will require a return to "feminine" values such as solidarity, complementarity, and balance, values similar to those that prevailed during the subsistence stage of humanity. It would be rather reductive to systematically contrast "masculine" and "feminine" values, but it is interesting to look at things from the perspective of their *complementarity*.

Since humanity's beginnings, masculine behavior has involved hunting, war, and the conquest and defense of territory, and feminine behavior has involved the organization and management of the home and the transmission of life and knowledge. Today, the environmental crisis, the dangerous powers of biology, and the challenges of education are bringing feminine values to the forefront again in discussions of the great issues facing society. The rise of these values is not only a matter of feminism or of women's attaining positions of responsibility in industry and politics—a necessary rebalancing of power—but also involves a new way of looking at the world and acting on it, one based on cooperation rather than competition. This view of the world is now shared by a growing number of men.

Men base their domination on strength, reason, and power. Women more readily rely on intuition, persuasion, and influence. Men's logic contrasts with women's feelings, emotions, and sensitivity. These qualities are never completely black and white in reality, but the broad masculine and feminine characteristics remain and are expressed in behavior. Masculine values are favored in the technological model of competition and conquest that is typical of industrial growth societies. But the transition to symbiotic society calls for biological and ecological concepts, those involving communications, transversality, and networks, and this reveals the need for new, feminine, values. Witness the increasing global influence of the roles and perspectives of women on the major issues of tomorrow's world (in the areas of biology, the environment, education, and health). From bioethics commissions to ecology groups, from consumer organizations to parents' associations, from assistance to the elderly to peace organizations, women's action is opening up alternative paths toward symbiotic models of social organization. Solidarity, complementarity, respect for diversity, action in networks, taking the long view, and frugality are modes of action often favored by women, and they are also necessary for the implementation and functioning of symbiotic mechanisms between human beings and the organizations they work in or the societies they live in. Frugality, for example, will be an essential quality for building the future in a world of overabundance and destitution. Just as nutritional dietetics helps to balance an individual's life, industrial societies have to create a "diet-etics" of information (to avoid infopollution) and a dietetics of en-ergy (to reduce waste). Frugality is not deprivation; it is a reasoned lifestyle choice that leads to planetary solidarity.

More than a decade ago, I suggested using the term *bionomics* to describe the art of managing life.* Bionomics involves the manage-ment not only of personal life, but also of the collective life of the so-cial organism of which we are the cells. Symbionomics is the appli-cation of the principles of bionomics to the complexifying evolution that is leading to the emergence of the cybiont and the planetary brain. In family and social life, being economical is a virtue; in order to build a successful future, we now have to learn to be *bionomical*— a lifestyle very much in keeping with the feminine approach in hu-man evolution.

The emergence of these new values—which I am calling femi-nine for the sake of simplicity—seems to me to be essential now for progress toward greater solidarity, justice, balance, and peace in the world. They represent other ways of seeing nature and society and other ways of acting, exerting control, and transmitting knowledge, ways that are intrinsic to the behavior and thinking of women. I will even go so far as to say that these values will become essential for the construction of tomorrow's society and the survival of the planet.

The integration of feminine values into a world of powers and conflicts created by men can contribute to a radical renewal of po-litical imagination. Feminine values can help free political leadership from the concentration of power and wealth on which it generally bases its legitimacy and from the use of violence as a manifestation of its authority; it can separate political power from the control of technological or military means of destruction. Feminine values, which tend to be expressed in networks, can contribute to creating a new equilibrium with government action, centralized decision mak-ing, and bureaucratic structures. They bring a new logic and a new culture to our preparation for the future. The *complementarity* of

---

* "La Sagesse du Corps," *L'Expansion*, September 21, 1979, p. 129, and *La Malbouffe*, Paris: Olivier Orban / Seuil, 1979, p.127.

masculine and feminine values is an essential condition of a real social symbiosis and a new culture of complexity.

THE FRACTAL CULTURE OF SYMBIOTIC HUMANITY

At one time, culture involved the display of knowledge, and privileged people, the cultural elite, had an encyclopedic knowledge of
many subjects: art, literature, history, and technology. The culture of
the cultivated involves knowing something about everything; the
culture of the expert involves knowing everything about something.
Today, culture involves a capacity to integrate separate elements and
facts into a coherent whole that can, in turn, be integrated into one's
life and actions to give them meaning and direction. Tomorrow, the
demands of culture will be even greater, and will involve the collective life and thought of the cybiont. The tools of culture will no
longer be limited to the book, the media, and entertainment, but
will include the prostheses of our brains (computers and communications tools), networks, and collective electronic memory. These
tools will open the way to a fractal, hypertextual culture—fractal because each individual will create a seed of the totality according to
the "density" of his or her culture, and hypertextual because its form
will be connectivist, linked in an infinity of connections with other
levels of fractal culture. This form of culture, personal and global, individual and collective, respectful of diversity and of each person's
temporal density, is the basis of the relationship between symbiotic
humanity and the social macroorganism. The encyclopedic culture
of the "gentleman and scholar" will give way to the fractal culture of
symbiotic humanity.

The cartesian approach fragmented knowledge into a large number of separate disciplinary territories. In the industrialized western
countries, this fragmentation led to a schism between literary culture and scientific culture, which is particularly pronounced in certain countries such as France. A distinction persists between the natural and the artificial and between culture and technology. This
fragmentation, this split between the natural (the human) and the
artificial (machines), has led us to believe that the best way to man-

age each of them and guide their evolution is to govern human beings by means of laws and machines by means of equations. The management and control of people and machines were thus based on a fragmented analysis of complexity. In a country like France, this may be seen in the predominant political and technocratic role played by the major schools of administration in managing the affairs of the state and that played by the major engineering schools in managing technology.

Today the real-time management of human societies and the copiloting of evolution require a new culture of complexity. Of course, biology and ecology provide a partial basis for such a culture: levels of organization, feedback, regulation, adaptation, networks, and cycles. But the need for a systemic, more generally symbionomic culture, the kind of culture I have tried to present in this book, will make itself increasingly felt. The unified theory of the self-organization and dynamics of complex systems, the hybridization of the natural and the artificial, the "mechanization" of the biological and the "biologization" of the machine are major trends that fuel and reinforce this need.

The convergence and gradual merging of biology, mechanics, and information technology is more than a mere scientific or technological change; it is laying the foundations for the new symbionomic culture. As I have shown, this is evident in the emergence of new scientific and technological sectors such as biotics, molecular electronics, nanotechnology, industrial ecology, ecoengineering, artificial life, and neural networks. These sectors will play a crucial role in the new culture. Systemic, symbiotic culture is also being introduced into organizations. In the past 25 years, systems theory has won acceptance in business administration, urban planning, the construction of large networks, ecology, and medicine. The reconfiguration of businesses, the reticulation of organizations, the flattening of hierarchical structures, and the emergence of the "polycellular," "intelligent," "virtual" company are signs of the paradigm shift we are experiencing. The paradigm shift, in turn, is catalyzed by the new information and communications technology and by the penetration of biological and ecological culture into structures that arose out of the mechanistic views of the nineteenth century.

The new culture of complexity includes the values of symbiosis. It promotes the integration of differences and respect for diversity. It connects the natural and the artificial in a broad vision of nature and civilization. The cybiont and symbiotic humanity are the thought models for this synthesis. However, this new culture introduces different relationships to time and duration. A fractal culture is the seed of an entire culture, just as a fertilized egg is the germ of a complete living organism. Each individual can experience a distinct fractal culture in his or her own temporal sphere. But whatever the level or degree of density, each person and each people carries a whole culture, and not just a part of an alienable culture or subculture. A hypertextual culture connects with other nodes and links in the planetary neural network that is being created before our eyes. Although evolving at an accelerating rate compared to the unchanging scale of clock time, the network, through its complexification, is densifying time. The new culture of symbiotic humanity is a catalyst of the future.

LACE, MOSAICS, AND CATHEDRALS: FRACTAL COMMUNICATION

This cultural revolution will have an enormous impact on our view of our material and immaterial environment and on the organization of societies.

The causal, disciplinary, linear view of the world that physics has given us has led to a preference for straight lines, regular curves, squares, spheres, and triangles. We seem to be obsessed with the rectilinear, with simple controllable shapes like those we see in highways, railroads, high-tension lines, the design of everyday things, and the regular structures of urban planning. A civilization in thrall to speed and efficiency favors straight lines and flat shapes, and ultimately generates monotony. However, throughout history, when people have had time, they have produced fractal structures, patterns and works of art of great conceptual and structural complexity, harmonious jumbles of interlocking patterns and colors that provide riddles for the eye and brain—mandalas and tapestries, intricate laces and persian carpets, mosaics and cathedrals, and Renaissance, impressionist, and cubist paintings. The infinite variety and complexity of the forms of nature are much more readily perceptible through esthetic sensitivity than through reason. The markings of insects and animals consist of interlocking fractal shapes, as do the patterns of gardens and mountain ranges, foliage and forests, cities and towns, and the contours of rocks, shorelines, and clouds. It is by imitating or transposing these forms that people invented means of communication to connect us symbiotically with nature.

I once heard Benoît Mandelbrot, the father of fractal structures, analyze the Garnier Opera as a fractal structure that is balanced at every level of observation. The striking harmony of the whole when viewed from a distance is seen, when viewed more closely, to be based on an arch, a door, the motif of the door, and even the door handle. This meaningful "nesting" of successive levels, each level in harmonious relationship with the next, in continuity with our individual perception of the world, fills us with wonder and connects us to the work and to nature. It may be the secret of the beauty of a landscape, a painting, or a symphony.

Through his computer analysis of works by Bach and Mozart, Kenneth Hsü, a Swiss engineer, discovered that each musician has a characteristic "fractal signature." The analysis of a few notes is enough to determine the musical and temporal "shape" of a piece, which can then be immediately attributed to its composer. What secret, art, or intuition did these musicians draw on to create their particular melodic and rhythmic arrangements? A similar phenomenon may be seen in impressionist paintings. The basis of the composition, the harmony of the colors, and the proportions of the forms are fractally present on a surface the size of a postage stamp, and then extended to the whole work, not through a process of *diffusion*—just to fill the space of the painting—but through the formal *reconstruction* of a whole that is consistent with itself, whatever its area. The paintings of Cézanne, Van Gogh, Corot, Renoir, and Vuillard are living examples of nature's fractalization, connecting us, through eye and emotions, to the deep texture and balance of nature. The same is true of works by Patinir, Breughel, Uccello, Carpaccio, Klimt, and Chagall. Throughout history, we find the same striving on the part of the artist to help viewers recreate the painting for themselves, so that on each occasion they discover anew its forms, colors, and underlying structures. Our active participation leads us to repeatedly reexamine an original in a museum, despite our unlimited access to copies. Artists are the heralds of alternative visions of the world. The fractalization of nature in image and sound is a powerful mode of *active* communication that we should draw on for education and general communication.

Fractal communication will be one of the most efficient vehicles for conveying ideas and concepts, replacing traditional linear, sequential communication. A speech, for example, instead of being organized in terms of an introduction, an exposition in three parts, and a conclusion, would be presented in harmoniously interlocking interrelated modules. In fractal communication, there is a consistency—even a *redundancy*—in words, images, models, and analogies. A message may be conveyed in one striking sentence (the "sound bite" so common in politics), repeated and reinforced in successive modules that interlock like nested drawers or elements. Thus, the message can be cut or divided up without losing its power or the wealth of its information, and reconstructed by the receiver. Advertising ought to adopt this approach if it wants to avoid banality and prevent viewers from being saturated through repetition.

Exhibitions should also use a fractal mode of presentation. An exhibition is a hypermedia presentation that includes text, audiovisual elements, games, models, or interactive programs through which visitors acquire information and knowledge at their own pace. Each element of the exhibition should refer to the whole, and the whole to each element. A fractal exhibition must be immediately understandable at the highest level, and then at the level of greater detail, remaining consistent through each interaction. Navigation in the *hypermedia* of a modern exhibition can take place through successive approximations of the total message, creating an intellectual ergonomics that favors the acquisition of knowledge.

It is this form of communication (which I try to apply to my own nonspecialized writing) that should gradually become the basis for the fractal education of the future. Through it, the "seeds" of understanding are transmitted, so that knowledge can be reconstructed by students using their own individual approaches, methods, and tools.

LONG TIME AND SHORT TIME: EDUCATION AND TELEVISION

Education is at the center of all strategies for building the future. It is a global concern, one of the great challenges of the third millennium, an essential process of survival, adaptation, and evolution of the human species that will have to be carried out while fully respecting diversity and freedom. Without education, there can be no conscious, responsible participation in the governance of the societies of tomorrow. Without relevant information being available to every actor involved in change and regulation, there can be no effective social feedback, and therefore no liberating symbiosis.

Fragmented knowledge leads to fragmented education. The arbitrary division of knowledge into distinct areas favors a Taylorist educational process. The curriculum is presented according to a set timetable, the subjects taught are cut up into disjointed sectors and transmitted sequentially, and the whole process is organized in levels validated by examinations. Traditional education takes place in linear time and does not take into account the different densities of time, of respiration, or of natural periods of calm and intensity.

The paradigm shift we are experiencing (from the analytical to the systemic) calls for other methods of education. The teaching of basic data and the rudiments of reasoning has to be supplemented with methods that promote the *integration* of knowledge. Rather than the encyclopedic approach of the systematic acquisition of information, we need to use a systemic method that allows students to integrate new information and place it in context. Learning to learn does not just mean preparing fertile ground so that the seeds of knowledge can grow and flower; it means above all managing and placing in hierarchical order what one already knows in order to make it operational and give meaning to one's actions.

This approach implies that subjects to be taught should no longer be divided up to be readily assimilable by everyone and controllable by the few, but that knowledge should be *reconstructed* from "seeds." Just as a fractal image is built up gradually by successive iterations of a simple equation, the new education should help each person reconstruct the relationships among the various hierarchical levels of knowledge. The symbionomic education of the future will have to be both fractal and synthetic—fractal to break up the linearity of the curriculum and create interdependent modules for different periods and ages of life and synthetic to allow students to assemble these modules into a personal structure that enriches their conception of life and the world.

Fractal education is light, open, and empowering. Its duration is no longer necessarily fixed, but depends rather on progress, experience, and motivation. It is based on the acquisition of the means and methods of accessing information, the development of creativity, the learning of reasoning procedures, and the systemic integration of knowledge. Fractal education provides the operators, the keys, the modules, and the seeds of complexification. It can thus be carried out in places other than schools. It helps each individual construct and reconstruct a personal sphere of knowledge instead of merely acquiring juxtaposed areas of information.

Since fractal education draws on the tools of information and communications technology, it can supplement the role of television, the omnipresent emotional medium and the main rival of traditional linear teaching. The speed of transmission of ideas, lifestyles, and behavior through television provides a contrast to the rigid practices of schools, and brings out the sharp opposition between the long time of education and the short time of current events. The culture of the mediasphere is ephemeral, yet it persists in memory and consciousness. Each new event has a stronger emotional charge and replaces preceding events. The monotony of scenes watched hundreds of times against the same backdrop (disasters, terrorist attacks, fires, floods, resignations, scandals) is mitigated only by the emotional personalization of the people involved.

The basic ingredient of good television communication is emotion, not reason. Television has thus gradually become "telemotion." The approach to subjects is often superficial, and form is put before content. The practice of zapping gives viewers the illusion of conscious choice while they are often responding only to transitory reflexes of boredom. Studies of young children have shown how zapping, music videos, advertising, and replay influence the concepts of long time and short time and the reversibility or irreversibility of time. Young people "scan" a page (as a video camera does) in early reading, rather than follow the lines. With the replay function of VCRs and video games, it is possible in a split second to revive a dead person, rebuild a smashed house, or reassemble a wrecked car. This manipulation of time, which transforms each player into a demiurge, is not applicable to real life, which is not "zappable." This explains the difficulty of young people, accustomed to the reversibility of a controllable, timeless world, when engaging with the responsibilities and constraining irreversibility of real life.

Television is a reflection of the world, both the source and the mirror of information. An amazing catalyst of behavior, habits, practices, and lifestyles, it has proven a powerful tool for the transmission of culture through the elements, rules, laws, and practices that can bind together or fragment a community. Television operates in a much denser time than schools, books, or the traditional press. When following events that involve millions of people, it almost functions in real time. An event, an idea, or an attitude can create chaotic oscillations that are amplified or abandoned, and that are capable of causing unpredictable (divergent or convergent) phenomena. Television is the dematerialized vehicle of emotions that amplify and motivate actions. The peak of emotion is death, and seeing the deaths of others takes away the fear of one's own death. The evening news will open with the live presentation of death whenever it has the images. We have become "telethanatophiles," enjoying the distant deaths of others.

Research undertaken at the University of California by Larry Cahill and James McGaugh shows that the ability to remember images and situations is reinforced by the stress created by fear or anxiety. The more shocking or frightening a scene is, the better people remember it. To prove this, volunteers were shown two different versions of the same story. One version was "neutral" and the other contained dramatic, bloody, or anxiety-producing material. Some of the volunteers were given propanolol, a substance that inhibits the effects of the natural stress hormones adrenalin and noradrenalin. One month later, the volunteers were given a detailed questionnaire to test their memories. The results showed that emotion reinforces memory: the group that had taken the drug remembered more details of the neutral version, while the other group remembered the more dramatic version much better.

This neurobiological property seems to be a condition that favors survival in the animal world; a creature will have a better chance of survival if it remembers dangerous situations it has encountered. It appears that certain types of television programs have systematically built their audience (and their ratings) on this biological mechanism. A reinforcement loop has developed between writers and audience, promoting sensationalism. The emotional charge of the images is used to reinforce the retention of a succession of similar dramatic sequences that might otherwise become monotonous and lose the viewers' interest. Good news is not as easily remembered as bad news. "Good news is no news," Marshall McLuhan said, and he had no knowledge of these biological experiments.

This work sheds new light on the debate about the effects of violence on television. Violent images are more easily remembered by young viewers than neutral images because of the production of stress hormones. A culture of violence can thus be established, which profoundly and unconsciously influences people's actions.

By enhancing people's lasting retention of dramatic sequences, television conveys an image of a world that is falling apart. The repetition of images of disaster and death gives the impression that there is no hope. This means there is a hidden face of the world that television does not see. Without close-ups of faces, emotions, emergencies, there is no news. A good television subject is a human drama showing good guys and bad guys, with sensational images shot at a specific time and location—unity of time, place, and action, just as in ancient Greek tragedy. In this context, processes, structures, organization, networks, plans, explanations, and reasoning are invisible, relegated to what is now the hidden face of the world. The eye of the television camera has blind spots, creating the impression that the world is in a state of permanent tragedy. Any progress seems impossible, any improvement doubtful, any constructive effort doomed to failure, any attempt at reconciliation vain.

And yet television also transmits a culture of the future, a culture that can motivate people to act to change things. We are capable of doing so—and it is not relentless optimism that causes me to say this, but rather faith in humanity and the human capacity to adapt. I admit I am tired of the general lack of respect for optimism, as if it were an incurable defect. Of course, I am opposed to the passive optimism that says "everything will work out for the best in the end." My optimism is born of my feeling that I am able to change things in cooperation with others. Optimism is the intelligence of the future.

Fractal education creates and fosters the seeds of change. It empowers everyone at his or her level of competence. It provides a complement to an omnipresent, emotional television that leaves one face of the world hidden, and lays the rational foundations for an optimistic construction of the future.

VIDEO GAMES: INTERACTIVITY AND HYPERMEDIA

Video games are another aspect of interactive culture. What we are now seeing is a real social phenomenon. In the United States, the video game market is bigger than that of the movie industry and is even catching up with that of the recording industry. Video games are not merely a fad. We can no longer ignore them; we have to ask ourselves how they can be used for educational purposes. The challenge for modern educators is to provide a smooth transition between the use of games as recreation and as an intellectual investment; this is the field of educational game software, one that is growing fast. The success of this strategy will probably depend on the intellectual contribution of the generation that has grown up with these games and can use its creativity to develop new types of educational media. Paradoxically, this could lead to having teaching materials and textbooks written or produced by students themselves.

Young video game players may be inventing a new culture of complexity and interaction. This culture is still in a rough state; it is in its infancy, to say the least. It could either move toward a passive, sterile habituation, or open up new paths to knowledge. There is a growing gap between the proponents of a literary, sequential approach and those of a global, hypertextual approach. Our cultural tradition is essentially literary; text is our basic reference. Even mathematics requires the textual statement of a problem, and the legal system is based on the text of laws. We have learned the alphabet, reading, writing, logical analysis, and verb conjugations. Our ways of thinking flow quite naturally into sentences and lines, paragraphs and chapters, from page one to the end. This traditional approach is analytical, linear, and sequential. With the explosion of the image, which we see mainly in television and cinema, reason gives way to emotion, and the rigor of analysis to superficial impressions. The process becomes encompassing, emotional, and sensory. But in going from the material world of things to the immaterial world of waves, signs, and symbols, we lose our natural ability to interact with our environment. Passivity in front of the television is sometimes paid for with violent collective behavior in the streets or on the highways.

Well established at the heart of the immaterial world, video games are based on *interactivity*. Their imaginary worlds lend themselves to all kinds of modifications, strategies, and deviations. Fingers on the console, the player has a feeling of controlling the world. Without prior training, without any rules of conduct, millions of children in the world are discovering electronic interactivity and creating their own personal ways of navigation in the world of multimedia and hypermedia, a world in which every choice immediately leads to new opportunities that are sanctioned or rewarded according to the rules of the game until the eventual loss of electronic life. From a Manichean point of view, video game players are both manipulators and manipulated. But it would be better to try to understand what is behind the central concept of navigation in hypermedia and by extension in the hyperspaces of complex multidimensional knowledge.

Video game players who navigate through hypermedia spaces have to invent their own rules in relation to the rules of the game. But this routine, often sterile experience does not lead them to navigate in other places or to other knowledge spaces. They choose no course, possess no compass or chart, and are guided by no marker or beacon. As such interactive systems develop and improve, the role of teachers, educators, and game developers will be precisely to provide the tools needed for future navigations. We have a great responsibility: we can guide this evolution or we can continue to cheat with images and sounds. It used to be that seeing was believing, but today we can no longer believe what we see. It is too easy to modify digital images, and with virtual cloning a person can be duplicated without his or her knowledge and, theoretically, "cut and pasted" into any type of situation. This image manipulation technology and young people's propensity to explore virtual worlds should induce us to create the foundations for training in "image literacy." With Internet interactive video or interactive multimedia television's 500 channels and services now being available in the home through cable and the telephone lines, and with hypermedia navigators rushing to embrace them, this type of training and copiloting is more necessary than ever. If we allow this opportunity to pass, a generation of navigators will find themselves adrift in the hyperspaces of superficiality.

The culture of the worlds of the future will thus come through many channels: traditional education, print and electronic media, gatherings, events, entertainment, television, interactive games, and networks, the combination of which builds relationships, creates procedures, gives rise to new ways of thinking, influences action, and constructs a collective memory—all part of the quintessential role of a culture. The emergence of a symbionomic culture has important consequences for schools, for the organizations of society, and for creation and action.

RECONFIGURING THE SCHOOL

The school has felt the full impact of the "mediamorphosis" (the explosion of communications technology) and the paradigm shift from an analytical to a systemic approach. A reconfiguration of the school is essential and urgent. We need to rethink the classroom, technological and methodological tools, and the role of the teacher, or else the situation of the school will become untenable within the next two decades. Marshall McLuhan's prophecy that young people would burn down their schools could, unfortunately, come true. In a way, it is already being borne out in school violence, attacks on teachers, and the little attention paid to life in elementary and secondary schools. We cannot ask teachers to be conveyors of knowledge, managers of the curriculum, classroom discussion leaders, and guardians of discipline and order all at the same time. There is too much competition from the media and show business so familiar to young people from television and music videos. Not everyone can be interesting, charismatic, a gifted communicator, and knowledgeable in his or her subject area. In addition, the competition from technology will become increasingly strong. CD-ROMs, computers with their capacity for simulation and connection to networks, and video games with new educational game software provide more educational substance than a school course of average quality. Does that mean teachers should be replaced by programmed machines? Should the schools be filled with quickly outmoded technological hardware? Should we jump from one medium to another (audiovisual, computers, videodisks, the Internet, etc.)? Or do we need, rather, to protect schools from technological invasion and make them havens of reflection, oases of serenity, relying on old-fashioned methods (paper, chalkboard, maps, and written exams) to instill reasoning, logic, and discipline, thus making the school the exception to the rest of the world, as Alain Finkielkraut has provocatively suggested?

As long as we have material bodies living in the *here and now*, there can be no virtual school. Of course, various means will be used to supplement teaching, both online, through networks, in particular using interactive multimedia television, and offline, on CD-ROMs and DVD. Certain kinds of (diploma-granting?) universal electronic schools will certainly be created on the hypernetworks of the future. But the classroom will long remain the cornerstone of education, because only there does a physical and social encounter take place, an immediate exchange of information, a form of collective learning mediated by the teacher. This type of structure, which is complementary to networks, has to be preserved. The future lies in finding a balance between virtual school and real school. A reconfiguration of the learning process is needed, involving the intelligent, measured use of new technologies for transmitting knowledge.

What will the classroom of the future look like? It will first and foremost be an environment that is open to the world. Using various image dissemination channels, and exploiting the possibilities of interactivity, current events (the facts that determine the future) will be discussed and incorporated into the curriculum. Computers will be used extensively, but in a "transparent" way—not for the machines themselves and their programming, but for their uses—primarily as "connectors" for networking with other classrooms and accessing information databases, as macroscopes for simulating speeded-up or slowed-down evolutionary processes, as tools for creating multimedia presentations, and as storage for various kinds of information the class needs on an ongoing basis. Of course, computers will also be used for other, more traditional applications such as writing, calculating, or managing. Teaching will be based on fractal education, the transmission of "complexifiable" seeds of knowledge as required, with students advancing at their own individual pace according to their abilities and motivation. Teachers will be mediators, catalysts, facilitators. Their role will be Socratic: showing the paths to knowledge, providing examples, acting as resource centers for both human and information resources. The reconfigured classroom will be a relay point, a node in a broad network that includes other, complementary, means for the transmission of culture and knowledge—science centers, exhibitions, interactive multimedia television, CDs, games, books, entertainment. Nobody will have a monopoly on education. The fractal education of the future will be the result of a symbiosis of many systems and networks.

THE LAMARCKIAN TRANSMISSION OF CULTURE

The transmission of the new culture will take place over generations. It is already percolating gradually through society by many different routes—schools, of course, but also the family, traditions, habits and ways of life, books, entertainment, the world of culture, and the media, and now, the electronic media, computers, and networks.

The transmission of a culture is analogous to the passing on of acquired characteristics, but it is social heredity, without genes or

DNA. It involves an inheritance that exists in books, plans, codes, practices, images, and collective memories and that is perpetuated through education in schools, families, and various groups, and amplified (or inhibited) through the relay of television. This is a Lamarckian transmission of acquired characteristics, and it is extremely accelerated compared to Darwinian biological evolution.

The basis of biological evolution is the three-part process of mutation, competition, and selection. Random variations occur in the programming of living things (DNA). This results in new species that are more or less suited to the environment in which the species are in competition. The fittest survive, are selected—or rather self-select—and transmit to their descendants the genetic code for survival and competitiveness, the new mutant genes. This process takes place in parallel within the DNA of billions of individuals in competition for limited resources. Biological evolution, as we have seen, is comparable to a huge parallel multiprocessor that seeks solutions to problems by trying out potential solutions and storing those that work in memory. This is how the diversity of the living world, biodiversity, is created.

According to Lamarck, the pressure to survive, expressed in animal behavior, leads to adaptive modifications of the organism that are transmitted to succeeding generations. A famous example is the giraffe's neck, which he believed had grown as a result of the animal's efforts to eat the leaves at the tops of trees, thus ensuring the survival of the species. Unlike Darwinism, Lamarckism introduces purpose into evolution—life as a whole "knows" where it is going—and with it the specter of an all-powerful creator. This approach, of course, did not stand up to scientific scrutiny. Moreover, it required a complicated biological mechanism that would decipher the information acquired by an organism and transmit it to the developing embryo by reprogramming the DNA codes—which would be much too expensive in terms of information and energy to be preserved through biological evolution.

However, in the case of cultural evolution, Lamarckism comes to the fore again. Fire, the wheel, writing, the automobile, the telephone, television, and the computer have all resulted in the reprogramming of the codes of the human societies using them, leading to other inventions, modifications, and adaptations. Culture and technology are one; they are two sides of the same coin. Evolution, learning, and collective memory are the basis of culture. The chipped flints of early humans were both cultural and technological tools. The cultural transmission of information already exists in insect societies: ants invented collective culture. What is transmitted from one generation of ants to the next is a spatial and temporal structure (the architecture of the colonies, the tools, the social organization, and the distribution of tasks over time). There is no memory storage or cultural learning at an individual level, and yet there is transmission of information on a collective level. Memory is inscribed in the physical environment of the colony; each trail has a history, which is discovered anew by each ant, and the network of trails constitutes an external memory that is perpetuated. This is a Lamarckian process of the transmission of characteristics acquired by the community. In the same way, in human societies, history is a powerful cultural catalyst that reinforces the cohesion of a people. Education, learning, adaptation, technological tools, communication, and evolution are the ingredients of a culture and its transmission.

The cultural environment and the technological environment have coevolved throughout the history of the human species. In this technical-social evolution, the Darwinian mechanism of mutation, competition, and selection is replaced by that of invention, competition, and market, which is similar to, though not an extension of, the Darwinian mechanism: generation of variety (mutation, invention), competition among populations (living species, ideas, products, companies, organizations, societies), and self-selection (natural selection, competitive exclusion, isolation in a time bubble). The major difference between these types of evolution lies in their speed. In technical-social evolution, the dematerialized nature of the media and the parallelism and reticulation of the operations densify time. Biology uses a slow, unwieldy process: creatures have to be born and die, and it takes generations to reinforce or eliminate an "invention." In technical-social evolution, a person modifies a patent, adapts a machine, and puts the product into mass production. A software program is both the coded medium and the action carried out in a computer. One instruction modifies a whole process.

Biological evolution with genes and organisms, and technical-social evolution with inventions, machines, and organizations, both form superimposed layers. The more dematerialized they become, the faster their evolution (compared with an "external" time scale). Today, new layers are being laid down, or, more precisely, concentric layers with increasing temporal densities are forming *within* those that already exist, nested spheres whose evolution, measured in terms of the traditional time scale, seems to be accelerating when one moves from outside to inside.

This is true of the cultural evolution of the mediasphere. The book had already externalized knowledge, making it independent of time and space. The press and television are both sources and mirrors of cultural information (in the broad sense). In this case, the mechanism of technical-social evolution—invention, competition, and market—is replaced by another—event, emotion, public opinion, and behavior modification. This, too, is a form of Lamarckian cultural transmission, but it occurs in an even shorter cycle—months, weeks, sometimes even days or hours. This is why the electronic media are so fond of events and images with a strong emotional charge; they give the impression that history is being made before our eyes and that the media are playing a preeminent role in it.

Television, as we have seen, is a catalyst in Lamarckian evolution. An event, amplified by the temporal presence of a large audience, modifies behavior. Transmission by the television mediasphere is a chaotic mechanism: an unforeseeable event can create an overall reaction that is completely disproportional. This amplification effect persists in the collective memory and determines future behavior, for example, at election time or, in a more everyday context, in purchasing decisions in the marketplace.

With the emergence of amplifiers for the individual brain (personal computers and hypernetworks), cultural transmission is accelerated yet further. Reactions on the Internet—individual and collective feedback—are even faster than those of public opinion as measured in surveys and amplified by the media. This trend will only be reinforced by broad public access to the information highways. Direct connections between brains and networks will in the future create a new space for expansion, a concentric temporal sphere even denser than preceding ones: the introsphere. This raises the old problem of time in a radically new way.

EMERGENCE, MUTATION, REVOLUTION

Human beings, their societies, their machines (mechanical or electronic), and their coevolving infrastructures and infostructures, connected by communications networks and regulatory loops, now form a series of indissociable nested systems, a new global living organism: the cybiont. But the cybiont is, in fact, made up of competing subsystems that are developing at different rates. The perception of these different rates is essential for harmonious evolution.

Our view of time and duration as applied to complex systems and chaotic, expanding evolutionary processes is still linear and one dimensional. We tend to think that evolutionary processes follow curves that can be extrapolated and that they take place in a pure, perfect, empty universe that has no direct impact on the evolution of the systems within it. In reality, the evolution of the cybiont's subsystems may be represented by bundles of curves describing nonlinear phenomena, with varying degrees of curvature depending on the rate of evolution. On a given date, all points coexist in a cross section of present time, but they obviously have different evolutionary potentialities (see the figure below).

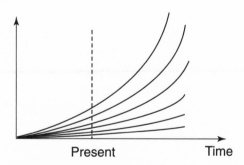

Present   Time

It seems that the density of information, a sort of informational critical mass, creates a "time bubble" with its own evolutionary constants. Just as the mass of a star "curves" space-time according to the theory of relativity, a critical mass of information of very high density—the result of multiple interactions, parallel processing, and branching communications networks—"densifies" time. Evolutionary processes could therefore be represented by "time bubbles." Although they coexist at a given moment, the bubbles have very different internal speeds and thus different potentialities for evolution, self-selection, and competitive exclusion. This introduces another dimension into the discussion of complex evolutionary phenomena. Intuition (the "sense of things in motion," according to Bergson) will be able to distinguish evolutionary potentialities and foresee situations better than analysis, which is blind to the information "density" of an evolutionary bubble.

Innovative ideas and information flow from human society as hot lava flows from a volcano. The lava gushes at high speed from some craters and flows slowly out of others, creating successive superimposed layers. Some layers remain hot and malleable, while others solidify. There are many different rates of flow, but the volcano as a whole is an entity whose components all coexist at a given time. Likewise, layers or strata of processes evolving at different rates coexist in society: technologies, economies, and ways of thinking. Among humans, those who become solidified in a layer cannot discern the seeds of change brought to the surface by the hot, flowing lava: the ideas, initiatives, actions, and achievements that are creating the world of tomorrow.

At the heart of symbionomic evolution there seems to be a new approach to time. The combination of the laws of self-organization with the exercise of human responsibility creates a particular space-time whose *density* is now challenging our traditional concept of duration and the flow of time. In describing the processes of evolution, I often use the terms "acceleration," "autocatalysis," "self-organization," and "emergence," as well as more common ones such as "revolution," "mutation," "crisis," and "break." These terms imply a particular relationship to time and duration, as if they were permeated with an additional temporal dimension. This constant implicit reference to duration seems opposed to the traditional time of clocks; it involves phenomena measured *by* time but in conflict *with* time. Seconds, minutes, hours, days, months, and years are too restrictive and rigid to express the profound nature of these fundamental concepts. We say that new properties "emerge," that improbable structures "auto-catalyze" and "self-select," and that evolutionary processes "acceler-ate" in relation to an unchanging ocean of time. These expressions, which are often used in biology and chaos theory, are revealing, as if the characteristic dynamics of these phenomena were imposing their laws on time. Why wouldn't time itself change? The standard time scale might dilate "from the inside" or contract "from the out-side." A new relativity of time could be born, enriched by the expe-rience of biology and the information sciences.

Emergence, mutation, and revolution can also be observed in the light of rapid accelerations resulting from sudden phase transitions. These phenomena are typical of the Internet's fast development, and can be seen as autocatalytic systems creating dense time bubbles and fostering the emergence of new properties. Just as a liquid will abruptly turn into a vapor when its temperature rises above a spe-cific threshold, autocatalytic systems will experience sudden essen-tial changes when a critical level of complexity is reached.

In *At Home in the Universe*, Stuart Kauffman discusses the auto-catalytic molecular systems from which life emerged, and he illus-trates the phenomenon by means of a simple network made of but-tons and threads.* Imagine 20 buttons spread out on a table. First, the buttons are randomly paired off with pieces of thread, then the pairs are joined. Gradually, the buttons become interconnected in increasingly large clusters, using increasing numbers of pieces of thread. As Kauffman puts it, "When there are very few threads com-pared to the number of buttons, most buttons will be unconnected. But as the ratio of threads to buttons increases, small connected clus-ters begin to form. As the ratio of threads to buttons continues to in-crease, the size of these clusters of buttons tends to grow." A phase transition suddenly occurs when the ratio of threads to buttons reaches 0.5, and a giant cluster is formed. The rate of growth of the giant cluster then slows down as the number of isolated buttons and

---

* Stuart Kauffman, *At Home in the Universe: The Search for Laws of Self-Organization and Complexity*, Oxford: Oxford University Press, October 1995.

small clusters decreases. When this growth is plotted on a graph an S-shaped curve emerges.

Now, I propose to replace the buttons with Web sites (nodes) and the threads with Internet links (edges). Instead of 20 sites, let's imagine millions of Web sites and millions of links. Beyond a given ratio of links to Web sites (0.5?), a phase transition must occur (as illustrated below).

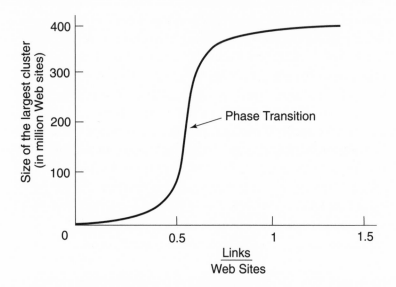

With 400 million users, 170 million host computers, and an average of 50 links per site (bookmarks and e-mail addresses), new properties will certainly emerge. What about with 2 billion users, 800 million host computers, and 500 links per site? With such a giant electronic cluster of interconnected brains and machines, what will these properties look like? Probably a new form of macrolife becoming progressively conscious of its own existence and self-maintenance.

INFORMATION AS POTENTIAL TIME

We ought to look for a new approach to time in the relationship between time and information. Could it be that the (perceived) speed of the flow of time is related to the speed of production of information.

I propose to consider information as potential time, as a reserve of time. The more potential time we create, the more we compensate indirectly for the outflow of universal time. To justify this proposition, I will have to return to the analysis provided in *The Macroscope*, which I briefly summarize as follows.*

We are confined in what I have called chronocentrism, the prison of time. We can explain the world only from cause to effect. We have thus associated linear causality and chronology, with causes always preceding effects. In the case of the Big Bang, for example, beginning with a first cause, the building blocks of matter were created, and they continued their divergent evolution in an explosion of variety. This type of explanation by causes, this reduction of complexity by means of analysis, is the traditional scientific approach.

But cybernetics has opened another path. In a feedback loop, causality is circular: the arrow of time turns back on itself like a snake swallowing its tail. Effects can precede their causes. The direction of before/after is reversed, and chronology is disrupted. Purpose and teleology arise out of the behavior of a self-regulating system. The teleological approach favors convergent evolution, like that which results from any intelligent act. Pushed to its limits, this convergence would lead to the Omega Point (Teilhard de Chardin), the ultimate concentration of dematerialized spirit.

Explanation and involvement. Knowledge and meaning. Causality and purpose. Determinism and teleology. Materialism and spirituality. So many mutually contradictory alternatives related to the problem of time. It is the concept of time flowing in one direction that creates the opposition, the universal time measured by clocks, the time of increasing entropy and disorganization of the universe according to the second law of thermodynamics—and the time, too, of our lives progressing toward death, which we project onto the time of the evolution of the world.

But there is a kind of evolution that seems to be the opposite of this: the evolution of increasing complexity and the creation of orig-

---

* *The Macroscope, pp. 202–224.*

inal information, which we see in biological evolution and technical-social evolution, a kind of evolution that appears to "climb the slope that matter has descended" (Bergson). The well-known second law of thermodynamics could be countered, in the terms I use in this book, by a *principle of symbionomics:* the self-organization of matter into systems of increasing complexity.

Biological evolution, working through the information contained in genes, has produced potential time. Human beings have taken over from biological evolution and are using information to create a time capital that can be used today or by future generations. A scientific publication, a plan, a library, a data bank, a culture, or a work of art is comparable to a reserve of potential time. This time capital bears "interest" in the form of time, accelerating the evolutionary process through autocatalysis. The creation of an original requires duration, but making a copy is practically instantaneous. The act of creation is always historic; the act of copying is commonplace. The former capitalizes time, while the latter only updates an existing reserve.

To try to overcome the dichotomy between divergent and convergent evolution, I have proposed to superimpose them in such a way as to bring out their complementarity in the context of the principle of time conservation.

Conservation of time would then come about through the maintenance of a balance between speed of organization and speed of disorganization of the world. When evolution began, the flow of entropic degradation was preeminent. The activity of man, however, helped to oppose it with an increasingly intense flow of new information (see the figure below). (*The Macroscope,* page 221)

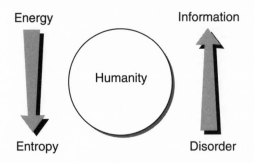

A new situation has arisen because of the speed at which human beings are producing original information. This information increases complexity, and complexity generates potential time: it adds time to time; it creates time *within* time. A system of high complexity (such as a living cell or a computer network) traps time, creating its own time bubble that represents the environment of its evolution.

Until now, the speed of the generation of complexity and information was not sufficient to compensate for and balance the speed of entropic disorganization. Clock time predominated. Today, with the power of information technology, the establishment of hypernetworks, and mass memory storage, the density of time is changing. The cybiont "thinks" in the hyperdense time of the introsphere.

For the sake of argument, to help visualize the densification of time, I imagine that there are time particles or "chronons," particles of duration that exist along with photons (particles of light), electrons (particles of electricity), and gravitons (particles associated with the gravitational field). Just as light is sometimes an electromagnetic wave and sometimes a particle, time would exist either in the form of a wave (duration) or a particle (the chronon). This is why we are able to think about and experience time either as a flow or as a juxtaposition of moments, but not both. There seems to be a kind of exclusion principle involving time. According to the exclusion principle in physics, if you know the position of a photon or an electron, you cannot know its energy state, and, conversely, the information on its energy state excludes the precise measurement of its position in space. A choice must be made between wave and particle. The same applies to the representation of time as flow or as moments.

Could chronons in a flow have different intensities? A flow of electrons in a wire is electric current. The intensity of the current (the number of electrons per unit of time) is proportional to the difference in potential (voltage) between the terminals of the circuit—in other words, to the reservoir of potential energy that produces the force generating the flow. Similarly, the flow of water (the volume of water per unit of time) in a pipe connected to a tank by a valve is proportional to the amount of water in the tank and its height.

A reservoir of information, as I have said, is analogous to potential time. In keeping with this image, it may be seen as generating a flow of chronons proportional to the quantity and the quality of information stored. The intensity of this flow would be measured per unit of conventional time. But today, the accelerated production of information is increasing the flow of chronons per unit of time; the intensity and density of the flow are increasing. Time capital produces a flow of chronons proportional to its critical mass. One of today's "heavy" chronons may be equivalent to 1000 chronons of the Middle Ages, yet we are still using the same universal standard of measurement. Should we now talk about an amount of information per unit of time, or about an amount of potential time per unit of information created—bits per second or chronons per bit?

The parallelizing of sequential time also contributes to the densification of time. Parallel computers, networks of neurons, anthills, markets, stock exchanges, and telematics networks are multiprocessors that convert sequential time into parallel time. The amount of information available for each person, as measured in bits per neuron and processed by the prostheses of the brain, is increasing exponentially. The intensity of time (the flow of chronons) is increasing. Time bubbles form and evolve according to their own dynamics. The creation of original information and the networking, parallelizing, and storage of information in data banks "curve" space-time, producing a basin of attraction and an attractor.

FRACTAL TIME

The creation of potential time needs to be placed in the context of chaos theory. In a chaotic system, a large number of agents produce and disseminate information in parallel. The complex systems that they create form so many time bubbles, which evolve simultaneously. In a hypernetwork like the Internet, each user densifies time from within, expanding cyberspace. The interest produced by this capital is reinvested back into it cumulatively. Using cyberspace means reinvesting information in this time capital and increasing its value. The creators of hypernetworks are remunerated in information. Unlike thermodynamic capital (energy), which is irreversibly converted into entropy as it is used, symbionomic capital (information) increases in value with use. It constantly produces more interest: it "radiates" chronons.

The French astrophysicist Christian Nottale has proposed that the universe should be represented as a fractal structure. According to him, the same reasoning and mathematical equations cannot be applied to the first seconds of the Big Bang and to the billions of light-years of the age of the quasar. In his view, the universe consists of a series of fractal niches, each requiring specific methods of calculation and reasoning.

In my view, each time bubble created by a complex system (living organism, society, or cybiont) is a *fractal* time bubble; it reflects the macro and the micro. Like any fractal structure, it is a seed containing the overall structure. Symbionomic time is not linear, but fractal. Each time bubble created by a complex system has a different density of time. These different times coexist, and their evolution is measured by the same universal time. Thus, a teenage Internet surfer, a Peruvian peasant, a Wall Street speculator, a Polynesian fisher, a TV journalist, and an African shaman are all contemporaries, but each lives and evolves in a fractal time bubble of a different density.

The symbionomic view of a world made up of time bubbles in evolution differs radically from the traditional conception of evolution as a linear process pursuing its course in a standard universe, like Zeno of Elea's arrow in flight. The traditional view corresponds to Aristotle's definition (time is the measure of motion) and that of Newton (there is a universal time and an absolute space), supplemented by the laws of thermodynamics (the irreversible time of the conversion of energy) and the theory of relativity (relative space-time). But it does not deal with the complementarity of entropic time and symbionomic time. Human creativity feeds on the degradation of energy into entropy, but it "saves" time in the great reservoir of information. Symbionomic evolution compensates for the flow of entropic time; the two flows, in opposite directions, balance each other.

This, I believe, is a key to understanding the paradox created by concepts related to time (emergence, self-selection, autocatalysis, evolutionary acceleration, and temporal closure). According to the symbionomic approach I am proposing, there is no single space-time common to all living things, but rather a process of coevolution of autonomous fractal time bubbles. There is actually no acceleration of evolution (billions of years for the appearance of life, millions of years for humanity, dozens of centuries for civilization, half a century for computers, etc.), but rather a densification of time bubbles and the "diversion" of some of them from the main flow of conventional time. Hence the paradox of the apparent autonomy and independence of the phenomena of emergence, autocatalysis, and self-selection. Or the paradox of the apparent linear, sequential nature of evolution, consisting of juxtaposed periods, constantly accelerating, and culminating in humanity, the "arrow" and now the pilot of this generalized process that encompasses prebiotic, biological, and technical-social stages.

The image of breaking the sound barrier illustrates this point. A stationary airplane generates sound waves that radiate out at a speed of 1088 feet per second. These waves are similar to the waves created by a stone falling into the quiet water of a lake, except that they are in the form of spheres radiating out. When a moving airplane approaches the speed of sound, the waves pile up in front of the nose of the aircraft, creating a compression wave. This is the sound barrier. When the speed of the airplane exceeds the speed of sound, it breaks the sound barrier, and sound bubbles form behind it (see the figure below).

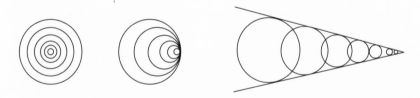

The time bubbles I have described are like those sound bubbles. They form contemporary sets, organized hierarchically according to their temporal density. The creation of new fractal bubbles within those that already exist corresponds to the phenomenon of *emergence*. When their high temporal density suddenly reveals their presence within the low-density bubbles, a mutation or explosion occurs. What is called a "technological revolution" (the industrial, biological, or digital revolution), the "explosion" of a sector, or a "decisive mutation" represents the opening up of a time bubble within our universe of reference. There is a sudden collective awareness of the existence of a complex system in accelerated evolution. There is a perception of a higher density of time and of the particular "curvature" of our familiar space-time as a result of the formation of a critical mass of information. The terms "revolution," "mutation," and "explosion" describe the nonlinearity of these phenomena, their exponential acceleration, and the conditions for the locking in of a sector through the action of virtuous circles (the law of increasing returns).

An example is the communications "explosion." The concentration of networks, information technology, and multimedia densifies time so much that the sector as a whole self-selects and emerges from the lower-density background as a signal stands out against background noise. A similar phenomenon in the context of the origin of life is the emergence of a set of molecules forming an autocatalytic network. The first living systems arose by closing themselves in time bubbles distinct from the undifferentiated background of the primeval soup, and evolved through the internal production of other, still denser bubbles.

LIVING OFF THE INTEREST ON TIME CAPITAL

Basic scientific research and paradigm shifts can also be examined from this point of view. Research is not a linear, sequential process like a river flowing from a source (discoveries) to an outlet (industrial applications); it is a fractal process. In the sphere of existing knowledge (information capital, time capital), which is expanding quite rapidly, a singularity arises—a new idea, the results of an experiment, the basis for a new theory. This fractal point is a tiny, almost invisible sphere, a potential space of new knowledge. It feeds on information, progressively adding the results of experiments, and creates new niches for raising questions. The sphere grows bigger and a time bubble emerges; as in any process of fractalization, this phenomenon is repeated on different levels. The bubble densifies from within and expands further. The new field of research, which was initially invisible, gives rise to new niches for applied research and industrial development, and a proliferation of publications and studies. Basic research has thus led to the formation of a new space of knowledge within the existing space.

This is how paradigms are born and die. The fractal point of a new vision of the world appears within a sphere of official knowledge. This point grows into a fragile, almost invisible sphere without any real influence on the recognized paradigm. The internal pressure of the established views seeks to eliminate it, but, as in the case of research, the bubble of the new paradigm densifies from within. It increases its volume by feeding on new contributions, until it occupies all the space available in the old sphere. The old paradigm is dead.

Symbionomic evolution produces time capital that generates interest. This law can be applied to time management in our personal lives. We all have trouble organizing our time; overworked, overloaded, and overwhelmed, we are always running short of it. Each new activity requires the elimination of an existing activity, since the time available is not expandable. Having time to spare is an unattainable dream for the vast majority of people in positions of responsibility. One of the reasons for this is the division of linear time into specific sequences: minutes, hours, days, weeks, weekends, months, holidays, years, training periods, occupational life, and retirement. Such time can neither be compressed nor expanded. On the other hand, if we adopt a nonlinear type of time management, we can generate niches for new activities without necessarily eliminating any of the old ones. In order to do this, we have to invest time in the creation of time capital (a library, a computer, a file management system, the Internet, an artistic creation, etc.), which generates interest. The interest may take the form of time gained—for example, by using a computerized database for personal documents—or time as use value, compressed or expanded as desired. It creates new niches for expansion and encourages synergy with other niches, enhancing the value of the original capital with a minimal investment of time. Time capital that has been well invested bears interest, providing a time income to live on and eliminating the need to draw directly on life capital, the linear time that is ordered sequentially and synchronized from outside by one's company or society. Personal computers and properly organized access to the Internet are powerful catalysts in the creation and preservation of this time capital. They are essential tools for all people who want to manage their time, in order to be more efficient, of course, but especially to give life greater meaning.

The planetary processes of coevolution between the biosphere, the technosphere, the ecosphere (economic and ecological), and now the introsphere take place at different speeds in their increasingly dematerialized spheres, within superimposed evolutionary layers. It is therefore essential to take into account the variety of situations and the amplifying effects of the temporal divergences in human societies. On a global scale, the isolation of the most developed societies in their high-density time bubbles raises the problem of exclusion. Competition among time bubbles of different densities leads to the elimination of those with the lowest densities. In a world of scarce resources, the accelerated appropriation of vital flows by the few gradually eliminates others from competition. How can we share financial, energy, food, and knowledge resources in a fragmented world, while respecting cultural diversity and personal freedom? Living in different fractal bubbles means living behind temporal boundaries. The densities of time flows are mutually exclusive—it is as if two people, one on a high-speed train and the other riding a bicycle, are trying to exchange packages. Yet sharing is essential if we want to avoid the irreversible processes of competitive exclusion between communities, peoples, and nations. The cybiont is beginning to develop and evolve in a hyperaccelerating time bubble, and it is up to human beings to prevent imbalances that could imperil the future of humanity.

THE CYBIONT AND HUMANITY IN THE THIRD MILLENNIUM

One of the greatest challenges for the future will be to integrate humanity into a larger whole; to create a planetary being with a higher level of organization, a being that is already emerging as a result of human action and is constructing humans in turn; to participate consciously in the new origins of life. However, it is very difficult for us to accept or even to conceive of something larger than ourselves that is neither political nor religious in nature—the categories in which we have traditionally confined ourselves. Any human attempt to create a living being quickly calls up the image of Frankenstein's monster. We have a visceral fear of the consequences of creating an entity that could surpass us. And yet this is the direction in which humanity is now moving. The cybiont is a macroscopic living being that obeys the laws of macrobiology and symbionomic evolution; that is, it is a physical, organic, natural creature. It is being born, and yet it is created. It lives, and yet it is moved from within by the human cells that control its functions. But those functions are gradually escaping human control. Humans are accepting a loss of part of that macro-control in order to better fulfill their local responsibilities. This raises the big question that is implicit throughout this book: how can we preserve human freedom within the context of the general laws of self-organization? How can we make autonomy and symbionomics mutually complementary? The answer, in my view, is the conscious construction of a planetary symbiosis between humanity and the cybiont and between the cybiont and Gaia. Hence the importance of understanding the natural laws that partially determine this process of evolution.

The biosphere, technosphere, noosphere, and introsphere are the successive stages of dematerialization, stages that are in constant acceleration, given the fluidity of the material. These spheres consist of increasingly dense bubbles of space-time that, in turn, create within themselves an infinite variety of new fractal bubbles in a succession of nested concentric spheres—Russian dolls of an ever deeper and denser space-time. If the noosphere is a technological structure of interconnection, the introsphere is a medium, a self-reflective collective preconscious mind. The symbiotic human being of the third millennium, connected biologically to the cybiont's planetary brain, is a neuron—but a neuron that is able to think both the whole and the part, both the introsphere and his or her own consciousness. A network brain is thus being formed, fluid, adaptable, in permanent reconfiguration. Donald O. Hebb's view of the human brain can be applied to the planetary brain of the cybiont.*

Reconfiguration takes place throughout the process of dematerialization, from the biosphere to the introsphere. In concentric layers, information is integrated into higher levels: signs into information, information into knowledge, knowledge into culture. The contents of these successive layers are transmitted in different times (see the figure below).

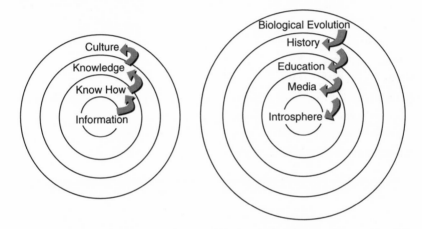

The signs contained in genes, and their modification, exist in the duration of biological evolution. The transmission of a "species culture" takes millions of years. Human information and actions take place in the time of history, which is a powerful factor in cultural transmission, influencing people and giving them a sense of cohesion and common destiny. The knowledge and information of a lifetime are transmitted through education, by means of books and examples of behavior for emulation, and here time contracts to the scale of a generation. Education, which involves Lamarckian cultural transmission, reconfigures brains and their environments. Faster still is cultural transmission by the media, the time of television news, with the power of images and emotions that are readily remembered—reconfiguring the planetary brain by transmitting a volatile, demate-

---

* Donald O. Hebb, *The Organization of Behavior: A Neuropsychological Theory*, John Wiley: New York, 1949.p

rialized culture at the speed of light. But even faster, in densified time, is the neural interconnection of the global hypernetworks. Today limited to exchanges of texts, sounds, and images, they will soon include direct brain-to-brain transmission through biotic interfaces that are currently being created. The speed of neural communication will create the conditions for the emergence of a self-reflective planetary co-consciousness. The cybiont will begin to think.

Biological evolution, history, education, media, and interpersonal communications networks are thus the accelerating stages of a type of cultural transmission that is now constantly reconfiguring the cybiont's planetary brain. The power to control the whole process lies in large part within the introsphere, the most recent and deepest layer of this evolution. Broader functions are emerging without hindering those that occur at the lower levels. Symbiosis is based on subsumption; the art of governance in the future will lie in the capacity to conceive and implement functions that have been subsumed for the good of humanity.

We are seeing new approaches in the social sciences and humanities. Once isolated in an artificial world of signs, codes, and laws, they can now be integrated into the powerful and unified current of symbionomics. Just as biology was transformed by input from the physical sciences, the humanities are being renewed by the contribution of biology and the sciences of complexity. The methods and tools of physics have enriched the life sciences, giving rise to the biological revolution and molecular biology, genetics, and neurobiology. We can expect to see a comparable revolution in the social sciences. The methods and tools of the sciences of complexity, the contribution of chaos theory, the massive use of computers, simulation, and *in silico* experiments will shed new light on the social sciences and reconnect them with nature. This does not mean reducing sociology to biology, extrapolating from biology to human societies, or attempting to discover "sociobiological" laws with questionable applications, but rather enriching the social sciences with the contribution of the basic sciences. The traditional boundaries between hard and soft science are becoming blurred: an invigorating current is flowing in both directions between analysis and synthesis—as it does between subjects and objects, the natural and the artificial, the material and the immaterial, and the real and the virtual. Physics, chemistry, biology, sociology, ecology, and macrobiology each represent a fractal glimpse of a whole reality perceived at various levels of observation.

Human social action will also be renewed in this context. Traditional politics, as we have seen, is giving way to new methods of participatory management of complexity. Governance and the principle of subsumption demonstrate this. Control by means of a vertical, top-down hierarchy is gradually being replaced by bottom-up, transverse methods that are characteristic of networked societies. The new laissez faire approach that has come primarily out of American neoliberal thought favors bottom-up control almost exclusively: intelligent agents following simple rules will be able to self-organize. But this approach is dangerous; it fails to consider the ideas, values, or ethics underlying such major orientations. Competition among ideas is as important as competition among products and organizations. The market cannot be a multiprocessor, a regulator, and a radar device all at the same time. The governance of the future will make the various methods of control and management (bottom-up, top-down, and transverse) complementary.

Dematerialized cultural transmission, reconfiguration of the planetary brain, new humanities and social sciences, governance, and the emergence of a collective intelligence mark the stages in the advent of symbiotic humanity. This creative convergence of new spacetimes of greater density will require humanity to make a crucial choice in the coming decades: to embrace the densification of the moment or to strive for solidarity in the harmonization of the multiple times of evolution. The basic rules of symbionomics can shed light on this choice.

THE 10 GOLDEN RULES OF SYMBIOTIC HUMANITY

These 10 rules summarize and contextualize the principal laws discussed in this book. They can be translated into actions, strategies, or policies at various levels of organization of society.

1. *Foster the emergence of collective intelligence:* Many agents following simple rules and connected through communications networks can collectively solve complex problems. Collective intelligence is catalyzed by interconnections, individual creativity, the acceptance of rules and codes, participation in an overall project, and the transmission of culture.

2. *Establish coevolution among people, systems, and networks:* Relationships that form in the context of coevolution among individuals, organizations, and machines favor mutual adaptations of structures and functions. The adjustment and regulation of evolutionary processes through better knowledge of the dynamics of systems, and synchronization and coordination of operations, create favorable conditions for coevolution.

3. *Create symbiotic relationships at various levels of social organization:* Drawing on the natural mechanisms of symbiosis, seek conditions that favor the equilibrium and harmonious development of relationships based on the mutual benefit of the partners, such as the division of tasks according to skills, the economy of metabolisms, and the sharing of communications networks.

4. *Build organizations and systems in successive functional layers:* One of the basic rules of biological evolution is the stratification of structures and functions. If a system functions properly at its own level and gives the organism (or the organization) an evolutionary advantage, it is preserved through natural selection. Complex systems involving people, machines, and networks should not be built from scratch solely from engineers' plans; rather, they should be allowed to grow and complexify by the layering of interdependent functions and structures. If a subset proves satisfactory, it should serve as a base for the next layer.

5. *Regulate complex systems through top-down (hierarchical) and bottom-up (democratic) control:* Uncoordinated microinitiatives can lead to anarchy and directives imposed from the top to dictatorship. The governance of the future will be based on the complementarity of top-down and bottom-up control, the former to establish the main symbiotic directions, such as the maintenance and development of partnerships, and the latter to promote the emergence of collective intelligence and creativity.

6. *Implement the rules of subsumption:* The art of subsumption consists of making one's individuality part of a greater whole that benefits the individual and gives life meaning. Giving up some of the individualism (or sovereignty) that hinders relationships among people and among nations makes it possible to create balanced symbiotic relationships. Everyone benefits from rules that are recognized by all, so that we can all attain a higher level of freedom and responsibility.

7. *Stay at the edge of chaos:* Computer simulations of the self-organization of complex systems and their evolution over time bring out the importance of a transition phase between sterile turbulence and rigid order. The art of managing complex systems is based on the ability to keep them "at the edge of chaos," balanced between the Charybdis of disorder and the Scylla of inflexibility. It is in this fragile, unstable zone that the structures, functions, and organizations of the world of tomorrow can come into being. The secret is to accept the risks of change while preserving the stability of structures and functions.

8. *Favor parallel forms of organization:* Parallelism of tasks should be implemented in the processes of creation, production, and regulation, just as it is in the living world. The analytical, Taylorist approach inherited from the nineteenth century has hindered the development of human networks that operate like multiprocessors. With the advent of powerful personal computers and global telecommunications networks, it becomes possible to parallelize many social functions. The divisions between sectors are disappearing, and redundancy of operations enhances security.

9. *Implement virtuous circles:* Traditional economics focus on the analysis of mechanisms that lead to diminishing returns such as market saturation, profit squeeze, or the effects of competition. But the mechanisms that lead to the self-selection of a species or the creation of a market are autocatalytic in nature; they are virtuous circles. As a form of encouragement, it is necessary to create development "niches" to amplify the circles and communications networks to enhance synergy.

10. *Fractalize knowledge:* Modern communications, education, and culture can no longer be based on a linear, encyclopedic conception of knowledge. The production and transmission of complex, interdependent knowledge requires a fractal, hypertextual approach to the organization of information. The fractalization of this knowledge creates seeds that can be reconstructed by each person, using his or her own approach.

THE VALUES OF A NEW HUMANISM

Symbiosis and coevolution also call for new values. Human responsibility for evolution, including the evolution of so-called artificial life-forms, must be based on something other than power, competition, economics, or traditional religion. Evolution toward symbiosis is a never-ending process, getting closer and closer to its objectives without ever attaining them. A humanistic morality can emerge from symbiosis, but for this to happen, we will have to give up some of our privileges. For states, this means accepting a transfer of individual sovereignty toward greater cooperation and solidarity in supranational endeavors with other states. For governments, it means accepting a lessening of omnipresent control so as to promote individual initiative and collective problem solving. For human beings, finally, it means accepting a partial loss of individualism for the sake of a greater whole that is capable of providing increased security, well-being, and power.

In this context of co-control, copiloting, and coevolution, we will need to rely on shared values. If humanity is to give computers and networks some control over the complex systems of which it is a part, if governments are to give people responsibility for the control of certain social functions, what does this mean in practice?

What course should we take? The function of governance in the future will consist in large part of regulating major economic, energy, and social flows—and even regulating the regulators, establishing cybernetic mechanisms for the real-time monitoring of the cybiont's major metabolic functions. What direction should then be given to symbionomic evolution?

Meaning implies direction; to give meaning to one's life is to give it direction and purpose. Politics, science, art, and religion contribute, depending on individual inclination, to giving life meaning and direction. Action, knowledge, emotion, and faith are powerful engines of the will to live, as is the desire for power and influence, money, and honor, or the need to create. But politics, religion, and science, major forces that shape the world, are separate domains, with distinct and often incompatible values.

Politics today has been appropriated by a specialized class, trapped in its desire for power and its own contradictions, creating its own demons in corruption, compromise, and media hype—a class that has started to discredit itself. But no alternative is yet available; there is no possibility of informed citizens taking back certain forms of power while awaiting the emergence of the transverse power of interpersonal networks.

Science, the principal avenue to knowledge, is also subject to power games that undermine its integrity. The desire to dominate, faith in triumphant reason, and the attraction of the business world sometimes distort results and often influence thinking.

The religions of the world intuitively discovered the great values of convergence: respect and love for one's neighbor, joining together in a greater whole that inspires both awe and love, and preparation for a future that depends on individual behavior. But the rituals, the dogma, the inquisition, and, more recently, various fundamentalist movements have stifled the natural spontaneity of faith and destroyed the hope for a religious practice that works harmoniously with universal laws.

Politics, religion, and science can converge, however, in the vision and construction of a new form of life, the creation of a planetary macroorganism, the next stage in the evolution of humanity. A humanistic morality, not revealed but emergent, can arise from the need to guarantee human freedom and responsibility within the framework of the natural laws that have gradually been brought to light by science. Politics, science, and religion, the traditional paths of action, knowledge, and faith, can coexist and be renewed within a symbionomic perspective. What links them is a new conception of time. A revealed, transcendent, immanent, or emergent religion is related to our conception of time as are the concepts of acceleration, mutation, and revolution discussed earlier. Linear, sequential, repetitive time that "fills" space no longer corresponds to the reality of the nonlinear, parallel, creative time of the cybiont. Fractal time, as we have seen, has various degrees of density and is bipolar: it can be explanation or involvement time, observation or action time, copy or creation time. But it contains two aspects of the same reality, two complementary visions of the world, divergent and convergent, a beginning and an end simultaneously present in the same fractal spacetime. Human creation is creation of the world, whenever it occurs and whatever its nature. An original work preserves time. Creation saves time. This can be the source of a humanistic morality. Promoting and respecting an original work, valuing difference, opening up to the creations of others, contributing to the production of something greater than oneself without ideological or religious constraints, this to me is the base on which a humanistic morality for the future can be built.

Before concluding, I must ask a last question. Is the cybiont beginning to think? And if so, where is the seat of that thought?

The cybiont is a planetary supraorganism of which human beings are the cells, and the machines, organizations, and networks of humans are the tissues, organs, and communications and regulatory systems. But the cybiont's planetary brain is evolving more quickly and in a denser time than the rest of the social macroorganism. This is why I have placed particular emphasis throughout this book on the interface between the human brain and the networks, the formation of the introsphere, and the influence of the cybiont's mind. Just as transportation and, later, communications networks and the technology associated with them have profoundly influenced the evolution of developed and developing societies, the cybiont's planetary brain will gradually exercise a decisive influence on the evolution of human society as a whole.

Where, then, is the seat of this planetary thought? Nowhere in particular, and everywhere at the same time. Our brain is a chemical, ionic machine, a parallel processor, a fluid network that is constantly being reconfigured. Hormones from the brain are found in other organs and tissues of the organism. While located in the head, the brain is coextensive with the whole body. It also extends to the personal bubble of communication and action that each person creates around himself or herself. Through connections with computers and networks, each brain is integrated into the planetary brain.

The real question, then, is not where the cybiont's thought is located, but how human beings can benefit from it. Will people be conscious of its thought? Does a neuron in my brain know what I am thinking? Does a cell of my blood or my liver contribute "consciously" to the functioning of my body? We would answer no to these questions without hesitation. The ant or the bee that is programmed to carry out specific tasks has no overall awareness of the results of its actions. The overall strategy of the anthill or the hive, a collective macroorganism, is beyond it. Would the same be true for symbiotic humanity?

Already today, public opinion, the collective consciousness, and the shared television culture are the precursors of a perception by each individual brain of the embryonic mind of the cybiont. Tomorrow, the interconnection of brains through the networks will reinforce the feeling of belonging to a supraindividual entity. Still reserved for a privileged class of the world (as the telephone, the automobile, and the color television once were), connection to the planetary brain by personal computers and networks will become widespread. Until there are biotic interfaces.

Unlike cells of the body, ants, or bees—cogs within a larger whole that remains forever unknowable to them—symbiotic humanity will be fully conscious of the shared thought of the cybiont. It will be conscious of it because the cybiont's mind emerges from its own thought and because humans themselves have established the perceptual relays for global thought.

The big question will be the harmonization of different times. The lifetime of a civilization is in the order of 5000 years. A person's lifetime lasts less than a century. The lifetime of the cybiont exists in the contracted time of the week or the month. The constant acceleration of time raises the problem of the equivalence of past and future time scales. Do they have the same value? They do for us, certainly, but do they for the cybiont? A human life may represent only a year for the social macroorganism. The neurons of the Earth can span close to a century, but the planetary brain they feed may evolve by the hour, because it is a different form of life, a macrolife confined in an increasingly dense time bubble. Furthermore, a similar process could take place with respect to a possible connection with other cybionts in other galaxies, creating a thinking universe made up of interconnected planetary brains. It would be as if the Big Bang were happening *in reverse*, by the implosion of information rather the explosion of energy.

At the end of this journey far into the third millennium, centuries beyond the year 2000, it seems to me that implosion and explosion, end and origin, are present in every moment that passes, as in a fractal seed that contains both the whole and the part. The two ultimate entities of knowledge and action are energy and mind. The world is explainable when explored in the course of the degradation of energy. To explain is the universal quest of science. The information science acquires is paid for in entropy, by the increase of the disorder of the universe. When explored in the course of creation or individual and collective action, the world gradually reveals its coherence. While science explains, action involves. Knowledge and action combined give the world a meaning that can nourish a humanistic morality or a religious faith.

The universe thus appears as a consciousness that forms by becoming conscious of itself. Energy and mind are the two faces of a single reality, and the boundary separating them is none other than time.

Conclusion

THE YEAR 2500: BACK TO THE FUTURE

Having started with molecules and natural laws, we now find ourselves in the middle of the third millennium, with the cybiont and symbiotic humanity fully alive. The year 2500 is as close to us today as is the year 1500, when trade, banking, transportation, printing, weapons, and the art of the Renaissance were already coevolving. In 2500, what will have become of communications networks, personal computers, and direct interfaces between the brain and machines? After the progress computers have made in only 15 years, what will they be able to achieve in 500 years?

The acceleration of evolution, as I have tried to show, is not an independent phenomenon occurring in the static context of a neutral space-time. Symbionomic evolution creates potential time, contracts space-time, and forms increasingly dense time bubbles. To measure the consequences of such an approach to the future, and to remain faithful to the course I have set for myself, I have tried to condense in fractal form the basic themes of this book.

The sciences of complexity provide a unified view of nature. Symbionomic evolution, the general theory of the self-organization and dynamics of complex systems, enables us to plot possible courses for the evolution of human societies toward the birth of the cybiont and symbiotic humanity. The life of the planetary supraorganism and the scenarios it gives rise to lead, in turn, to strategic choices and methods of managing complexity that apply to the present. Human responsibility can be exercised within the deterministic framework of natural laws. Governance and subsumption are the keys to this new symbiotic alliance. The analytical, systemic, and chaotic meet in a rational and sensitive interpretation of the world.

Through the laws, codes, and constraints voluntarily established by human societies, interactions among the many agents acting at various levels of organization can lead to the emergence of a collective intelligence. The political copiloting of the future, the art of governance, will be to regulate the major flows in the world, to catalyze the emergence of intelligence, to manage complexity, and to copilot evolution.

The industries of the future are already being created: information industries, bioindustries, and ecoindustries. New disciplines are coming into being—biotechnology, biotics, molecular electronics, neobiology, macrobiology, network sciences, cognitive sciences, bioinformatics, and a renewed discipline of social sciences. These are the methodological and technological tools of the revolution of the third millennium.

But the great challenge of the future will not be technological, it will be human. How will the industrial societies, worlds in constant acceleration, isolated in their fractal time bubbles, continue to develop without leaving the less fortunate societies by the wayside? How can we prevent the irreversible action of the mechanisms of competitive exclusion from widening the gap between the privileged minority and the impoverished majority? The great choice that will undoubtedly arise for humanity in this century will be whether or not to slow down the headlong rush of the privileged, and organize society and the planet for the good of all. The great choices of governance will not involve the acceleration of growth and the reinforcement of competition, hegemony, and power, but rather the planetary sharing of knowledge and wealth so as to preserve cultural diversity and freedom. The great choices of tomorrow will not concern the synchronization of times according to a standard decided by an elite, but the harmonization of times, of the different densities of fractal bubbles, the specific constants of evolution, and appropriate response times. Just as different times coexist in our bodies, the cybiont will live by the harmonization of superimposed times. Sharing, solidarity, temporal harmonization, and respect for differences will be the new rule, the new way of life of symbiotic humanity.

THE FIFTH PARADIGM

The Copernican revolution allowed humanity to step out of its confining geocentrism. Human beings were no longer the center of the universe. This was the birth of the first paradigm.

The Cartesian revolution made the universe accessible through reason. The power of analysis and logic made human beings masters of science and technology, the artisans of a changing world. This constituted the second paradigm.

The Darwinian revolution put human beings fully back into nature, freeing them from anthropocentrism. This was the basis of the third paradigm.

Today's systemic revolution has reintegrated knowledge into a coherent whole and given humanity back its role in the universe. It characterizes the fourth paradigm.

The fifth paradigm is in the process of coming into being. The sciences of complexity and chaos theory are producing a synthesis of the analytical and the systemic. Symbionomics is giving rise to a unified approach to organizations and time, leading to individual and collective human action. The natural and the artificial, art and technology, culture and civilization are now joined together in a coherent whole. There is no need for fundamental biological mutations to transform the human species or create a "superman." The future belongs to human societies organized in symbiosis with their natural artifices. The conception and planning of the cybiont for the good of humanity, through improved knowledge of natural laws, will be the new horizon for humanity in the new millennium.

Why should we resign ourselves to a vision of the future that is necessarily linked to the spatial and temporal destiny of the universe, as if our future were already written there? That universe is foreign to me. I confess that elementary particles, quarks and muons, quasars, galaxies, and black holes do not motivate or guide my everyday actions. The grand opera of the universe does not inspire me! I prefer the vibrant life of the cybiont that is now being born—the constant acceleration of its evolution, the conviviality of the networks, the budding promise of planetary solidarity among human beings, the still-utopian hope of a sharing of wealth and knowledge, the collective responsibility for environmental protection. I prefer immersion in the depths of shared time—real time—and exploration of the density of the fractal time generated by creative activity, the fragile capacity given me to imagine and create.

Everything that gives human beings the ability to innovate makes them masters of their future. Creation saves time. When parallelized, saved time densifies duration. Salvation is in the moment, dilated from within. The future of the world, a minuscule point in a cold, remote universe, no longer belongs only to sidereal space. The future of the world is in human time. Humanity is a point of convergence in this increasingly significant time that is its own. This is the time of the cybiont and, perhaps, the time, denser and deeper still, of the cosmic superorganism that will succeed it.

A collective leap into the depths of the moment rather than dilution in the infinite duration of the expansion of the universe.

Glossary

Artificial Life The human manufacture of life-forms that can develop autonomously and independently.

Autocatalysis A reaction that is self-amplifying and self-reinforcing.

Biofeedback An information feedback loop going from the body to the brain.

Biomimetic Relating to a structure or function that imitates life.

Bionomics The art of managing life.

Biosphere The living environment and the collectivity of beings of the planet.

Biotics A new science that combines biology with computer science. It applies principally to the creation of links between the human brain and computers.

Chaos The unpredictable manner in which certain systems behave, despite the deterministic laws ruling them.

Coevolution Evolution involving successive changes in two or more interdependent species or systems, be they biological, technical, or social.

Combinatorial Chemistry A new field of chemistry in which billions of new molecules can be simultaneously manufactured in parallel.

Complex System A complex system is characterized by the number of its constituent elements, by the nature of the interactions among these elements, and by the number and variety of connections among them. Examples of complex systems include a cell, a city, and an ecosystem.

Compression A computer process by which a message, image, or sound is reduced in size so as to take less disk space or less space on communications networks.

Cybernetics The science of communications and control theory concerned with the regulation of organisms and machines.

Cyberspace An electronic space-time created by the emergence of communications networks and multimedia computer interconnections.

Cybiont A planetary macroorganism currently in evolution. A hybrid biological, mechanical, and electronic superorganism that includes humans, machines, networks, and societies. In this book, it appears under several designations: living planetary macrocell, social ecosystem, and macroscopic living being.

Digitization A computer process that converts sounds and images into numerical digits. The data can thus circulate within networks and be processed by computers as a common machine language.

Dissipative Structure A system "jump" or sudden transition to a higher level of complexity or order, absorbing the energy perturbing the lower levels in the process. This is an evolutionary change; it resists the natural tendency toward entropy, and, thanks to a constant flux of energy and information, retains its organization over time.

Ecosphere The collectivity of all natural and artificial ecosystems.

Ecosystem A system of interdependent living species; by extension, a system of interdependent living beings and machines.

Emergence The sudden appearance of structures, ideas, and original systems.

Feedback An information circuit by which corrective or regulatory information is transmitted from the output of a device or system back to its input.

Fluctuations The ebb and flow of physical or biological phenomena or forms; in time, fluctuations may become oscillations.

Fractal Forms or structures consisting of identical patterns that are repeated at any scale on which they are observed. The concept can be applied to the organization of this book, to communications, education, culture, and time.

Fractal Culture A culture bearing the seeds of its own development.

Fractal Education A form of education that fosters the use of learning methods, principles, and tools, rather than the rote memorization of encyclopedic knowledge.

Fractal Time A concept of time encompassing both duration and instantaneity. Fractal time has a variety of densities.

Gaia The name given to the Earth by James Lovelock. Gaia is a metaphor that compares the workings of the planet to that of a self-regulated machine or a living organism.

Genetic Algorithm A computer software category that draws on principles akin to those of biological evolution (mutation, selection, amplification) to find solutions to a given problem.

Glial Cells Brain cells that serve to support, repair, and nourish neurons or nerve cells.

Governance Governance is a possible form of government for the future. This term designates the adaptive comanagement and networked management of all government action.

Homeostasis From the Greek *homos* (same) and *stasis* (to stand). The capacity for dynamic stability in complex systems, living organisms, or ecosystems. Homeostasis involves preserving an equilibrium through a set of regulations. A homeostatic system resists change and transformation.

Hypertext A traditional text contains information set out in a linear and sequential manner (lines, paragraphs, pages, etc.). A hypertext is an associative network allowing the "reader" to shift between elements of information. With hypertext software, users need only "click" on to words or pictures to access the related information.

Information Highway A communications network with a rapid flow of information on very high bandwidths.

Infostructure By analogy with infrastructure, the term refers to the heavy structures required by the communications networks.

Intellectual Ergonomics An applied science concerned with the efficient and controlled interaction between humans and machines.

Intelligent Agent A software that offers advice or even acts as a personalized intellectual assistant to the user.

Intelligent Telephone A technological hybrid with the merged capacity of a portable phone and a hand-held computer.

Internet International meganetwork of interpersonal communications via computer. The Internet is the first international information highway.

Introsphere The subsconscious of the planetary brain. A virtual sphere of internalized collective consciousness spread out through communications networks.

Leveled Hierarchy The organization of complex systems into successively interlocking building blocks (atoms, cells, societies) and forming hierarchical layers.

Lock-In The exclusive occupation of a system or sector through autocatalysis and self-selection. A succession of virtuous circles (increasing returns) can lead to the lock-in of a sector, which then becomes closed to all other evolutionary influences.

Macrobiology The new biology of macroorganisms.

Macrolife The life of a planetary macroorganism.

Macroorganism A living organism made up of an extremely large number of individual agents (living beings and machines).

Macroscope A method and tool for the observation of the infinitely complex. Through its capacity for simulation, the computer has become a macroscope.

Media Immunity A form of public protection or "untouchable" status achieved through a strong media response to an individual's words or stance.

Mediamorphosis The revolution in communications that came about as a result of the newly developed powers of multimedia computers and communications networks.

Modem An electronic device allowing computers to communicate through telephone networks.

Multimedia The convergence of platforms and processes for communication through text, sound, and images.

Multiprocessor An electronic processor or computer capable of processing information in parallel, rather than in a strictly sequential mode (one instruction following another).

Natural Artifice A product or structure that is created by humans, but is part of the natural course of evolution.

Neobiology A new scientific discipline concerned with the study of artificial life.

Noosphere A term coined by Teilhard de Chardin referring to the slowly developing sphere of human consciousness and intellectual activity. Beyond the biosphere (all living things), the noosphere designates all dematerialized productions.

Paradigm A theoretical framework resting on a set of shared fundamental principles. A new paradigm emerges when a new theoretical framework and set of references develop.

Regulated Adaptive Development Extending the idea of "sustainable development," this expression highlights the necessary symbiosis between the economy and ecology. It also underlines the importance of governance, its regulations, and adaptive mechanisms.

Retroprospective A method of forecasting that uses future scenarios to analyze current trends.

Self-Organization The spontaneous organization of matter.

Self-Selection The selection of a system or an element through a set of autonomous reactions.

Subsumption The act of subsuming (from the Latin *sumere*, "to take up"). Subsuming means thinking of an individual object as part of the whole.

Supramolecular A grouping of molecules that forms natural or chemically engineered organized structures; for example, the envelope of a virus, a cell membrane, thin layers, etc.

Symbionomics A unified theory of the self-organization and dynamics of complex systems. Symbionomic evolution is a general evolution toward increasing complexity and organization, extending to all matter, life, humanity, and society.

Symbiosis An association between living species that is mutually beneficial to all partners; by extension, an association between living species and macrobiological systems or organized forms, including machines.

Systemic Approach A new approach that organizes knowledge in such a way as to make action more effective. The systemic approach is related to the study of systems and their evolution over time.

Technosphere All tools, processes, and machines (mechanical and electronic) that produce, reproduce, and maintain the social organism.

Unimedia A field created by the convergence of digital media. A new form of electronic writing for the communications of the future.

Virtual Reality A computer process by which users can create artificial worlds, and within which they can grasp objects, modify shapes, or act on their environment.

Bibliography

Axelrod, Robert, *Donnant donnant*, Paris, Odile Jacob, 1992.

Barnaby, Franck, *The Gaia Peace Atlas*, Londres, Gaia Books Ltd, 1988.

Brown, Lester R., *L'État de la planète*, Paris, La Découverte, 1994.

Changeux, Jean-Pierre, *L'Homme neuronal*, Paris, Fayard, 1983, et Hachette, coll. «Pluriel», 1984.

Cohen, Jack, et Stewart, Ian, *The Collapse of Chaos*, Londres, Viking, 1994.

Debray, Régis, *Manifestes médiologiques*, Paris, Gallimard, 1994.

Dertouzus, Michael L. *What Will Be*, New York, Harper Collins, 1997.

Drexler, K. Eric, *Engines of Creation*, New York, Anchor Press/Doubleday, 1986.

—— et al., *Unbounding the Future*, New York, Quill - William Morrow & Co., 1991.

Dyson, Freeman J., *The Sun, the Genome, and the Internet: Tools of Scientific Revolutions* (Nypl/Oup Lectures), Oxford University Press, (April 1999).

Gleick, James, *La Théorie du chaos : vers une nouvelle science*, Paris, Flammarion, coll. «Champs», 1991.

Hagel, John, and Marc Singer, *Net Worth*, Harvard Business School Press, 1999.

Kauffman, Stuart F., *The Origins of Order*, Londres, Oxford University Press, 1993.

——, *At Home in the Universe: The Search for Laws of Self-Organization and Complexity*, Oxford University Press, (October 1995).

Kelly, Kevin, *Out of Control*, Londres, Fourth Estate, 1994.

——, *New Rules for the New Economy*, Viking Penguin Publishers, 1998.

Lamarck, Jean-Baptiste de, *Système analytique de connaissances positives de l'homme*, Paris, PUF, coll. «Quadrige», 1988.

Lévy, Pierre, *Les Technologies de l'intelligence*, Paris, La Découverte, 1990, et Seuil, coll. «Points Sciences», 1993.

Levy, Steven, *Artificial Life*, Paris, Penguin Books, 1992.

Lovelock, James, *Les Ages de Gaïa*, Paris, Robert Laffont, 1990.

Margulis, Lynn, et Dorion, Sagan, *L'Univers bactériel*, Paris, Albin Michel, 1989.

Mazlish, Bruce, *The Fourth Discontinuity*, Londres, Yale University Press, 1993.

Morin, Edgar, et Kern, Anne Brigitte, *Terre-Patrie*, Paris, Seuil, 1993.

Myers, Norman, *The Gaia Atlas of Future Worlds*, Londres, Robertson Mc-Carta, 1990.

Negroponte, Nicholas, *Being Digital*, New York, Knopf, 1995.

Nottale, Laurent, *L'Univers et la Lumière*, Paris, Flammarion, 1994.

Piaget, Jean, *Le Comportement, moteur de l'évolution*, Paris, Gallimard, coll. «Idées», 1978.

Quéau, Philippe, *Le Virtuel, vertus et vertiges*, Paris, Champ Vallon/Ina, 1993.

Rheingold, Howard, *Virtual Reality*, New York, Summit Books, Simon & Schuster, 1991.

Rifkin, Jeremy, *The End of the Work: The Decline of the Global Labor Force and the Dawn of the Post-Market Era*, Putnam, New York, 1995.

Rosnay, Joël de, *Les Origines de la vie*, Paris, Seuil, 1966 (épuisé).

——, *Le Macroscope*, Paris, Seuil, 1975, et coll. «Points», 1977.

——, *Le Cerveau planétaire*, Paris, Olivier Orban, 1986, et Seuil, coll. «Points», 1988.

——, *L'Aventure du vivant*, Paris, Seuil, 1988, et coll. «Points Sciences», 1991.

——, *Les Rendez-Vous du futur*, Paris, Fayard/Éditions n° 1, 1991.

—— et Rosnay, Stella de, *La Malbouffe*, Paris, Olivier Orban, 1979, et Rothschild, Michael, *Bionomics*, New York, A John Macrae Book, 1990.

Segura, Jean, «La réalité virtuelle», in *La Recherche*, n° 265, mai 1994.

Serres, Michel, *Le Contrat naturel*, Paris, François Bourin, 1990, et Flammarion, coll. «Champs», 1992.

——, *Atlas*, Paris, Julliard, 1994.

Seuil, coll. «Points Actuels», 1981.

Shapiro, Carl, *Information Rules, A Strategic Guide to the Network Economy*, Varian, 1998.

Stock, Gregory, *Metaman*, Londres, Bantam Press, 1993.

Tapscott, Don, and Art Caston, *Paradigm Shift: The New Promise of Information Technology*, McGraw-Hill, Inc., New York, 1993.

Teilhard de Chardin, Pierre, *Le Phénomène humain*, Paris, Seuil, 1955, et coll. «Points», 1970.

Toffler, Alvin, *Les Nouveaux Pouvoirs*, Paris, Fayard, 1991, et coll. «Livre de poche», 1993.

Varela, Francisco J., *Autonomie et Connaissance*, Paris, Seuil, 1989.

Virilio, Paul, *L'art du moteur*, Paris, Galilée, 1993.

Waldrop, M. Mitchell, *Complexity*, Londres, Viking, 1993.

Wilson, Edward O., *Consilience: The Unity of Knowledge*, Knopf, (April 1998).

Index

293

About the Author

Joël de Rosnay, Ph.D. is Director of Strategy for the Science and Industry Complex in La Villette, Paris. Prior to joining the Science and Industry Complex, he was Director of Research Applications at the Pasteur Institute in Paris from 1975 to 1985.

Dr. de Rosnay received his doctorate in organic chemistry from the Pasteur Institute in 1965 and worked as a research associate in biology and computer graphics at MIT. He also served as Scientific Attaché with the French Embassy in the U.S. and Scientific Director of the European Enterprises Development Company, a venture capital group specializing in the finance and launch of technological companies.